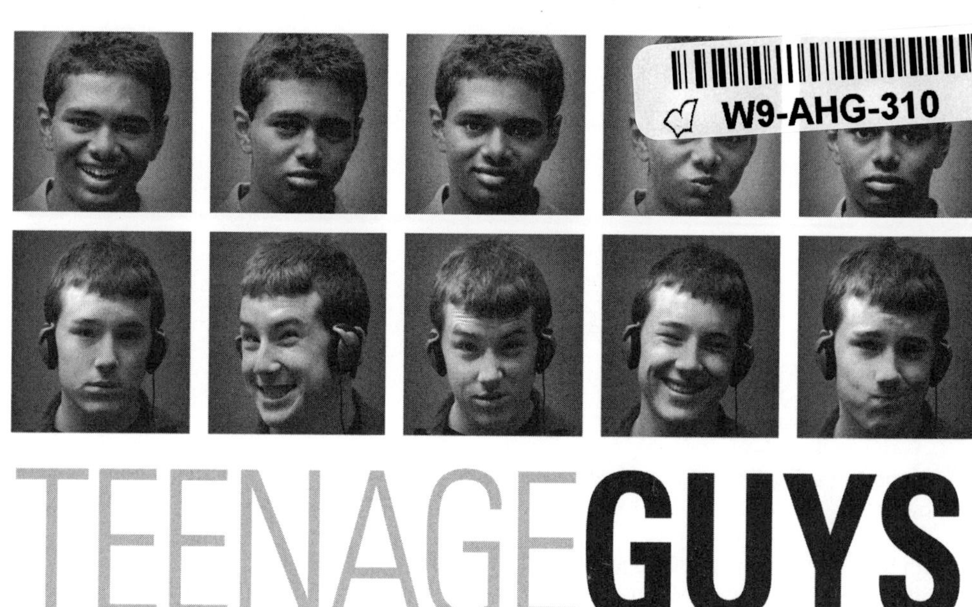

TEENAGE**GUYS**

Exploring Issues Adolescent Guys Face and Strategies to Help Them

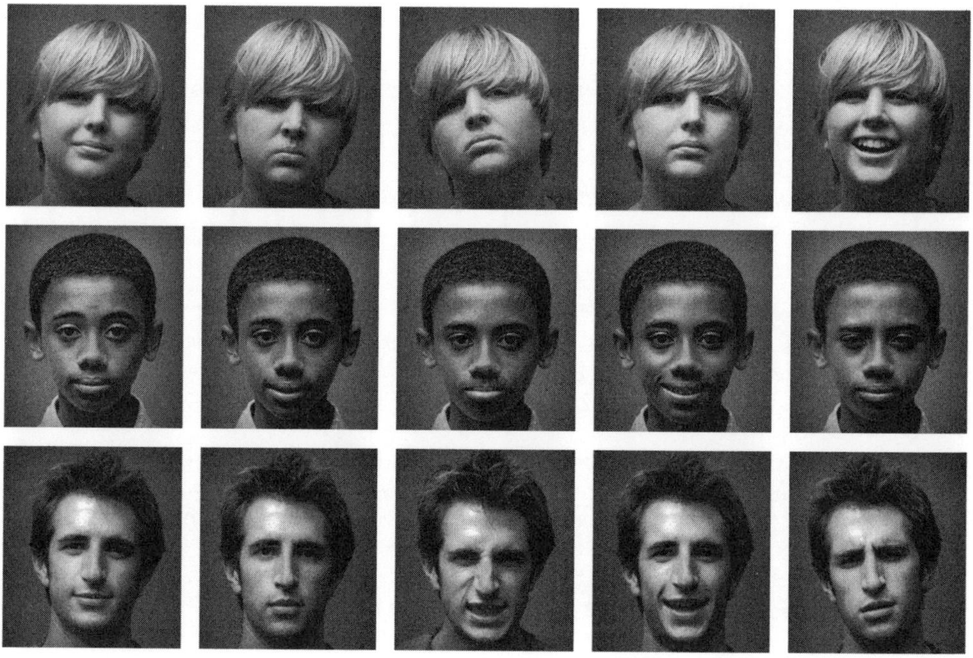

Steve Gerali

ZONDERVAN™
GRAND RAPIDS, MICHIGAN 49530 USA

ZONDERVAN.COM/
AUTHORTRACKER

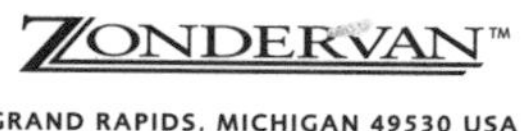

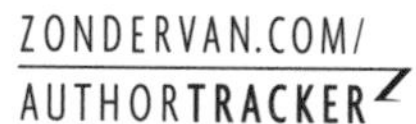

Youth Specialties
www.youthspecialties.com

Teenage Guys: Exploring Issues Adolescent Guys Face and Strategies to Help Them

Youth Specialties products, 300 South Pierce Street, El Cajon, CA 92020 are published by Zondervan, 5300 Patterson Avenue Southeast, Grand Rapids, MI 49530.

Library of Congress Cataloging-in-Publication Data

Gerali, Steve.
Teenage guys : exploring the issues that adolescent guys face and the strategies to help them / by Steve Gerali.
p. cm.
Includes bibliographical references.
ISBN-10: 0-310-26985-7 (pbk.)
ISBN-13: 978-0-310-26985-4 (pbk.)
1. Church work with teenagers. 2. Teenage boys. 3. Adolescence. I. Title.
BV4447.G46 2006
259'.23--dc22
2006000896

Web site addresses listed in this book were current at the time of publication. Please contact Youth Specialties via e-mail (YS@YouthSpecialties.com) to report URLs that are no longer operational and replacement URLs if available.

Creative Team: Dave Urbanski, Laura Gross, Heather Haggerty, Janie Wilkerson, and Mark Novelli
Cover design by Burnkit
Printed in the United States

06 07 08 09 10 • 10 9 8 7 6 5 4 3 2 1

ACKNOWLEDGMENTS

Thanks to the Azusa Pacific University Men's Chorale and director Harold Clousing for letting me tag along on tour. You guys provided great insight: talking, being honest, sharing your stories, and being the men of God he's made you to be. I pray God makes you wise men. You guys are great!

Thanks to the Azusa Pacific University Men's Soccer Team and coach Phil Wolf. Being the team chaplain has really blessed my life. I've loved watching you guys become men of integrity. Your ambition to win the prize Christ sets before you—more than just winning the game—is what makes you strong men.

Thank you Pete and Marianne Gerali. I can say with confidence that this book would not have been written without your generosity and hospitality. You provided the perfect writing environment.

To Rosa Sabatino, my scribe. Thank you for the work you did to make this happen. It was a long journey, but it's completed. I didn't forget!

Thanks to my D-group: Brian Belting, Craig Thompson, Eddie Bernhardt, Nathan Sautter, Scott Ingersoll, and Seth Van Essen. I love you guys—you are the best "sons" a man could ever have.

Finally, this book about guys is dedicated to the beautiful girls in my life: my daughters, Andrea and Alison, who help me keep things in perspective. *Adore* is too weak a word for what I feel for you two. And to my wife, Jan—my friend, my love, and my partner. Many teenage guys have become great men who walk with Jesus because of you.

—Steve Gerali

CONTENTS

Section 4: The Teenage Guy's Emotions (Emotional Development)

Section 5: The Teenage Guy's Mind (Intellectual Development)

Section 6: The Teenage Guy's Family and Friends (Social Development)

INTRODUCTION

ADOLESCENT GUYS: NEVER A DULL MOMENT

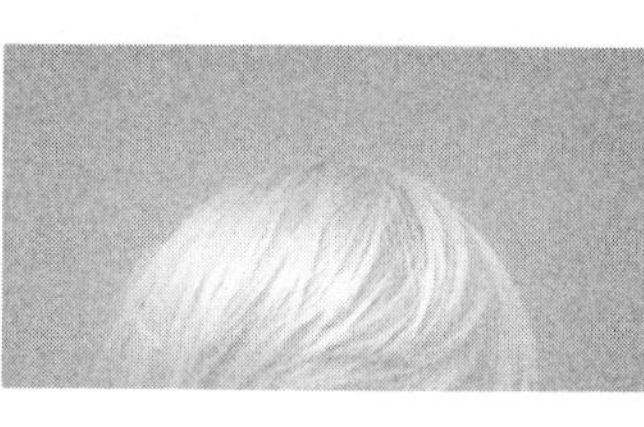

I'm sitting on a plane heading back to my home in Los Angeles. I've just completed researching this book, and it's been an adventure of a lifetime.

All my life I've been in youth ministry. The people who know me would say my forte is mentoring and developing boys into men. But despite my experience and abilities, I thought it would be advantageous to get a fresh, hands-on, intimate, and contemporary perspective into the hearts and lives of some young men.

With notebook in hand, I went on tour with the Azusa Pacific University Men's Chorale for two weeks. I boarded the bus with 65 guys, ages 18 to 22, because I wanted to engage in a firsthand experience—without retreat—of being "one of the guys." As they pushed, shoved, and wrestled their way onto the bus, part of me began to wonder if I would survive this research project. (I couldn't remember being in such a confined space with so much testosterone since my own college days.) Yet another part of me resonated with excitement over this adventure.

The men in this chorale group had ambitions to become *godly men*, and my goal for our time together was to hear their hearts. *Godly men*—those powerful, culturally loaded words became the center of my study and the major theme for this book. I wanted to gain insight from their perspectives, cultural imprints, ideals, behaviors, values, biases, norms, conceptions, and day-by-day interactions that cause them to struggle with what it means to be *men*, and then what it means to be *God-honoring* men.

So for two weeks, 24 hours a day, I invaded their conversations, watched their interactions, solicited their perspectives on many issues, served as the butt of their jokes, participated in their games, and listened one-on-one to their concerns, hurts, desires, dreams, and hopes. In the end, I experienced in a raw, new way their passion for a vibrant relationship with Jesus Christ.

We were on that bus an average of three to four hours a day. It was like sitting in a locker room on wheels, but I had a captive test group. Gradually they revealed to me the issues that men their age struggle with. I saw them tackle these issues and integrate and internalize values regarding every aspect of their beings: physically, intellectually, socially, emotionally, and spiritually. They were uniquely and distinctly—GUYS.

MALE LIBERATION

Navigating from boyhood to manhood was never a concern in Western culture until the 20th century. As that century rolled on, gender similarities became a focal point in the unisex movement of the '60s. Then the women's liberation movement of the '70s and '80s changed gender-identity development even further by defining the male-female difference as "separate, but equal," creating a greater sense of androgyny in our society. In light of this shift in perspective, masculine development needed some more attention.

THE WILDMAN MOVEMENT

This quasi-men's-liberation movement swept the nation in the mid '80s. Adherents hosted weekend retreats where men could get away and wrestle with their conceptions and misconceptions of masculinity. It liberated men from their stereotypical roles and expectations.

Men redefined what it meant to be men. They were released to pursue their passions by getting in touch with their "feminine side," as it was called. They discovered how their parents—particularly their fathers—played a part in shaping their views of masculinity. This opened the door to dealing with woundedness or the "father-wound" that each father inflicts on the psyche of his son. This male-liberation movement generated other themes, including rites of

passage and rituals into manhood, male bonding and intimacy, reconstruction and redefinition of masculine roles, an accepted androgyny, and male sexuality.

The movement's masculine template was often rooted in masculine archetypes and metaphors taken from history, literature, and mythology. Some were labeled Wildman, Warrior, King, Child, Sage, Hero, and so on. Authors who influenced this men's movement such as Robert Bly, Sam Keen, Herb Goldbloom, and John Lee borrowed from and expanded on the works of early psychoanalysts, particularly the late Carl Gustav Jung, a Swiss psychiatrist.

Jung's work on masculinity integrated heavy spiritual (although not solely Christian) overtones, most likely because Jung's father and grandfather were both pastors. Nonetheless, Jung's work became the springboard for this movement, allowing men to be well rounded, balanced, fully integrated, and liberated.

THE CHURCH RESPONDS

The church had some difficulty with the men's movement because of its spiritual overtones and rituals. The church viewed Wildman retreats as being voodoo-like, occult getaways where men were brainwashed into becoming savages who ran naked through the forest while screaming and banging on drums.

Well, we've come a long way since then. The church discovered some of the truth found in the men's movement. It revealed that there actually are distinctions between men and women. This has given rise to a number of Christian books on men and rites of passage into manhood. It has also given rise to Christian organizations such as Promise Keepers that, like the earlier men's movement, challenge traditional and societal templates of what masculinity is and should be and then exchange the generic spiritual component for positive aspects of Christian character.

But the struggle remains. I've resolved that it will always be that way because God has created his people to be progressive, open-ended, and always changing. As he continues to "make all things new," our collective perspectives and expectations of masculinity will continue to change and be remade.

I realize that God is also remaking women. As a matter of fact, I believe a woman's identity development is much more together than a man's. But the disclaimer of this book is that this is a book about GUYS. Many things we discuss may have some gender overlap, but for the sake of staying on task without having to walk a politically correct tightrope, I'll just say from the start that this book will only deal with the masculine.

GUY STUFF

My tour with the Men's Chorale set me on a journey to observe aspects of the masculine. These millennial, postmodern guys were raised in homes where values, roles, and ideas about manhood were influenced by the history I've just explained. Many of them had read *Wild at Heart* by John Eldredge or one of the *Every Man's* books. Many had been on some type of father-son bonding retreat or similar event. Some of these young men even experienced a rite of passage into manhood. And this was regardless of whether the relationship between father and son was good or bad because the dads were concerned about their own roles in their sons' masculine identity development. (Many dads are working through their own father-wounds and don't want their sons to experience a similar trauma.)

Yet in spite of the amount of preparation they'd received, almost all of these young men were still wrestling with what it means to be a man, and more specifically, what it means to be a man who follows after God. But it's a good struggle because it keeps men in community and constantly looking to Christ

for definition. It means every older man plays a role in a younger man's life to influence him toward becoming a *godly man*.

While on tour I began to connect with a student named Jared. He was a senior, and he'd been involved with the Men's Chorale for years. He'd even served as its president, just like his dad did when *he* attended the university.

Jared is bright and engaging and exhibits a strong, unassuming, relational style of leadership. He's the kind of guy you hope your daughter brings home. But in addition to his many outstanding qualities, he has a compassionate heart and he loves Jesus. I believe his father shaped him to be this way.

The year prior to this tour, Jared's dad passed away. I wanted to know more about Jared's story, and he'd agreed to share it with me sometime. So as we stepped off the tour bus one day, Jared grabbed my shoulder and asked, "Hey, do you think we can go talk now?" I agreed.

As we sat in a coffee shop, Jared told me about the goodness and sweetness of his relationship with his dad. He began to unveil his heart about how difficult it was to deal with his dad's death. Soon the conversation became more emotional. I knew this wasn't the best place for us to talk, so we quickly left and began to walk. Our walk led us into the Seattle Convention Center. We rode the escalator to the second floor where we found a secluded bench to resume talking.

Jared continued to tell me about the quality of his dad's character. He described the ways he thought he was like his dad and the ways he wanted to be like his dad. We even talked about how he thought he was different from his dad—but in a better way. As Jared retold his dad's story and how it shaped his own story, we cried together. He told me he'd never talked about his dad this way before. "I miss my dad,

and I'm afraid," he said. "I feel like now I have to do things on my own. I just want him to be around so we can talk about guy stuff."

Guy stuff.

With only two words, Jared nailed the essence of the ongoing evolution of the masculine, from generation to generation. We need to know and define and talk about guy stuff. While Jared was emerging as a godly man in every way, he still needed compasses—mentors, confidants, and coaches who would continue what his dad had begun. At that moment Jared couldn't see how God wouldn't allow just one man—his dad—to be the solely sufficient model of a godly man in Jared's life. Instead, God was raising up a community of men who would step in and connect with Jared in countless ways. Even if his father hadn't died, this would still be true.

God works through his people. He'll work through men to develop the masculine in other men. Yet he won't allow that help to come through a single human source, lest we become too reliant on one person.

I asked Jared if he would have had this type of emotionally charged, intimate conversation with his dad. He said no because he'd never faced so great a loss while his dad was still alive. But as Jared recalled his dad's loving nature and strong guidance, he realized his dad would have done the same thing that I'd done. He recognized that, like his dad, there were other men who weren't afraid to engage the deepest emotional and spiritual core of masculinity. Other men who weren't afraid to stand in the gap and be examples of godly men to a following generation. Jared would not be without godly men in his life to talk about the guy stuff.

"Do you think God would deprive you of anything you need to become the man he wants you to be?" I asked. The light went on for Jared.

MASCULINE IN COMMUNITY

With my intense focus on mentoring guys into men (both professionally and academically), it's ironic that I'm the father of two daughters. My home life has been filled with estrogen! Even our pets were females. I played dolls, had my hair done, danced, participated in countless fashion shows and dress-up games, watched chick flicks, went on shopping dates, made emergency grocery store runs for feminine hygiene products, lived through prom dress traumas, primped, pampered, and ran the emotional gamut with the beautiful women in my life. And I wouldn't change a second of it. I adore my incredibly beautiful, now college-age girls. They are by far the greatest treasures of my life.

But I had always dreamed of having a son. And to make matters worse, I'm 100 percent Italian (both sets of grandparents came to America from Italy). In Italian families it's believed to be essential that men sire male children to perpetuate the lineage and family name. In addition, I'm the oldest son in my family. So the patriarchal heritage that fueled my desires for a son only made the letting go of that dream more difficult.

One day my wife and I were talking about our daughters—how proud we were of them and what a great gift they were from God. Then she said she was glad God didn't give us sons. My heart was cut—why would she say that? She acknowledged my shock but continued by saying she was glad God hadn't given us sons because our girls had my undying devotion and undivided attention.

"God has given you so many sons," she said. "I'm afraid that if he had given us a boy, our son might have been deprived of what our girls get from you." At that moment I realized God wasn't going to deprive me of what I needed, either.

My talk with Jared that day was just what I needed as a dad, as well as what he needed as a son. It was what we both needed as *men*. We sharpened each other. We redefined the masculine. I look back at my life and see the many men who were there to work through the guy stuff with me, too. Hopefully this book will help you understand how adolescent guys develop and how they can become godly men.

WHAT THIS BOOK IS

This book is designed for youth workers, parents, teachers, counselors, coaches, mentors—in short, anyone who loves and works with *teenage guys*. This book isn't a comprehensive guide on adolescent males, nor is it rigidly universalized to include all teenage guys. But there are problems, concerns, and characteristics unique to adolescent males. I want to take you into their minds, hearts, and worlds.

In addition, we'll also *craft strategies* to assist them in their development. Adolescence is a critical, rocky time in the life of any teenager. I believe teenage guys look for and deeply desire guidance and mentoring. More than former generations, this generation of adolescents has been exposed to the concept of mentoring through educational directives, life-coaching programs, counseling and psychotherapeutic interventions, athletic programs, and even through the media. (Even Frodo had Gandalf.) On a weekly basis, I encounter late adolescent guys who articulate their desires or needs to be mentored. This generation is ripe for meaningful engagement.

The strong undercurrent of this book is *mentoring*. The strategies you take away from this book will assist you in helping teenage guys navigate the storm of adolescence and emerge on the other side as God-honoring men.

God's blessings on you as you read.

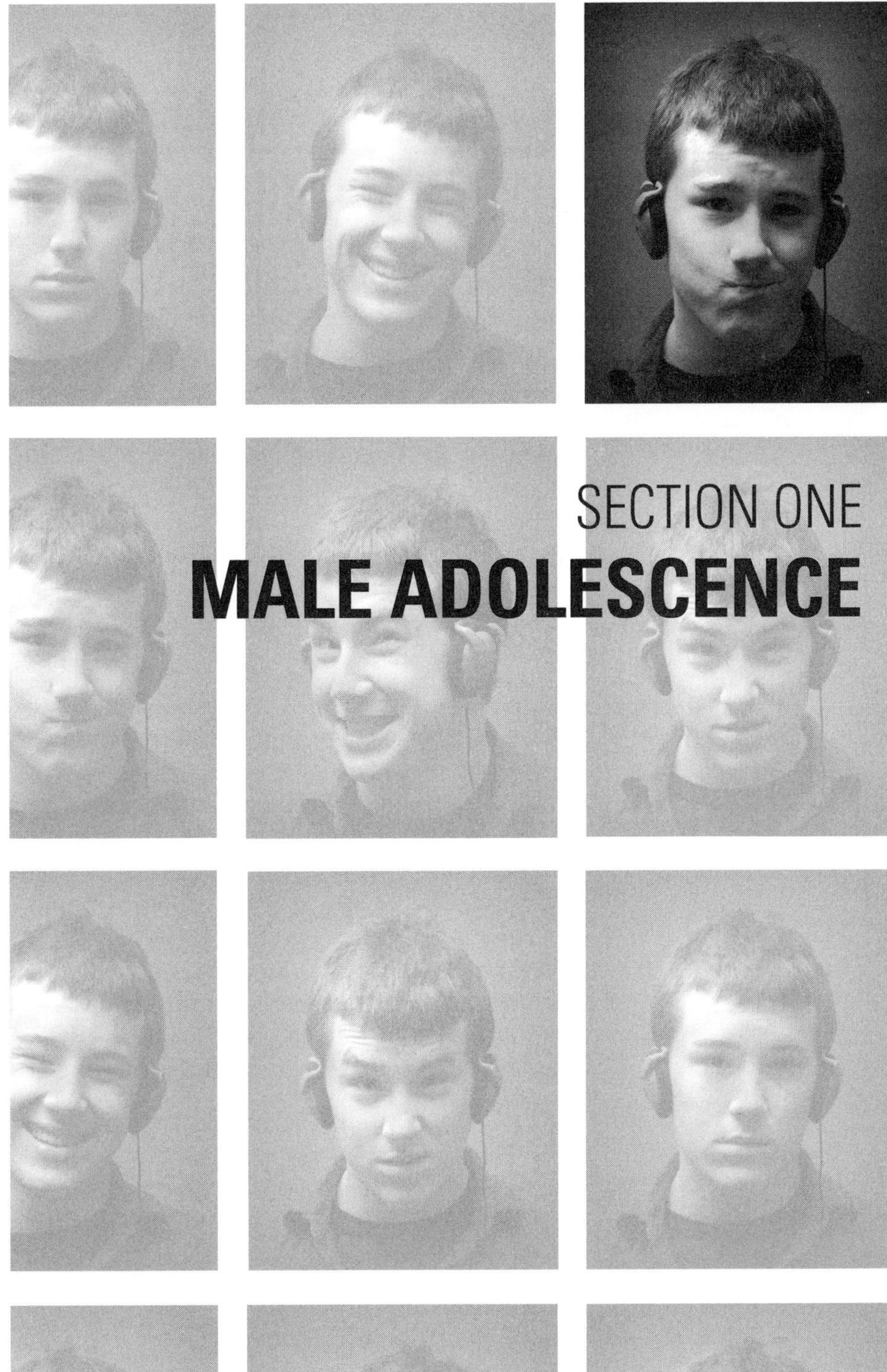

SECTION ONE

MALE ADOLESCENCE

1.1 UNDERSTANDING MALE ADOLESCENCE

I'd just finished speaking to parents of teenagers at a church-sponsored seminar when a very determined, seemingly panic-stricken mother hightailed it down the aisle to reach me before anyone else could. I knew she was stressed because she nearly plowed over some people on the way. When she reached my side, she looked fatigued and her voice was many decibels louder than normal. (I wondered for a moment if she thought I was deaf.) But I soon discovered this dear woman's plight.

"I need help!" she blurted before disclosing to me that she was the mother of four boys—ages two to 13. (It immediately began to make sense to me.) She described how her oldest son used to be a sweet little boy, but now he was *changing*. She drew parallels between him and her two-year-old, describing the many similarities between a child in the terrible twos and a child in the—her term for it—"terrible teens." She bombarded me with more questions than I could answer. Finally, she said, "I don't understand how teenage boys work; I wish my boy came with a user's manual."

"So you need to know how your teenage boy is wired?" I asked jokingly.

She quickly affirmed my observation and added that she was concerned that his wiring may be malfunctioning. This mother wanted her teenage son's user's manual to include an explanation of his wiring, tips on how to detect if and when the wiring goes bad, and instructions for how to rewire her son, if possible.

Guys are wired differently than girls from the beginning. But when adolescence sets in, it can appear as though their wiring has gone bad. In reality, it may be just a normal phase of growth. While they don't come with user's manuals, these days we have a better understanding of what makes a guy uniquely masculine and how to help him navigate through the storm and stress of adolescence and on into manhood.

STORM AND STRESS OF MALE ADOLESCENCE

The science of adolescence is a relatively new phenomenon, but adolescence has been recognized—although misunderstood—throughout history. The earliest records we have about adolescent boys are observations Aristotle made about the young adolescent males who were his protégés. He saw them as egocentric, idealistic, passionate, quick-tempered and easily angered, impulsive, overly optimistic, gullible, lacking self-control, and driven by their sexual desires. He also observed the strong, intimate connectedness—or brotherhood—they formed with their friends, which he noted was unlike any other period in a man's life (throughout childhood or maturity). He recognized that they were developing cognitively and entering into more advanced thinking stages. This led him to say, "They think they know everything."[1] Aristotle believed that adolescent boys "carry everything too far: they love to excess, they hate to excess—and so in all else."[2]

He wasn't too far off the mark in his observations. And they shaped Aristotle's instructional approach with adolescent males—one that fostered ethical and moral choice and self-determination. But while these distinctives were recognized, it wasn't until the Industrial Age that adolescence emerged as a distinct, formative life stage.

In 1902 developmental psychologist G. Stanley Hall published *Adolescence: Its Psychology and Its Relations to Physiology, Anthropology, Sociology,*

Sex, Crime, Religion and Education. Hall became known as the "father of adolescence" because he identified the developmental issues that create a transition from childhood to adulthood. He recognized and popularized adolescence as a formative stage in the developmental life span of an individual from ages 11 to 22.

Prior to Hall's pioneering work, the world viewed people as children until they could sire children of their own. The physiological phenomenon of puberty immediately made a boy a man. Hall theorized that the physical factors of puberty started a series of physical, psychological, and sociological changes that distinguished passive, effeminate boys into more assertive men. While not always evidenced outwardly, this internal aggressive shift in the makeup of boys into men was what Hall identified as "Sturm und Drang" or *storm and stress*.

The onset of this transitioning period was marked by puberty. (As a basic point of clarification, puberty is *not* adolescence. It's the event that marks the beginning of the developmental life span called "adolescence.") In Hall's era, puberty often began around the age of 11. Hall believed adolescence ended with the autonomy of the individual. This was marked by adult-like accomplishments such as marriage, starting a family, financial independence, acts of bravery and/or leadership, pursuing a career, and so on. Hall believed this most likely occurred around the age of 22 or 23. When a boy successfully navigated through the storm and stress of adolescence, he emerged at the other end a stable, autonomous man.

If we applied Hall's lines of definition to adolescence today, we'd have some problems. Puberty is starting earlier for most guys. They still begin puberty later than girls do, but most guys begin physically changing at age nine or 10. And at the other end, at ages 22 and 23, most people aren't ready or able to be financially autonomous yet (due to various

POSSIBLE CONTRIBUTING FACTORS TO THE EARLIER ONSET OF PUBERTY IN GUYS IN THE 21ST CENTURY:

View 1: We are healthier than the generations before us. We are more aware of diet and exercise and have made our children more aware of the same issues. Medical advancements have also put us in a more healthy position. This may allow the human body to develop at a less hindered rate, making puberty come earlier than in past eras.

View 2: While we may be healthier, we scientifically alter our food to preserve it longer or enhance its growth and qualities. Yet these chemicals may affect the onset of puberty, accelerating it at an unhealthy rate before its intended time.

View 3: Puberty is triggered by the release of hormones through the endocrine system that is primarily controlled by the hypothalamus and pituitary gland in the brain. Some believe a child's brain is stimulated to interact as an adult in certain situations, through

CONTINUED >

socioeconomic factors). They're not settled into their careers, nor are they ready to start a family.

Adult behaviors blur even more with technological advancements, leaving very little room for rites of passage in Western culture. Guys engage in video games and have access to adult-rated DVDs and online adult Web sites that expose them to adult sexual behaviors. They own and operate cell phones, computers, and personal handheld computers that give them the privileges and freedoms of adults without the usual responsibilities. Many parents fail to exercise parental controls over this technology. Or worse, even if the parents do implement some controls, teenage guys can find ways to get around them because they're more techno-savvy than their parents. As a result, teenagers are experiencing adult behaviors earlier, but they're still hindered from autonomous adult living.

In short, if we followed Hall's definition, then adolescence would run from ages nine to 35, give or take a few years. So for all practical purposes, today's social science community recognizes the years of adolescence as ranging from age 11 or 12 to age 22 or 23. We will use this timeline throughout the book (see fig. 1):

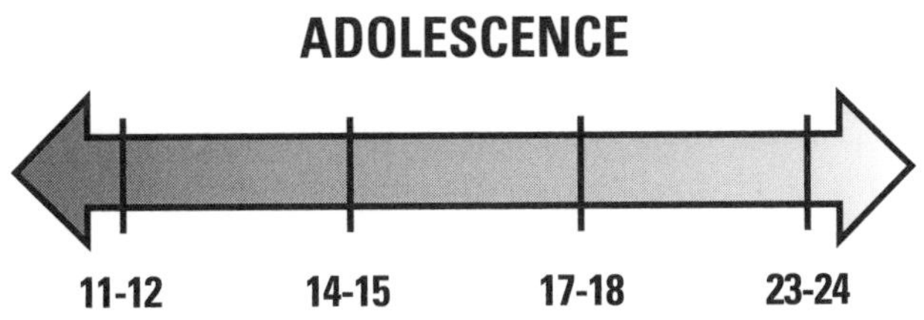

Figure 1

CONTINUED >

media exposure and life events. For example, kids watch prime-time television programs and are exposed to hours of adult themes and problem solving, whether it's healthy or dysfunctional. Kids are also given adult responsibilities (such as childcare for younger siblings, grocery shopping, and so on) because their parents work. Kids may also experience forms of independence due to shifting family structures and divorce. All of these activities prematurely stimulate areas of the brain toward more advanced functions, which may also trigger the release of growth hormones and result in the early onset of puberty.

View 4: There may be a combination of all of the above. While these factors may be influential, there is no conclusive evidence to substantiate any single factor.

AGE RANGES WITHIN ADOLESCENCE

It's easier for us to see how guys develop if we break down the timeline into three distinct age groupings.

Early Adolescence

Between ages 11 and 14 is technically termed *early adolescence* (see fig. 2). These are the middle school or junior high years, and this is often the time when guys begin to experience rapid growth in stature. Junior high guys are full of seemingly reckless energy, and parents and youth workers sometimes wonder if they have any real cognitive ability because they can be rude, obnoxious, and lack appropriate boundaries. At this stage they are becoming very *self-aware*, and they're learning about who they are. Since identity is being formulated, they tend to mimic societal norms regarding gender roles and masculinity, often with an awkward reluctance and lack of confidence.

On the other hand, early adolescent guys have profound moments. They can often surprise us with clarity of thought and wisdom that seems strange for their years. Yet they still fluctuate between little-boy and adolescent behavior. This is especially evidenced in their play. They still enjoy their little-boy toys and games, but they wouldn't be caught dead playing with them. It's also evidenced in their emotions. They still have a tenderness that is untainted by the bravado that will be internalized during middle adolescence.

Becoming more aware of girls but not being sure they like the opposite sex yet; discovering sexual pleasure through masturbation; having a limited attention span; not wanting to be around parents or family; learning that crying must be done in secret or not done at all; attempting to be funny or gross; roughhousing and swearing in front of their friends as an act of manly independence; and a budding spiritual sensitivity all mark this stage in a young teenage guy's life.

Middle Adolescence

Middle adolescence occurs between 14 and 17 years of age (see fig. 2). The high school years. These guys take on a new image as their stature begins to fill out, and this makes them much more *body aware*. And, depending on how their development progresses, they become more confident or less confident about their physical appearance. Regardless, most middle adolescent guys can find something they believe is abnormal about their physical appearance.

Most senior high guys develop a bravado that they'll eventually internalize as their masculine identity. This is defined by strength—both physical and emotional (meaning the suppression of emotion)—and status. It's also accompanied by a sense of invincibility and a heightened desire for adventure. (This feeling will become even stronger in the next stage.) High school guys often present themselves as detached from emotional situations, and they also lack confidence to make solid decisions. This often puts them behind girls their same age, resulting in the girls taking more control and leadership roles. Yet guys in middle adolescence become more confident in their cognitive abilities. (Have you ever wondered why senior high guys think they know everything?) While this age range develops new confidences, it feels unstable overall.

Hanging out with friends; playing hours of computer and video games; attempting new and more daring stunts on a skateboard, snowboard, or surfboard; dreaming about the perfect car and girlfriend (and trying to acquire both); worrying about future college plans; and attempting to discern and own spiritual truths mark this stage in a guy's life.

Late Adolescence

Late adolescence occurs between ages 18 and 23 (see fig. 2). A guy in this age range begins to personally define himself as a man; but because he must let go of childhood—more specifically, adolescence—many guys have a difficult time with this identity transition. Girls this age will more easily define themselves as adult women; but many young men want to stay kids a while longer. Ask any guy this age, and he'll tell you he's not a man!

Late adolescents' play becomes more adventurous, and their toys become more expensive and powerful. They're less inhibited about their bodies and more obsessed with defining them. They become more aware that they need to be responsible adults, which often means taking on some form of personal or group leadership position. Late-adolescent guys desperately seek out, consciously or subconsciously, strong male mentors. Many college-age males will attempt to identify with male role models as a frame of reference regarding their own manhood (this occurs more during this stage of adolescence than in the previous ones). They also become more aware of the deficiencies of their own fathers. If their father-son relationship is lacking a strong emotional connectedness, then this results in a *woundedness* that's become so popularized in masculine-identity literature.

This stage in a guy's life is marked by the internalization of values; strong male bonding; sexual awareness, desire, lust, and hormonal overdrive; a noted attentiveness to future planning; more intimate dating with the goal of mate selection; and at times a greater desire to be well-rounded ethically, morally, and spiritually.

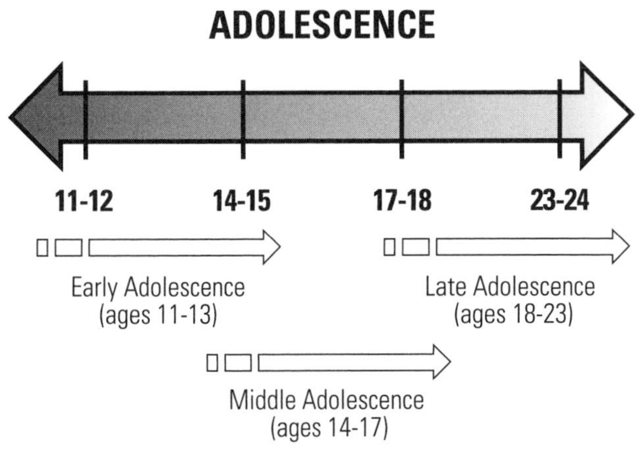

Figure 2

DEVELOPMENTAL TASKS

In each age and stage of adolescence, a guy must accomplish certain developmental tasks. A developmental task is the formation of attitudes, values, behaviors, and skills that will transition him from boyhood into manhood. It's the process of formulating a proper masculine identity. Developmental tasks become the series of hoops a boy jumps through on his way to becoming a man. These tasks often root themselves in changes in physiology, cognition, social expectations, and identity.

Nancy Cobb, author of *Adolescence: Continuity, Change, and Diversity,* states: "Because our sense of ourselves comes in part from our awareness of how others see us, cultural norms give shape to personal standards. Biological maturation contributes more heavily to some tasks, such as adjusting to an adult body, whereas cultural norms contribute more to others, such as developing social skills."[3]

DEVELOPMENTAL TASKS OF ADOLESCENCE

Robert Havighurst coined the phrase *developmental task* and identified the following as tasks of adolescence:

- Forming mature relationships with peers—same and opposite gender.
- Adopting masculine social roles.
- Accepting one's body.
- Achieving emotional independence from parents and other adults.
- Preparing for marriage and family life.
- Preparing for career and becoming self-supporting.
- Acquiring values that guide one's behavior.
- Exhibiting socially responsible behavior.

MALE YOUTH WORKER TIP

Be quick to notice and verbally affirm any character qualities that distinguish a guy as a qualitative, God-honoring man. Take him out for a soda and when you're one-on-one, disclose your agenda of affirmation regarding his qualities. A conversation like that becomes a *coming of age* moment for a guy.

PROGRAMMING TIP

Plan a variety of *rites of passage* rituals or ceremonies to mark the progression from early-, middle-, and late-adolescent boyhood into manhood. This gradual advancement will give your male students a more stable perspective on and greater readiness for manhood. (Chapter 6.4 is devoted solely to rites of passage.)

As a guy encounters these tasks in adolescence, it becomes essential for parents and youth workers to help him navigate through them. Although developmental tasks are somewhat sequential and dependent upon each other, many of them are worked on throughout adolescence. Each guy is different and navigates through these tasks at his own pace. Therefore, it's more important to know about the tasks of adolescence, rather than attaching them to a specific age in adolescence.

When a guy begins these tasks, we call this a *coming of age*. This is when a guy recognizes that he's crossed a line somewhere, leaving a part of childhood behind. Often, coming of age may be distinguished by an event, experience, conversation, or rite of passage. A *rite of passage* is a ritual or ceremony that marks the transition from childhood into adulthood. The Western culture has very few rites of passage for adolescent guys. The single most significant rite of passage may be the acquisition of a driver's license. Others may include graduation, voting in an election, and going to college, but these really don't affirm the shift of a child into manhood.

A HOLISTIC APPROACH TO ADOLESCENCE

Remember the mom who wanted a "user's guide" for her son? Well, she would have loved a holistic approach to the developmental process he's experiencing, which offers more information about each of the different dimensions that make up her son—and all people.

There are five specific dimensions to a person—biological (physical); affective (emotional); cognitive (intellectual); sociological (social), and spiritual (some refer to it as moral/ethical). This frazzled mom observed some physical changes in her son, but she didn't understand how those changes affected his identity. She needed to understand how her son was thinking, as well as what he was feeling. She also assessed him to be spiritually bankrupt because of his apathy, not realizing that he actually may have been spiritually on track, while his apathy was due to a sociological issue. Or maybe it wasn't an issue at all.

For now, I'll offer a quick overview of the dimensions. As we continue to examine how a guy is wired, we'll walk through each one in more detail throughout the remainder of the book.

The Biological/Physical Dimension

Except for the time between infancy and the toddler years, at no other time in the developmental process is a person's physiological change as dramatic as it is in adolescence. The process begins with *puberty* and ends in full *sexological* maturation. Guys experience many different physiological alterations that will ultimately affect their emotions, relationships, self-image, personality, and even their spirituality. When we examine this area, we'll discuss everything from the development of sex characteristics to the effects of testosterone on the psyche. We'll look at some myths and misconceptions about sexuality that the world and the church believe to be true. We'll also examine some physical problems and disorders that could affect a guy during adolescence.

The Affective/Emotional Dimension

Many books about raising a male child have been written with this dimension in mind. Guys are constantly bombarded with societal messages to suppress, ignore, or deny their feelings. This becomes very confusing for an adolescent guy because he's constantly running counter to the way he was wired. God created us in his image and likeness (Genesis 1:26). Being created like God means guys are created to be fully emotional. Thus, this frequently repressed dimension can lead to serious repercussions in the quality of a young man's life and relationships.

DISCLAIMER

"Normal development" is a relative term. The age spans and developmental process through which a guy changes are as unique to him as he is unique from everyone else. The breakdowns in this book are ballpark observations that experts have identified for centuries. If you believe your adolescent guy isn't developing normally, be patient—he may be a late bloomer. If you believe he's way outside the realm of the experts' observations, then consult an expert in adolescence.

THE BOOK OF PROVERBS INFORMS THE DEVELOPMENT OF THE SOCIAL DIMENSION OF A GUY

The book of Proverbs is written from the perspective of an older man mentoring a younger man. The mentor continually helps the protégé see the effects of his alliances and relationships:

- Proverbs 1:15 (NASB)—"My son, do not walk in the way with them. Keep your feet from their path."
- Proverbs 2:20 (NASB)—"Walk in the way of good men, and keep to the paths of the righteous."
- Proverbs 13:20 (NASB)—"He who walks with wise men will be wise, but the companion of fools will suffer harm."
- Proverbs 14:7 (NASB)—"Leave the presence of a fool, or you will not discern words of knowledge."
- Proverbs 18:24 (NASB)—"A man of too many friends comes to ruin, but there is a friend who sticks closer than a brother."
- Proverbs 20:19b (NASB)—"Do not associate with a gossip."

CONTINUED >

The Cognitive/Intellectual Dimension

We have come to understand that guys think differently than girls. Those differences are issues of perspective, many of which may have roots in cultural conditioning, genetics, or biblical values. We also know that, developmentally speaking, a junior high guy thinks differently than a senior high or college guy. Men move through an intellectual growth pattern. They go from being the concrete-thinking little boy to a mature-thinking grown man. In order to effectively assist guys through adolescence, we have to know how to assess where they are on an intellectual developmental grid.

The Sociological/Social Dimension

This area is where a guy's sense of self is formed. He'll challenge, internalize, shape, and mold his personal masculinity. His views of women will also be formed here, as he begins to understand his own gender better. He'll begin to engage in adult-specific behaviors that he perceives as making him an adult male. Much of the input he receives will be from others—his friends, family, church, community, and so on.

An understanding of identity formation in the sociological dimension of an adolescent guy is critical. Too often youth workers *think* they understand this social dimension just because they hang out with kids. Helping a boy become a man requires more than just hanging out with him. While that relational aspect is critical in creating an authoritative voice in the kid's life, it isn't enough to deliberately shape his identity. Examination, observation, critical assessment, and sometimes modification of the sociological systems that shape a guy must be understood. This systems approach means we need to help guys understand the influences that their friends and family have on their identity. In other words, we can't deal with the kid apart from the system.

The Spiritual or Moral/Ethical Dimension

This is the place where morals, values, and beliefs are formed. This is also where we'd deal with faith and spiritual formation. There has recently been an outpouring of Christian literature geared toward Christian men and their faith. Many organizations and denominations have also done an excellent job of informing a guy's spiritual development and needs.

Despite this positive trend, there is still a problem in the trajectory of these teachings. Most of the literature on men's spirituality is written to address the problem of a lack of leadership in general and, more specifically, a lack of *spiritual* leadership. This can often create a narrow perspective that ignores the multifaceted characteristics of a man's relationship with God, as demonstrated by the many diverse archetypes of men that are found in Scripture. In an attempt to goad men into a single style of spiritual leadership, these well-meaning books create a "Christian Strongman Syndrome" that often spiritualizes myths about masculinity and makes sacred these capitalistic, Western concepts of manhood by harmonizing them with Scripture rather than drawing them from Scripture. In the long run, this can become a spiritual poison in the development of a young man's spiritual formation.

I encounter many guys who feel as though their spiritual lives are worthless because they're wired more as "wise men" or as "conciliators" rather than spiritual archetypes of "warriors" or "wild men." I talk to young guys who are troubled with the concept that every man must have a cause and rescue a maiden. This wounds the spiritual commitment of celibacy for these men. I've also seen late adolescents learn to dominate or intimidate others in the name of spiritual leadership, following the example of many of the spiritual "role models" who do the same—and all in the name of being a godly *man*.

CONTINUED >

- Proverbs 23:6 (NASB)—"Do not eat the bread of a selfish man, or desire his delicacies."
- Proverbs 23:20 (NASB)—"Do not be with heavy drinkers of wine, or with gluttonous eaters of meat."
- Proverbs 24:1 (NASB)—"Do not be envious of evil men, nor desire to be with them."
- Proverbs 27:17 (NASB)—"Iron sharpens iron, so one man sharpens another."

And the list goes on...

The Christian Strongman Syndrome ignores the tenderness of Jesus. It fails to honor the way he draws people to himself and how he is moved to weeping by their pain and brokenness. It only sees spiritual leadership as an in-your-face-get-out-of-my-way-cuz-I'm-right-and-empowered model. An understanding of the spiritual dimension of a guy's life can help us mentor men into deep spiritual relationships with others and with God.

1.2 WHAT GUYS NEED

While it may not appear to be true, teenage guys are incredibly complex creatures. They have passions and desires. They're moldable and pliable. They have a fresh curiosity about life, seeing it through eyes of wonder. At times they are reckless; at other times, they're reserved. They're free-spirited, fun, and exciting. They have hearts that can be courageously strong, yet easily broken. They're growing and developing to be men. You gotta love 'em! And if you do, you need to understand them and know what they need.

1. Guys need to be known and understood. We need to know them better than they know themselves. We need to know how they develop; what cultural influences are bombarding their lives and identities; how they think and feel; we need to know their fears and joys. We must know about adolescence and masculinity if we really want to meet this need in guys. Once we get this part figured out, then we have an adequate frame of reference or foundation to know and understand the individual guy. Guys are cautious about being known personally and deeply because they're conditioned to be in control and on guard. *Known* means *vulnerable*, and that becomes a great divide to cross. But it's worth the time and effort because guys desperately desire to be known. They want mentors who will value them enough to look at every fiber and flaw, every quality and characteristic. They want to know they're loved and valued for who they are, who they're becoming, and who they *will* become. They want to be known enough so you can help them see their blind spots and be their ally and confidant.

2. Guys need a close connection to God. Spirituality and masculinity are a lot like oil and water. It's difficult to get them to mix unless one or both are refined. Despite this daunting task, guys have a very deep internal spiritual sensitivity. It grows out of an instilled desire to know their Creator. Guys have always felt a connection to majesty—whether it's the majesty of nature or the majesty of imagination and creativity. This pull toward majesty is an internal desire to know the ultimate majesty—Jehovah God. Deep within they know he loves and adores them, he stands ready to complete and empower them, and he stirs everything within them that makes them whole men. Yet this spiritual sensitivity is fragile and can easily be extinguished by other things that compete to fill the place of awe in a guy's life. So he must be spiritually guided. He must explore and see the awe of God. He must taste for himself and see that God is good.

3. Guys need validation and empowerment as unique individuals. We must be very careful not to pigeonhole a guy. We need to realize that a universal label can make him feel as though he isn't a man or he cannot become one. To make one issue "every guy's battle" or journey or need robs him of his uniqueness. It also makes him a freak of nature if he isn't like every other guy. We need to understand there's no universal type of guy, but there may be commonalities. We need to help guys discover their unique talents, skills, abilities, characteristics, flaws, needs, weaknesses, and so on. Then we need to empower them to be all that God is making them to be.

4. Guys need community. Guys are clan-oriented. They bond and form intimate relationships differently than girls. They need multigenerational community. Within that community, they need the closeness of other men who act as a compass for their manhood. They need a gang of close male peers to sharpen them like iron sharpens iron. They need this tribe of guys to validate them as masculine. In the context of community, they can see there are many different ways that men are men. They learn to celebrate the diversity of manliness. They need to see how they're normal, as well as the areas where they deviate from the norm. They need to experience the kind of heart connection they can have with other men that they can't get with women. If they cannot be intimate with the masculine on a tangible level, then they can never become intimate with an invisible God whom they perceive as being predominantly masculine in nature.

5. Guys need mentors. All throughout Scripture we see older men who come alongside younger men as mentors. David comes alongside Samuel and Jonathan. Paul comes alongside Timothy. Jesus comes alongside his 12 disciples. The entire book of Proverbs stands as an example of an older man who mentors a younger man in the ways of wisdom. Mentors proclaim to guys that they're valuable and worthy of investment. A mentor plays multiple roles in shaping everything from a guy's character to his thoughts and perceptions. Mentors fill the role of teacher, father, coach, confidant, example, refiner, encourager, shepherd, and on and on. A mentor imparts wisdom and looks for life's teachable moments in a guy. A mentor is concerned about the development of a guy's heart and character. A mentor empathizes with a guy and creates an intimate bond that lets a guy know he is known. A mentor allows the guy to struggle through tough issues without the fear of judgment. He loves at all times and doesn't walk out of a guy's life. He becomes the safe place a guy needs. A mentor models dependence upon and devotion to Christ. A mentor pushes the protégé into the presence of God.

6. Guys need to know how to work. Guys are raised in a culture that defines their value by their contribution. While we want to bust this ideology, we still want guys to learn how to work hard as an act of devotion toward and worship of Christ. Hard work builds responsibility. It helps a guy develop the dis-

ciplines he needs to do life fully. It generates in him a deep sense of purpose that ultimately plugs into the kingdom purpose of bringing glory to God, as he will hopefully learn a little bit later in life.

7. Guys need to lead and to follow. Leadership comes in many forms, from influence to position. In adolescence, guys are just beginning to develop some of their talents and abilities, such as leading. But leadership doesn't come naturally for everyone. Regardless, young men should learn to do both because at some point, guys will serve as an example to others—whether it's to their children or to others in their own peer group.

The United States, among many other nations, has been confronted with a crisis in leadership, especially in the church. Men aren't stepping up and taking the lead. This has created a knee-jerk reaction by many men to make leadership a masculine power trip. It's implied that men in leadership wield power, and we all know that "power makes the man." Thus, we have completely lost the concept of servant leadership. Today it's perceived as just a weak, less-than-masculine approach to influencing others. Yet this is the model Jesus demonstrates and demands that all men—and women—follow. A good leader serves. He knows when to take charge and when to relinquish the lead as others become empowered. Guys must take the responsibility of leadership, but they must also learn that a strong man is not a power monger but a servant.

A guy also needs to learn how to follow because he's constantly bombarded with messages that say being a man means he must be a rugged individual. This creates an internal mechanism that places the individual at the center of his universe. He grows up believing that his voice (his perceptions, beliefs, values, desires, passions, and so on) is the only authoritative voice that informs him. Even Christian guys learn this, and they take it a step further by spiritualizing their own voice, believing they have the only line of direct contact with God. They claim God is the authoritative voice in their lives because he tells them, and they obey. Fortunately, God has chosen to provide many authoritative voices—from his Word to the church, a community of believers. When guys don't learn to follow, they ignore authority and rationalize—or worse, *spiritualize*—their self-centered ambitions and behaviors.

8. Guys need to play. I know a family with five boys who were all involved in different sports: soccer, basketball, baseball, track, and tennis. Life was one practice after another for this family. So you'd think that by the end of the day, these guys would've had enough play—you would think! I watched the brothers interact one day, and everything became a game for them. They constantly challenged each other: who could spit the farthest; who could eat dinner the fastest; who could eat the most; who could win back Mom's affection after they'd just made her angry, and so on. They were always at play. And they were just being guys—guys *need* to play.

Many theorists have picked up on this innate characteristic in men. They've labeled it as a need for the hunt, for competition, or for adventure. These needs play out in a single God-instilled, masculine characteristic—dominion. Follow the logic: in Genesis 1:28, God gives humankind dominion over the earth. He puts men and women at the top of the food chain. Conquest, competition, and control become a part of the DNA. These innate characteristics, instinctual to humankind but exemplified in guys, all influence a guy's need to play.

Guys learn to release their aggression in a healthy way during play. They learn depth of character by playing fair, learning teamwork, and prioritizing important human values, such as, "Winning isn't everything," or "It doesn't matter if you win or lose, but how you play the game." They learn how to be gracious losers or winners, how to manage their disappointments, how to evaluate their skills and abilities

and change themselves. They learn respect, control, strategy, and discipline while having a great time.

The world teaches guys that they should win at all costs. They learn to fight, kill, and destroy, either as descriptors of or as a form of fun. Now the idea of having *dominion over* something quickly becomes *domination, humiliation, bullying,* or *warring*. Healthy play that brings out the best in guys and calls into question those destructive messages is the reason guys *need* to play.

9. Guys need the freedom to BE. Guys grow up having great expectations imposed upon them. They live in the shadow of a looming cultural press that squeezes them into the mold of what a man should be. This encoding often runs counter to the guy's image of himself. Much of this book will reveal the complicated encoding that presses a guy into a dysfunctional conformity of Western cultural masculinity.

Guys often internally question whether they're normal, manly, or if they're in denial of who they really are. Many guys grow up to be men who never know who they are. Therefore, they have difficulty with intimacy. After all, how can a guy give himself to someone else if he is constantly wondering who he really is? He is forced to suppress his feelings, to hide any signs of weakness, and to prove himself by doing things that run counter to his passions (such as being athletic, mechanical, or outdoorsy) or his morals (such as leading other guys to believe he scored with his girlfriend or showing no weaknesses or flaws). In short he becomes defined by what he does.

For a guy, action and behavior define his being. What he does determines who he is, rather than who he is (character, intrinsic qualities, and so on) mandating what he *does*. If you ask a man who he is, he'll say, "I'm—a police officer, a pastor, a teacher, an executive." He tells you what he does. He doesn't say, "I'm—compassionate, trustworthy, discerning, and so on." Boys need to be surrounded with men who will fight for their freedom to discover who they are *apart* from what they do (or are expected to do). Men need to model character (being) over action (doing). Young guys need to see men who are compassionate, meaning they will be moved to emotion (a code-breaking action that grows out of being) *and* action (doing things that are loving and caring). They need men in their lives who will model the freedom of being.

10. Guys need to be loved. Joe Ehrmann, the former defensive lineman for the Baltimore Colts, is one of the football coaches for the Gillman High School Greyhounds. Before the team goes out on the field, they work themselves into an adrenaline frenzy with a battle cry that exemplifies Ehrmann's strong influence over the masculine development of his guys.

The coach yells, "What's our job as coaches?"

The team roars back, "To love us!"

Ehrmann then prompts them with, "What's *your* job?"

The guys shout, "To love each other!"

Ehrmann, a man who makes teenage guys into men, realizes that guys need to be loved. He understands that the defining point for a man is not his strength, nor his sexual conquests, nor even what he's accomplished, but rather it's his love. The only way a guy can learn to love is to be loved.

Guys need male role models who will step up and love them and also show their love for others. Guys desperately desire to have loving men in their lives who will speak a multilingual love language. Spending time with a guy, showing him affection, verbalizing your love for him, serving him, and giving to him are all necessary parts of really loving him. When men do this with teenage guys, they destroy the cultural restraints that limit teenage guys. They model

what it means to be a man who separates a powerful loving relationship from a sexual one.

Often guys learn to confuse love with sex. They grow up with a love deficit and attempt to fulfill their needs for affection with sexual behaviors. Men who demonstrate Christ's love to teenage guys break that sexual connection guys tend to form between being and needing love. It also models that love is a powerful force with which to be reckoned because it comes from a masculine, non-sexual source.

As I mentioned earlier in point number four (Guys need community), I've always contended that it's difficult for men in our culture to be intimate and loving with an invisible God (whom they perceive to be predominantly masculine in nature) when they can't do that in a tangible way man to man. The early stages of the men's movement recognized this love deficit and saw this as being fulfilled by one's father. When a dad couldn't meet this need, it created a deep wound in a teenage guy's heart that he then carried with him throughout his life. It was believed that a guy's father was the only one who could meet this need because men still bought into the notion that love had strong sexual connections. Obviously, the only man who would love a guy without that type of overtone would be his own father. The point they missed is that love doesn't have to—nor should it—only come from a guy's father. Any man who desires to be like Christ and model Jesus to teenage guys will love them deeply.

Jesus said people would know his disciples by their love for each other. Thus, love becomes the defining mark for a Christian. Guys need to be loved as a means of fulfilling their deepest emotions and understanding that they're valuable. But guys also need to be loved because it models what a man should be and do.

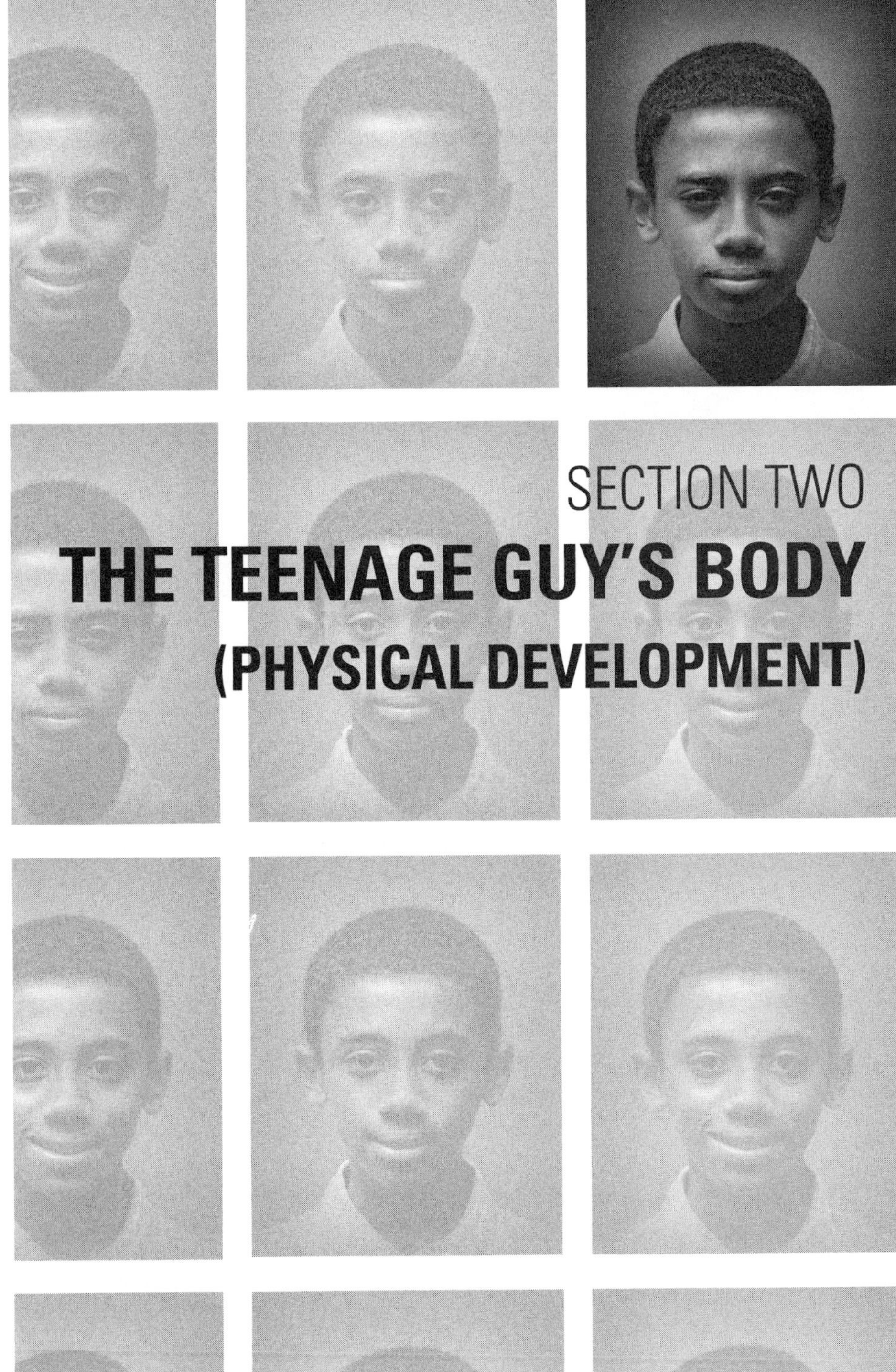

SECTION TWO

THE TEENAGE GUY'S BODY

(PHYSICAL DEVELOPMENT)

2.1 THE MALE BODY (PHYSICAL DEVELOPMENT)

Eleven days of a 16-day tour had gone by. The 65 late-adolescent guys of the Azusa Pacific University Men's Chorale had spent about 44 hours on a bus, and they were quickly becoming like caged animals. Occasionally they'd have an opportunity to stop and throw around a few Frisbees and footballs, but they needed another way to vent their pent-up aggression. This would be the night.

The scheduled concert had been cancelled. So in an attempt to alleviate the aggression and provide a "bonding" experience for the guys, we decided to take the entire group to…the Seattle Mariners/New York Yankees baseball game. There's something about being at a ballgame with your buddies—65 of them—that brings out the bravado in guys.

Our tickets were in the nosebleed section right above third base. Naturally, the guys were aware of the television cameras aimed at the fans, and they wondered if they were too far away to get their 15 seconds of fame. The goal of the evening quickly became apparent—get the entire group on TV!

The guys started by chanting and then yelling, which soon led to crowd-involvement activities. But the cameramen ignored them. Then a few guys took off their shirts and started to twirl them over their heads. And suddenly, with a total disregard of the 50-something-degree temperatures that night, the entire group was shirtless. It happened so quickly—it was like spontaneous combustion.

Then another interesting thing happened: other adolescent guys throughout our section of the stadium joined the fun. Now the rest of the fans were very aware that the APU guys were in the house. Younger guys from other sections came over to join them. When a new guy took off his shirt, the entire pride of guys roared with approval. Nobody around us was watching the ballgame. Instead everyone was having the most hysterical time of their lives, laughing, yelling, chanting, and coaxing every guy in the park to "take off your shirt!"

We found out later that the director of the broadcast didn't want to encourage further "nudity," so he decided not to put us on the air. But the guys finally made their TV debut during the last inning of the game—after they put on their shirts. And the entire section exploded in cheers when they appeared on the marquee.

ADOLESCENT GUYS ARE VERY BODY CONSCIOUS

You may have noticed this phenomenon: the older an adolescent guy gets, the more "clothing optional" his adventures may become. From birth, guys are conditioned to understand that part of being masculine means having little or no shame regarding their own nudity. Have you ever noticed that it's usually an older adolescent guy who moons someone or who's the first to skinny dip or streak? High school sports teams change and shower in locker rooms that aren't equipped for privacy. Men expose themselves in front of each other while standing at a urinal. And if young men venture off to college or enlist in the military, they soon learn that having any kind of privacy when you're nude is a luxury.

But it isn't this way with younger guys. They may be more reluctant to undress in front of their peers, or anyone else for that matter. Some studies reveal that many early-adolescent guys are as uncomfortable and dissatisfied with their bodies as their female peers.[1] Regardless of age, guys don't like to admit they're

YOUTH MINISTRY TIP

Females view a lot of guys as being perverted because they're comfortable with their own nakedness. The Christian community tends to have a difficult time separating natural nakedness from erotic nakedness, reducing nudity to an immoral act of sexuality or a shameful act of exhibitionism. We forget that when Adam sinned, he covered up out of *fear and shame*, exclaiming to God that he was naked. God's reply—"Who told you that you were naked?" (Genesis 3:11).

In *Wild at Heart*, John Eldredge writes about the emasculating effect our society has on the development of young men. He speaks of their need to be validated by their fathers or older men. A scene from the movie *A Perfect World* (Warner Bros., 1993) illustrates this well. A young boy, Phillip, is reluctant to bare himself in front of Butch, played by Kevin Costner. The boy says his genitalia are "puny," leading him to feel fear and shame. Butch beckons the boy to change his clothes and allow him to offer an honest appraisal. When Phillip does so, Butch says, "That's a

CONTINUED >

uncomfortable being naked; it's perceived as a weakness. They also don't readily admit to being *modest*. As a matter of fact, modesty isn't a concept that's applied to guys in Western culture. It's usually a nuance associated with females.

FASCINATION WITH FUNCTION

Both my brother and my sister have 12-year-old sons. When I saw my nephews at a recent family reunion at my parents' house, it was evident that these boys were in the throes of puberty. Being typical, early-adolescent guys, they weren't comfortable with the bravado of baring all, but they evidenced their body awareness nonetheless.

One evening all the adults were sitting in the dining room having a great conversation. We could hear bursts of laughter coming from the family room, along with flatulence noises. My 14-year-old niece walked into the dining room, rolled her eyes, and sat down with the more mature crowd. The noise and laughter continued. We soon discovered that the guys were watching a scene from *Kangaroo Jack*, a movie they'd seen many times before. The main characters are riding camels that keep breaking wind—so throughout the dialogue there are gaseous explosions. The boys were fixated on this and were laughing uncontrollably as they annoyingly replayed the scene over and over and over. And each time gas was passed, you'd have thought it was the first time they'd seen the clip.

My seven-year-old niece was also watching the video. Her response was one of frustration as she petitioned the boys to stop so she could watch the rest of the movie. Finally my brother and I stepped into the room and told the guys they'd watched that scene enough. As we walked out of the room, my brother asked me if it were possible for boys to know they can be guys without being gross.

It really isn't a matter of being gross as much as it is the fascination with the body and its functions. A guy's brain develops differently than a girl's (we'll discuss this more in depth in section 5). Guys think in a more objectifying (or concrete) manner than their female peers, as their attentiveness to their bodies' functions and changes centers more on the tangibles (such as burping, spitting, and passing gas) than the abstracts. They can intellectually connect that it's socially unacceptable to do these things in public, but they find there's a camaraderie surrounding these "edgy" behaviors when they're performed with other guys. This fuels bravado.

WHEN PUBERTY STRIKES

It's important for people who love adolescent guys to know about the complex physiological changes that are occurring in their bodies. Physiology is the most observable change, and it's also critical because it affects everything from a guy's identity to his emotions.

Guys start puberty around age nine to 11. This is usually about 12 to 18 months later than girls. Puberty begins when a guy's endocrine system starts to increase and decrease the production of hormones. A guy's body has always produced the hormones required for puberty. Yet through the creative mysteries that God instilled when he created guys, a biological alarm signals the opening of a floodgate of these hormones essential for physical growth and maturation. It's as if the endocrine system goes into high gear and takes over this innocent little guy's body.

But this isn't the first time this has happened. The first time was in utero. Guys' DNA is structured differently than girls'. The chromosomes in the DNA contain the genetic information that makes each of us similarly human, yet unique as individuals. We know from health class that a girl has an XX-chromosome configuration and a guy's DNA is comprised of an XY-chromosome combination. The Y-chromosome is the starting point of maleness. It's responsible for a male genetic patterning that determines his gender and may affect his gender

CONTINUED >

good size for a boy your age," which positively and confidently redefines the masculinity of the boy.

In a way, this same effect is played out with guys and their nakedness. Their bodies symbolize their manliness, and they realize they're changing from boys into men. But they also feel the emasculating effects of society. That's why adolescent guys become obsessive about working out and lifting weights. Their fascination with the physical is a natural outgrowth of their creative design.

Note: *I am* not *advocating that we allow or encourage guys to run around buck-naked!* I'm just suggesting we rethink how we expect guys to react to their fascination with nakedness apart from fear and shame.

IT'S A GUY THING

It never fails. You're on a retreat or at camp with your junior highers and the time comes for lights out. Immediately one guy starts to talk, joke, and then he pulls out the big guns—gas! And it comes in not one, but two forms: flatulence and belching. Naturally the entire room bursts into laughter. At first you overlook the event, understanding that "boys will be boys," but it continues. For the next hour or more you tolerate it; then you suggest that it stop and everyone get some sleep; and then you become overwhelmingly annoyed because you know this could go on all night! Be patient and persistent—patient in knowing that this is an inevitable fascination that early-adolescent guys have with bodily function, and persistent in holding guys to an acceptable social standard. They do outgrow it—though some do so sooner than others.

identity. While this is true, it still takes more than the Y-chromosome to *masculinize* a fetus.

The early development of a male or a female fetus appears to be the same. The formation of two gonads, or sex glands, will either be testes or ovaries. The genital tubercle or small bud at the base of the lower abdomen will either become the clitoris or the glans of the penis. Both genders have breast nipples along with other reproductive similarities that *feminize* the fetus. Every human being also starts with a feminized brain. The brain triggers the endocrine system and produces hormones such as estrogen and testosterone in both genders.

Toward the end of the first trimester of a pregnancy, the male fetus experiences an androgen bath due to the presence of the Y-chromosome.[2] Androgens are a grouping of hormones largely and more dominantly exhibited in the male. The primary androgen is testosterone. This testosterone wash masculinizes the brain and begins the differentiation process, resulting in different male and female prototypes at birth. The androgen bath may act on the brain to organize certain circuits into male rather than female patterns, such as the more aggressive and active play that's often exhibited in males over females throughout childhood. But for the most part, these patterns may lie dormant until puberty hits and the second androgen wash occurs, activating sexual maturation and sex drive.[3]

There is no conclusive way to measure the amount or total effect of the androgens released during the first and second washes. This can lead some to speculate that an androgen-deficient wash may be the biological anomaly linked to homosexuality. While one may deduce this, there is no evidence that supports or refutes this theory. (We will discuss guys and homosexuality in chapter 3.2.)

The second androgen wash starts with the hypothalamus. Located at the base of the brain, the hypothalamus serves as the command center in the grand

orchestration of the process of puberty. *The hypothalamic-pituitary-gonadal axis* (HPG axis) **(see fig. 4)** sets off a series of physiological events that change a boy's body into a sexually reproductive man.

When secondary male sex characteristics are evidenced and a guy becomes a functioning (as opposed to practicing), sexually reproductive male, then puberty is complete. His body will peak and the hormones used for this rapid growth process will maintain his sexual drives and reproduction **(see fig. 3).** For the most part, puberty ends around age 15 to 18.

THINK ABOUT IT!

Testosterone is the hormone that controls sex drive, as well as God-instilled sexual thought. During puberty a male teenager is experiencing testosterone overload, which is essential for his physical and sexual development. Because youth workers are so conscientious to present guys with a standard of sexual purity, we often give the impression that sexual thought is equivalent to lust. But we rarely define lust, nor do we validate sexual thought as being good. There is such a thing as pure sexual thought, and we need to help guys discover that fact.

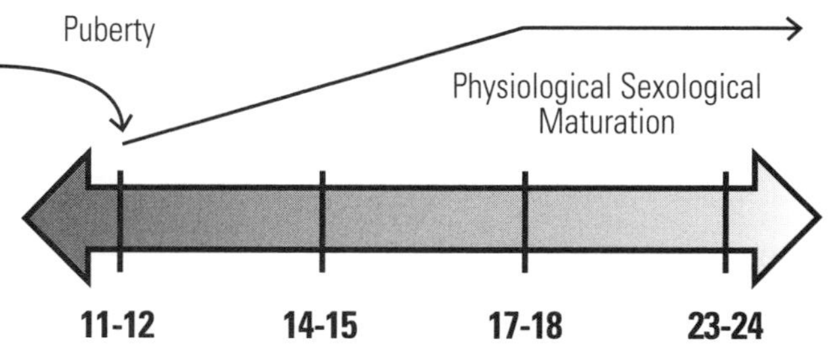

Figure 3

MANIFESTATIONS OF MALE PUBERTY

Secondary sex characteristics (the physical changes that occur in a guy's body apart from his reproductive system, giving him the physiological appearance of an adult male body) begin to appear before primary sex characteristics do. This fact often confuses youth workers and parents because they believe the words *primary* and *secondary* refer to sequence or to internal and external reproductive organ development in the male.

The development of primary sex characteristics involves the physical changes and maturation of the reproductive system or the primary sexual system—whether internal or external. This stage reaches its end

when a guy experiences his first seminal emission and ejaculation. This indicates that his reproductive system is functioning and he's a sexually reproductive male.

HYPOTHALAMIC-PITUITARY-GONADAL AXIS (HPG AXIS)

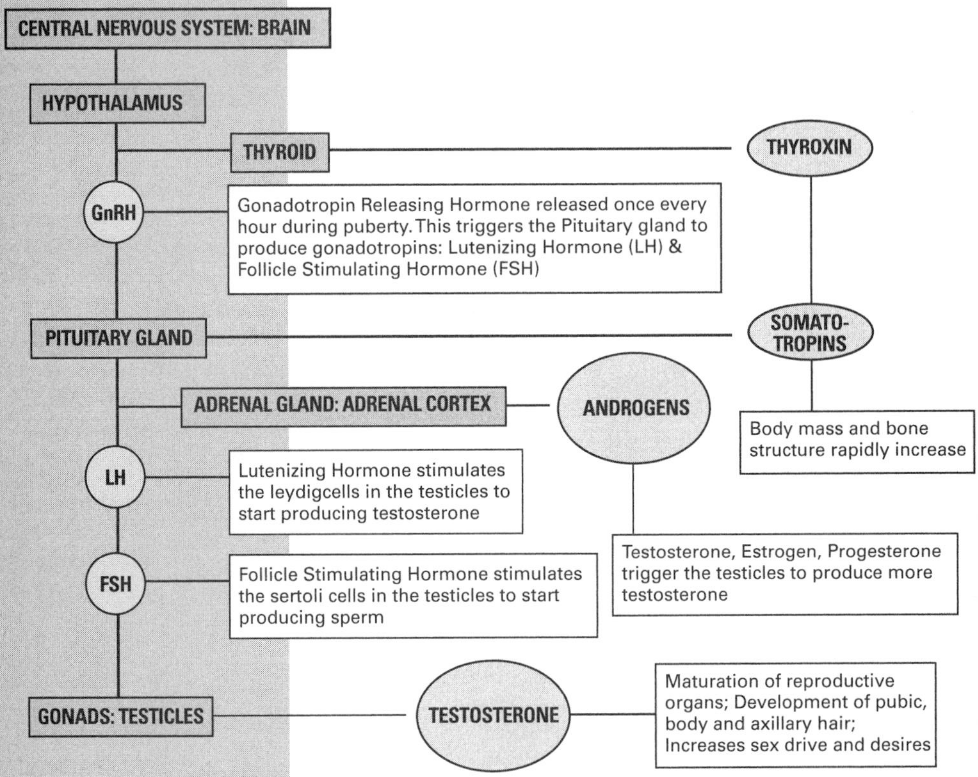

CENTRAL NERVOUS SYSTEM: BRAIN

HYPOTHALAMUS

THYROID — THYROXIN

GnRH — Gonadotropin Releasing Hormone released once every hour during puberty. This triggers the Pituitary gland to produce gonadotropins: Lutenizing Hormone (LH) & Follicle Stimulating Hormone (FSH)

PITUITARY GLAND — SOMATO-TROPINS — Body mass and bone structure rapidly increase

ADRENAL GLAND: ADRENAL CORTEX — ANDROGENS — Testosterone, Estrogen, Progesterone trigger the testicles to produce more testosterone

LH — Lutenizing Hormone stimulates the leydigcells in the testicles to start producing testosterone

FSH — Follicle Stimulating Hormone stimulates the sertoli cells in the testicles to start producing sperm

GONADS: TESTICLES — TESTOSTERONE — Maturation of reproductive organs; Development of pubic, body and axillary hair; Increases sex drive and desires

Figure 4

Now that we understand the process, stages, and facilitating agents of puberty, let's look at the physical outcomes. If you're a guy, this may take you down memory lane. Some try to forget this stage ever happened. If you're a female, then welcome to the complex, biological shifts that have occurred inside the men in your life. I trust both males and females will be fascinated by the mystery and wonder of a Creator God at work.

2.2 SECONDARY SEX CHARACTERISTICS

Nathan came bounding into my office with his completed application for our youth group's summer mission project. We were going to Venezuela to help renovate a Christian boarding school in the Andes Mountains. The applications were due in September, along with a covenant (signed by the applicant and his parents) that spelled out all the requirements during the months before the trip in order to keep a spot on the team.

Nathan was an incoming freshman. You could tell by his social and cognitive immaturity, but you would never know it from his stature. He was about two feet taller than other guys his age, and he was shaving, which put him ahead of some of our juniors and seniors. Despite these physical changes, his actions still reflected those of a boy about two years behind his age group.

Everything seemed to be in order with his application, and he was very excited to be considered for acceptance on the team. But as my staff put together the team roster, we came to the overwhelming consensus that Nate needed the team more than the team needed Nate. So we accepted him as part of our ministry team that year.

Nate responded with enthusiasm throughout the fall semester. He jumped through all the training hoops, Bible studies, Scripture memory, and countless hours of service. Then, toward the beginning of the spring semester, Nate became distant. He began to lose passion for the project, and he became uneasy

when confronted about it. Something just didn't feel right.

One Sunday Nate followed me back to my office. "I can't go on the team retreat next month," he said. I reminded him that he'd agreed to all the requirements of the mission project. He stammered to find some excuse, eventually throwing the blame on his parents. That didn't work because his parents had signed the covenant, too. I stood my ground; Nate left agreeing that he would resolve the problem before the retreat.

During a team meeting the next week, Nate became more disengaged as we talked about the details of the coming retreat. I confronted him after the meeting, and he said he was thinking of quitting the team. He began to grab for reasons, rationalizing that the money he was saving for this trip could be put toward a car he'd been dreaming of buying. I was convinced that something wasn't right, and I was determined to get to the bottom of it. I made arrangements to meet with Nate for lunch later that week.

As we talked I began to deduce that Nathan was afraid to go on the retreat. I did a quick mental evaluation and recalled that Nate had never been on any of our retreats or camps. He had conveniently been busy each time. I wondered if Nate suffered from enuresis (bedwetting), a disorder that some guys his age experience. Wisdom mandated it was best not to ask him outright, but to see if I could get more information from his mother.

The next time I saw Nate's mom, I told her about her son's desire to quit the team and asked if there was anything I should know. It would have been the perfect cue for a parent to privately disclose her son's problem, but Nate's mom seemed surprised. Nate hadn't indicated to her that he didn't want to go on the retreat, and she couldn't think of any reason why he wouldn't want to be on the team. I informed her that I would hold him to his commitment, and she dismissed it as immaturity.

At this point I should share some of Nate's family background. His parents isolated themselves and their children from the surrounding culture, believing it was evil. As a result there was no television in the home, popular music was banned, movies were avoided, and so on. Nate's mother suffered from bouts of bipolar disorder; his dad was very timid, self-absorbed, and socially inept. They held to some very extreme, nontraditional views regarding medicine, education, and the government. Consequently, Nate had never attended an organized school—instead, he was homeschooled. Not a bad thing, except for the fact that outside of a weekly youth group meeting, he wasn't allowed to take part in organized sports or other kinds of social experiences with his age group. His entire social frame of reference was his six siblings—four sisters and one brother 10 years younger than he. Needless to say, Nate did not have a typical outlook on life.

After observing the reaction of Nathan's mother, I knew the boy wasn't suffering from enuresis, and he wasn't giving me all the pieces regarding his dilemma. I pushed for an answer, and Nate finally began to reveal the truth. "I'm different from the other guys," he said quietly. I wanted to understand, so I asked what he meant. He went on to say he was different "down there," pointing to his crotch. Immediately I thought he meant he wasn't circumcised. So I asked him, but he didn't know what circumcision was. After I explained it, he said he *was* circumcised.

I didn't expect what came next: Nate said he was embarrassed because he had hair "down there." As we talked I became more enlightened. Nate had never been in any situation where he'd been required to disrobe in front of his peers, nor had he been to see a medical doctor for an exam. His only frame of reference on male physiology was his little brother at bath time. Because Nate was shaving and the other guys

in the group weren't, he thought they were all hairless like his little brother. Nate was greatly distressed, believing he'd have to change and shower in front of other guys who looked like boys when he did not.

I assured Nathan that he was normal. He didn't quite believe it; plus, he'd still never been required to undress with another person in the room. But I knew how to help Nate. There was a sports club right next to our church. I had a good relationship with the owner, and he allowed my staff and me to bring the kids there to swim, play tennis and racquetball, and use the facilities on a regular basis.

Nate and I decided to meet on Saturday morning and go over to the club. I also invited two other guys from the ministry team to join us—two guys I knew to be the least modest. These guys would start taking their clothes off before they got to the locker room door, snap their towels at each other's naked backsides on the way to the showers, and stand naked in front of the mirrors while they fixed their hair. Neither one of them had a problem revealing it all. And just as I suspected, they were true to form the day Nate came along. It didn't take him very long to see that he was normal and get past his inhibitions. After that Nate remained on the team and never missed another retreat.

You'd think that in the information age of the 21st century, something like this wouldn't happen. Yet there are guys like Nathan who fall through the cracks. When puberty hits, a guy's body goes into warp speed, hurling him into the twilight zone where some parts look like a man and others still have that boyish appearance. If he's informed, a guy may believe that some of the changes his body is going through are cool. But because the growth pattern is so irregular and unique from guy to guy, he may feel awkward, unusual, self-conscious and—like Nate—abnormal.

THE GROWTH SPURT

At about age nine or 10, a boy's body begins a period of intense growth spurts. Mothers tend to notice this first, primarily because they buy their sons' clothes. Often you'll hear them comment about how their boys are growing out of a pair of pants in as little as three months. This growth spurt, while many refer to it as pre-pubescence, is actually the start of the first stage of puberty—largely the stage when secondary sex characteristics begin to develop. We'll try to look at these characteristics in the order they often occur.

Bone and Skeletal Growth

God turns on a flood of hormones that causes a guy's body to begin changing in stature. Bones are the first affected; their size makes them susceptible to rapid and pronounced change. So small bones in the hands and feet begin to develop quickly, causing boys to become clumsy and awkward. They may also feel self-conscious because their fingers and toes seem abnormally long. Thus, early-adolescent guys with tiny bodies suddenly need to wear size nine or 10 shoes. And the last thing a guy needs is for someone to draw attention to it, but parents will inevitably comment about how their son is now wearing the same shoe size as his father.

Other places where there are small bones in the body are the face and ears. While the face is very slow to develop and becomes more dramatically changed in late adolescence, even an early-adolescent guy will begin to lose his boyish features as his face becomes more angular. One feature that does change more quickly during this first stage is the shape and size of his nose. This is often the primary feature that begins to draw the line of demarcation between boyish looks and adult looks. Often his nose will start to take on the genetic predisposition of his family, as opposed to the cute button nose of childhood.

More dramatic bone growth occurs in his ears. Those three little bones in the inner ear, which regulate accurate hearing, begin to change. No change in bone growth goes smoothly, but the changes in this area of the body may cause some problems for the guy. This, along with some attention problems due to his brain development, may prevent guys from being good listeners.

As the small bones continue to develop, his larger bones follow suit. Before the four-to-six-year period of puberty ends, a guy's height may increase anywhere from three-and-a-half to five inches per year. The most dramatic growth spurt usually happens around ages 13 to 15. Along with the lengthening of his bones, they will increase in density, adding to a guy's mass and weight in adolescence. Skeletal growth is also visibly marked with the broadening of a guy's shoulders, rib cage, spine, and hips. His torso takes on a more triangular shape—smaller at the waist and hips and flaring at the shoulders. The lengthening of a guy's torso accounts for more of his height increase than the lengthening of his legs. Just when his mom thought she could keep him in a pair of pants for more than three months, she discovers she can't keep him in shirts.

While all of this is happening, especially at the onset of puberty, a guy may experience growing pains. It's often believed they're caused by the rapid growth of larger bones in the skeletal system. There is no substantial evidence to support this. Many medical professionals believe these pains are the result of advanced bone and muscle growth, which causes the guy to be more active. The activity from exercising those muscles leads to pronounced pain, similar to the pain that comes after working out. Most guys experience these pains in their legs, but they may also complain of pain in their arms and back.

After this growth spurt, a guy's bone growth continues to increase, but at a slower and less pronounced rate until he reaches about age 20 to 22, where it finally levels off. At the end of adolescence (around age 18 to 20) a guy's body releases large quantities of the male sex and growth hormones again. This time a hormone called *somatostatin* is released. This hormone has an inhibiting effect on the guy's bone growth. In other words, the hormone surge he experiences toward the end of adolescence, while it increases his sexual drive, serves as a circuit breaker to shut down the bone growth centers.

Snap, Crackle, and Pop

This change tends to take place in the middle of puberty, right around age 13 or 14. Every guy who's gone through puberty can relate to having his voice crack unexpectedly while he's speaking. There's no way to guess when it will happen, and there's no way to arrest it when it does. It occurs often during early adolescence, and sometimes even in middle adolescence. But guys only remember that it happens at the most inopportune times, such as when they're called on in class or when they're talking to girls they want to impress.

Testosterone, that powerful androgen, has a strong and direct effect on the larynx and vocal cords. As a guy's body begins producing more testosterone, his larynx starts to enlarge. This happens about the same time his penis starts to enlarge and, in fact, it kind of parallels penile growth. There's no correlation between the two, except testosterone affects the growth of both these male body parts concurrently.

The enlargement of the larynx is sometimes visible—it's the spot on the throat called the *Adam's apple*. The vocal cords stretch across the larynx, generating speech as air passes through them, and the pitch of a young man's voice is altered as these cords are stretched and relaxed over the enlarged larynx. For the most part, this is an involuntary experience. The growth hormones thicken the vocal cords, and they also change a guy's muscle mass, which means the muscles surrounding the larynx become less con-

BE AWARE...

Many times an "early bloomer" can have some problems because people will judge a book by its cover. They see this guy who is more masculine in appearance than his peers, so naturally they expect him to be just as developed emotionally, socially, cognitively, and even spiritually. So you need to keep in mind that the 13-year-old who looks like a 16-year-old may still have the social skills of an 11-year-old.

The opposite is also true for a "late bloomer." At 15 he may still have the body of a 13-year-old but the mind of a 17-year-old. These guys are often patronized, but in the end they'll frequently emerge as socially confident leaders.

YOUTH WORKER TIPS

Phone Etiquette

When I was a teenager, I hated it when people called our house and mistook me for my mother. Relatives often share familial voice patterns that make their voices sound similar. So you can never be sure whether the person you're talking to on the phone is the adolescent guy you're trying to call or one of his female family members. So when you call teenage guys, get in the habit of identifying yourself first, then ask with whom you are speaking. Never trust your inclinations. By doing this you won't embarrass the guy or find yourself trying to correct your blunder.

A "SINGING" ALERT

Sometimes guys will just stand there and not sing during worship. Many youth workers interpret a guy's lack of interest or participation as a sign of a deeper spiritual problem. In reality, he may be afraid his voice will betray him. It's not low enough to hit all the notes, and it may crack if he tries to hit the higher ones. Either way he loses, so sometimes it's just easier to shut up! If this is the case, help your guys find an alternative to singing during worship time.

trollable as well. And all of these changes happen in such a small space—the throat. No wonder his voice cracks uncontrollably!

Sometimes a guy's voice is higher pitched than he'd like it to be. So while other parts of his body make him appear manly, his voice often makes him sound mistakenly feminine. Many times the voice cracking and the higher-pitched voice that doesn't correspond to the rest of his masculine development will cause him to remain silent when he's prompted to communicate. He may also choose not to participate during the singing time because he's afraid of what may come out of his mouth. This fear is often masked by an attitude of disinterest. Guys would rather take the heat and be labeled "apathetic and disinterested" than suffer the humiliation of being viewed as less manly when their voices crack. When a guy's larynx and vocal cords finish their growth, he emerges with a lower-pitched voice.

Bigger and Better

Another manifestation of male puberty is weight increase. There are many changes that contribute to this, one being the increased bone density. In addition, his muscles must change in order to accommodate the enlargement of his frame. So with an increase in stature comes an increase in mass.

During puberty a guy's weight may go up an average of 40 to 50 pounds. For some this means their body mass can be increased almost one and a half times what it was as a boy. A guy's peak weight increase parallels his bone growth spurt. During these few years he can average about a 20-pound increase per year.[1]

Increased muscle mass often provides more opportunities for a guy because he discovers he has new physical strength and improved motor control. The clumsy feeling he had while his bone growth ran wild is now replaced with a renewed confidence from his increased muscle mass. He also realizes that he can generate and sculpt his muscles. Guys wish to appear big and strong because they notice how body definition generates attention and respect. This natural desire may cause a guy to try anabolic steroids or other muscle enhancers. However, these substances can be very dangerous if not used under the control of a physician. In principle they're a synthetic form of male growth and sex hormones, but they can be harmful to a body that's still developing. The negative side effects include testicle shrinkage, loss of sex drive, and a shutdown of the bones' growth centers.[2]

A guy's weight and mass is also increased by the growth and development of his internal organs. A guy's heart and lungs steadily grow larger. This yields a higher systolic blood pressure and a lower resting heart rate, giving him a greater capacity for blood oxygenation.[3] Testosterone also increases red blood cell production. All of this gives him a greater capacity for aerobic-based activities. This is why guys are usually able to sustain exercise more efficiently than girls.

ANOREXIA IN GUYS

Anorexia is not just a female disorder. Guys can suffer from it, too. One in 10 teenagers with eating disorders who talk with mental health professionals are guys. The primary male candidate for anorexia is an athlete who competes in weight-class sports (such as wrestling and martial arts). Often these guys are allowed to drop weight to qualify for a lighter weight class. Other athletes who attempt to lose weight so they'll be faster—swimmers, runners, soccer players—can also be at risk. An anorexic guy is unknowingly destroying the muscles his body is attempting to increase, including his heart.

Wake Up!

Parents are always concerned that their son sleeps too much. Have you ever noticed how hard it is to get a sleeping teenager out of bed? The very thing they dreaded as little boys (going to bed) becomes the activity of choice—second only to eating. This is also part of God's ingenious, creative design. With all that's going on in a guy's body during adolescence, his heart and lungs need to be paced down so his body can develop accurately. Sleep becomes the pacing agent that gives these organs essential growth time.

A guy experiences a pubertal shift in his circadian rhythms (biological clock), to prefer later bed times and rise times. A teenage guy should get about nine and one-half hours of sleep each night. When parents hear this, they ask, "Well, then why doesn't my son go to bed at a decent hour?" The reason is

due to the same body process. During the evenings (when he's supposed to be sleeping), his body begins a cycle of releasing androgens into his system to stimulate sexual development. If he's already awake, this may give him a "second wind." We've all been there, done that, and survived it.

Hair, There, Everywhere

The development of body hair is the first real visible indication that puberty has begun. In fact, the word *puberty*, derived from the Latin word *pubescere*, means "to grow hairy or to be covered with hair." Testosterone is the hormone primarily responsible for generating bodily hair growth in both males and females. But because a guy's body produces almost 20 times the testosterone his female peers produce, a guy will naturally have more body hair.

The first place hair starts to grow is directly above the penis, at the base of the abdomen. At first it appears as fine, straight, and lightly colored hair; but as it increases, it will become more dense, curly, and dark. The presence of pubic hair begins about the same time the testicles start to increase in size. As puberty progresses, pubic hair will begin to fill the pubic region, a triangular area at the base of the abdomen above the penis.

About the same time he develops pubic hair, a guy's body will start to produce body hair on the lower portion of his legs and arms. Toward the middle of puberty he may find pubic hair spreading to his thighs and lightly on his scrotum. About two years after that, the body will produce underarm hair, facial hair, chest hair (starting around the nipple), and hair along the line from his bellybutton to the pubic region.

One of the interesting events I've observed among college (late-adolescent) guys is their newfound fascination with facial hair. The once fine, light hair his dad commonly called "peach fuzz" now starts to get

coarse. In the late-adolescent developmental stage, guys produce more hair around their lips, chins, and on the sides of their faces. Inevitably, guys at this age will create contests to see who can have the most facial hair by the end of a particular month.

I meet weekly with a group of guys I mentor. We've been meeting since their freshman year in college, and they're juniors now. We have a tradition, which began during their first year in school and grew out of this facial hair contest—"No-Shave November." The guys don't shave for the whole month! And when they go home for Thanksgiving, they look more...rugged.

Some guys may get really hairy before the end of late adolescence. Hair can grow on a guy's shoulders, neck, feet and hands, back, and buttocks. Many guys don't like this, so they'll shave or use hair removal methods and products to groom these areas. Despite their efforts, the hair still returns. (By the way, it's a myth that if a guy shaves unwanted body hair it'll grow back thicker or fuller. If that were the case, fewer men would be going bald.)

Try Being in Their Skin

Puberty also affects another organ of a guy's body—his skin. A very complex series of events make a person sexually attractive. God has designed more into the mating process than we'll ever know. Scientists have discovered there is attraction between males and females as the result of pheromones that are emitted from the body. These pheromones are a hormone-based chemical unconsciously detected through the olfactory system—by smell!

Puberty is the body's way of preparing a guy to be a sexually reproductive male. So naturally he begins to develop the physical capacity to emit odor, but this odor we can detect. Ever been around junior high guys for an extended period of time? Whoa!

TANNER STAGES OF MALE PUBERTY[4]

Because puberty doesn't begin or end at the same age for everyone, clinicians trust a scale developed by J.M. Tanner. The Tanner scale helps professionals assess a young man's maturation by dividing puberty into five stages and identifying the physiological changes that should occur in each stage.

Pubic Hair Stage

Stage 1 (Pre-adolescent): Vellus over the pubes is no further developed than that over the abdominal wall, i.e., no pubic hair.

Stage 2: There is sparse growth of long, slightly pigmented, downy hair, straight or only slightly curled, appearing chiefly at base of penis.

Stage 3: Hair is considerably darker, coarser, and more curled and spreads sparsely over junction of pubes.

Stage 4: Hair is now adult in type, but the area covered by it is smaller than that in most adults. There is no spread to the medial surface of the thighs.

Stage 5 (Adult): Hair is adult in quantity and type, distributed as an inverse triangle. There is spread to the medial surface of the thighs but not up the linea alba or elsewhere above the base of the inverse triangle.

The smell can be unbearable, and what's more amazing—they *don't* smell it.

Well, here's how it works: at puberty, hormone levels in a guy's body activate the sebaceous glands located under the skin. These glands produce a fatty substance called *sebum* that travels from the glands to the pores in the skin. This is what makes a guy's skin feel oily. There's nothing a guy can do to make it go away. Hygiene helps some, but it can't stop the production of sebum. The sebum can become oxidized along with skin pigment in the pores to block the opening of the pores. This can produce blackheads. Bacteria can also invade the area; this produces pimples. No matter how hard a guy tries throughout his adolescence, he cannot avoid getting zits! It's the cursed side effect of hormones. (It's interesting to note that elderly people who go through hormonal therapy may experience bouts of acne.)

There was a deodorant commercial that showed a beautiful woman dancing. She was getting a workout because you could see (from the camera close-ups) she was perspiring. The words came on the screen saying something to the effect of: "When a woman sweats—she's sexy." Those words faded and another set replaced it saying, "When a guy sweats—he stinks!" Guys sweat a lot during puberty because their sweat glands are also developing. It's important to note that little kids sweat when their body temperature rises. Perspiring is God's natural way of cooling a body down. But when puberty hits, the sweat glands grow causing a guy to sweat in less strenuous and varied situations, and more profusely than he did when he was a little kid. A young adolescent guy may not even realize he's sweating in some places—such as under his arms, around his crotch, and his feet—until he changes his clothes or someone brings it to his attention. He's clueless because this hasn't been his experience so far. In addition, his olfactory system isn't as developed as an adult's, so he may not smell what the adults do.

Guys also sweat because their circulatory system is becoming more advanced. Circulatory changes can cause his body to perspire. In addition, a guy may find that his hands and feet start to sweat when he gets nervous. The phenomenon behind this is that his adrenal glands are actively producing a hormone called *epinephrine*. This hormone is responsible for raising his awareness of physical threat or excitement. It causes his heart to beat faster, opens the airways in his lungs, and constricts the smaller blood vessels, such as those in his hands, feet, and forehead. The constricted blood flow makes his hands and feet feel cold and clammy—just what he needs when he's out on a date! Guys often worry about this, and it creates a dreadful cycle. They don't want to be sweaty on a date, but then the stress of trying to avoid sweating produces more epinephrine—which makes him sweat more. So tell the older adolescents to relax and the younger adolescents to shower.

2.3 PRIMARY SEX CHARACTERISTICS

Brian was a typical hormonally charged, sexually driven 17-year-old guy. We developed a great mentoring relationship and would meet at least once a week. One afternoon at lunch, Brian asked me, "If two people are really in love, does it matter if they have a marriage ceremony?" His rationale was that if both agreed before God that they love each other and are committed until death separates them, then that commitment to each other and to God should be enough. I gave a theological explanation, and he agreed, but it didn't quite hit the mark. Now I was curious to know what was really behind his question.

Brian became more serious than I'd ever seen him as he leaned across the table toward me. Naturally, I leaned in, too, because I knew he was about to say something unbelievably intense. Well, Brian told me he'd read in a magazine that most guys reach their sexual peak at age 18 or 19. So he now realized that his biological clock was ticking, and before the year was out he would have "peaked" without experiencing the joys of marital bliss. His idea was to make sure that he and his girlfriend were committed as a married couple so he could reach his peak in more ways than one.

Brian misunderstood, just like many guys do, that "peaking age" has to do with the effects of sex hormones on the physical development of guys—not with pleasure, virility, performance, or sexual stamina. From about the middle of puberty and the end of early adolescence to the beginning of middle adolescence, a guy will begin developing primary sex char-

acteristics—a process that begins after the secondary sex characteristics have begun to develop. Each guy is different, so while the sequence is the same, the timing and duration of development will vary from guy to guy. Throughout the process of puberty, his body will be affected by this steady hormonal production. At the end of the process, it will peak in a phenomenological way to end puberty.

Brian spent needless hours worrying about something he didn't need to worry about.

THE TIME HAS COME...

The stage through which a guy develops primary sex characteristics is all about the development of a guy's primary reproductive organs. This includes the internal development of his prostate, seminal vesicles, and Cowper's gland, as well as the external development of his testicles, scrotum, and penis. As we have already established, a guy's body begins to develop secondary sex characteristics in the form of stature, body mass, and pubic hair prior to the development of primary sex characteristics.

In early adolescence, hourly hormonal bursts happen while he's sleeping. Later on, his body will need more hormones, so he'll have these hourly hormonal doses throughout his sleeping *and* waking hours. These hormones are the same ones that give a guy his sex drive. As Michael Gurian wrote in his book, *A Fine Young Man*, this teenage guy is getting a minimum of about seven shots of "horniness" a day. His body is shooting these hormones through his blood stream every hour. If it doesn't, his reproductive development will cease or be compromised. Now you do the math—that's a *lot* of testosterone!

Because testosterone has this effect, we need to be careful to let guys know that their sexual drives are acceptable. Often we give the impression that sex drive and lust are one and the same. Sex drive just means a guy is going to desire and *think* about sex.

He will rehearse it in his mind, develop sexual tastes, and seek relationships with attractive partners (this is part of mate selection). While lust can and may be a part of these things, they're not always lustful.

This will be covered more in depth in section 3, but for now just note that there's an incredible amount of testosterone pulsing through a guy's bloodstream, and this hormone begins the process of sexual maturation in a guy's body.

TESTOSTERONE EFFECTS

Testosterone is the androgen largely produced in the male body. It affects guys in a variety of ways:

- It matures and regulates his reproductive system.
- It has links to aggressive behavior, although not all studies show this to be completely conclusive.
- It's linked to high-risk, sensation-seeking behaviors such as reckless driving, high adventure, and so on.
- It regulates sexual appetite, meaning it's responsible for sex drive and desire in both men and women. Because a guy's body produces more testosterone, his sex drives are more frequent and intense than those of his female counterpart.
- It can regulate healthy mood levels.

EDDIE'S PROBLEM

Eddie took his relationship with God seriously, and he was determined to become a man of spiritual integrity. One day he came into my office and burst into tears because he'd asked God to take away his lust problem, and God wasn't doing it. Eddie was discouraged and disillusioned on many fronts. First he had come to believe all sexual thought was lust. He didn't know that the testosterone in his body induced sexual thought. Because he was 18 years old, his body was in overdrive. Secondly, his ignorance regarding how his body worked made him question and doubt the power of prayer and the graciousness of God. I explained to him that God wouldn't take away a natural result of his sexual maturation process because those hormones were the very things keeping him healthy and making him grow. I also assured him he wasn't living in an addictive, sinful, lust trap, and that God hadn't abandoned him.

Guys carry a lot of guilt and baggage because of the reckless, incorrect information the Christian community has perpetuated out of a fear of sexual arousal. Guys will think sexually and feel sexual because of the testosterone pulsing through their bodies.

Testicles

The first primary sexual organs to develop are the testicles. They're responsible for the production of more testosterone and the manufacturing of sperm.

As puberty progresses, his testicles will start to enlarge. When they are completely developed, his body no longer uses testosterone as a primary source of sexual development, but it will continue to use it for reproduction and sexual appetite. Therefore, his sexual *development* has reached its peak.

Many guys become concerned because one testicle can become larger than the other. This is not a problem. A guy's testicles develop independently of each other. In time both will be about the same size. Another concern is that one testicle hangs lower than the other. This is also normal and essential. God designed it this way so a guy can walk, run, sit, and function normally. If the testicles were set parallel to each other in the scrotum, a guy would live a very painful life.

The Scrotum

This is the skin sac that houses the testicles. During puberty the scrotum will become a bit more elastic and the pigmentation of the skin will start to darken. This may occur before the testicles are fully descended into the scrotum. Toward the middle of puberty, pubic hair may begin to grow on his scrotum.

The scrotum plays a huge role in sperm production. In addition to being the protective covering around the testicles, it also maintains the right temperature for the testicles to manufacture sperm. When a guy's body starts to heat up, the scrotum will become more elastic, allowing the testicles to hang lower or farther away from the heat source—his body. If the temperature is cold, the scrotum will constrict, bringing the testicles in closer to a guy's body. This is why guys experience "shrinkage" after they've been swimming.

As a guy's scrotum develops during puberty he may experience some discomfort while wearing tight underwear or pants. Wise parents may want to

TANNER STAGES OF MALE PUBERTY[2]

Because puberty doesn't begin or end at the same age for every guy, clinicians trust a scale developed by J.M. Tanner. The Tanner scale helps an adolescent professional assess the maturation of a guy by dividing puberty into five stages and identifying the physiological changes that should occur in that stage.

Genital Stages

Stage 1 (Pre-adolescent): Testes, scrotum, and penis are about the same size and proportion as those in early childhood.

Stage 2: Scrotum and testes have enlarged, and there is a change in the texture of scrotal skin and some reddening of scrotal skin.

Stage 3: Growth of the penis has occurred, at first mainly in length but with some increase in breadth. There has been further growth of the testes and the scrotum.

Stage 4: The penis is further enlarged in length and breadth, with development of glans. The testes and the scrotum are further enlarged. There is also further darkening of scrotal skin.

Stage 5 (Adult): Genitalia are adult in size and shape. No further enlargement takes place after stage 5 is reached.

buy boxers for their son at this time—just to see if he likes them! He will.

The Penis

This is the last external organ to develop. On average a guy's penis will grow about three to four inches during puberty. Teenage guys tend to worry about the size of their penis. It's reassuring to know that when most men are erect, regardless of size when not erect, their penises become about the same size.

They also tend to pick up on the message that says manliness is dependent on penis size. Some guys can internalize these messages without ever talking about it. As a result they can struggle with fears and esteem issues in painful silence. Parents, mentors, and youth workers should combat these myths by breaking the silence and discussing these issues. Sometimes all it takes is for a guy to hear a trusting voice of authority confirm the truth.

As the penis grows, the skin pigment will become darker. This may alarm a guy and his thoughts may range from thinking he has a medical problem to notions that women won't accept him because he's ugly.

While a guy's penis is developing, he'll experience frequent *erections*. This may become awkward, especially for younger guys who already believe they are the center of the universe. If they're erect, guys may feel as though the entire world can see the bulge in their pants. Many times the nervousness of the guy only draws more attention to himself (but not to his pants), but he believes he's been compromised. Reassure teenage guys they don't have to worry—their crotch is not the focal point. On the other hand, there have been occasions—such as when a guy is wearing swim trunks at camp—when it can be noticeable. A guy might not want to stand or move from a veiled position if this occurs.

Sometimes frequent erections happen without sexual stimuli. This is the result of the testosterone levels in a guy's system. It can happen if his pants are too tight or loose; if he has to urinate; if he gets nervous; if his adrenaline gets going; when he cools down after a sport (which is horrible if he's required to shower after a game); whenever his circulation gets pumping and his muscles relax; in short—when the wind shifts! In a Christian culture where sex is not talked about or where it's mostly talked about in negative terms, a guy can feel guilty for having erections.

I recently had a conversation with a 26-year-old male youth worker who asked how he should advise a 15-year-old regarding masturbation. In the middle of the conversation, he disclosed that he used to feel guilty about having so many erections while he was growing up. He'd been told that sex is a good thing, but he never knew his erections were a normal and frequent occurrence for teenage guys. And he couldn't talk about it because of the embarrassment he felt, so he just lived with the guilt and thought he was sexually perverted. We need to talk about these things with young men, especially if we believe it's a common-sense issue. Otherwise our silence carries moral value that is damaging.

YOUTH WORKER TIP

Ever find one of your male students being a wise guy at inappropriate times or when it's out of character for him, primarily when you've asked him to do something that requires him to stand or to leave the room? Don't take it personally; he may be waiting out an erection. It's possible that he's only giving you grief because he knows that if he stands up or walks away, someone will take notice. His rationale is that it's better to smart off and hope it goes away than to stand up and suffer the humiliation. Just be sensitive—chat with him while still expecting that within a few minutes, he will do exactly what you've asked him to do.

The Circumcision Effect

Beginning in the '80s and '90s, many parents didn't elect to have their male children circumcised. (Some insurance companies don't see this as a necessity and therefore don't cover the procedure.) As a result there are more and more uncircumcised guys now living in the United States. This can have a defining effect on them.

One 22-year-old guy told me he wasn't circumcised when he was born (he was an '80s child). He said this was always an issue for him because he was embarrassed about being the *different* guy in the locker room. It made his participation in sports

TREND CHECK

In studies done in 1992 and 1993, it was estimated that fewer than 15 percent of boys around the world were circumcised, compared with 80 percent of the guys in the United States. Only 40 percent of the boys in Australia and Canada, and six percent of the guys in Great Britain were circumcised.[3]

difficult. He even told me he didn't believe his college roommates (who were also his teammates in a college sport) knew he wasn't circumcised because he still avoided totally disrobing or showering in the team locker room in front of them.

Whichever way the trend shifts in the future, the guys in the minority (whether circumcised or not) may feel inferior or strange. This may become an issue that youth workers will have to be sensitive to. Once again, listening, reminding a guy that he's normal and healthy, and celebrating uniqueness can help a guy navigate this uncertain time in his life.

INTERNAL REPRODUCTIVE DEVELOPMENT

The internal male sex organs include the prostate, seminal vesicles, epididymis, vas deferens, and Cowper's gland. Each begins to grow in size and function during puberty.

As the testicles mature, they make billions of sperm. In a single 3.5cc ejaculate, there can be close to 200 million sperm. It's estimated that as a guy matures, his body begins to produce several hundred million sperm each hour.[4]

There is a popular Christian book that was written for guys that explains very dogmatically that the production of semen doesn't need to be passed through masturbation or intercourse because God takes care of the increased production of semen by allowing a guy to have a nocturnal emission. When that isn't possible, it says God has designed it so the semen will be released in the urine. If semen is being released into a guy's urine this is a dangerous disorder known as *retrograde ejaculation*.[5] If this persists, it can lead to infertility since a natural orgasm doesn't occur. Semen does not pour into the bladder so that it can be released through urination. This myth is only propagated to keep a guy in a bondage regarding their true sexual function.

Emissions, Ejaculate, and Orgasm

Anywhere from age 12 to 14 (two years into puberty), a guy will experience his first ejaculation. The first time is known as *spermarche*, and it parallels a girl's first menstruation or *menarche*. This term is only used for the very first experience that marks the onset of an ongoing sexual function. From this point on, a guy will experience *ejaculation* primarily through deliberate masturbation (from self-exploration) or accidental masturbation (while washing himself). It may also occur through nocturnal emission (commonly called *wet dream*). But regardless of how it happens, it's a sure thing that he'll experience it. For some guys it's a marked experience. For others it may happen a few times before he realizes what it is.

When a guy's body starts to produce sperm and semen, it becomes a nonstop process that will follow him until his death. A girl's body contains—from the time of her birth—all of the ova she will release until menopause. But a guy's body is different because he continually produces sperm and semen. His reproductive system stores these fluids and, in time, needs to release them. If it doesn't, then they will eventually dissipate or dissolve and be reabsorbed back into his system because sperm and semen are largely composed of protein. This can create a dilemma because an adolescent guy's body is making sperm and semen faster and in greater quantities than it can dissipate. But it can be painful for a guy to have his prostate, seminal vesicles, or epididymis engorged or what's commonly referred to as *blueball*. (This can also happen after a guy has a sexually charged experience, such as going on a date.)

When the sexual fluid storage areas of the male reproductive system engorge, his body kicks into sexual high gear by releasing more testosterone, and this peaks his sexual drives. Basically this is his body's way of urging him to do something about it before he experiences greater physiological prob-

lems (such as bacterial infections). This is one explanation as to why most guys masturbate. It's almost instinctual for guys to do this as part of the sexual maturation process, and it may be a natural way to keep them healthy and in a sexual cycle. About 95 percent of all guys masturbate, about a four to one ratio over women.

Now before we go any further, let me put a disclaimer here: the Christian community is divided regarding the morality of masturbation. Scripture is silent on this subject, which makes it a wisdom issue. There are three very distinct theological views, all of which have scriptural supports.[6] I'm not going to explore those in this book, but if you are serious about mentoring teenage guys, then you really need to think through this issue.

With that in mind, I'm not advocating one view over the other. I just want to level the playing field and create a greater understanding of teenage guys and their struggle with this issue. Because a guy's body is producing semen and sperm at such a high rate, and because testosterone also controls a guy's libido, some guys can chart a regular cycle in which their bodies need this release. A guy discovers intentionally or accidentally that masturbation relieves the sexual tension and brings pleasure in the process.

A second way his body can experience relief is through nocturnal emissions. It's a myth that nocturnal emissions are common occurrences. Some guys can experience them on a regular basis. I've talked to men who've had them so often they can almost compare it to a woman's clockwork menstruation. (By the way, these guys are not the norm by far. Some of them claim to never have experienced masturbation, which would make sense since their body has a built-in emission clock. It's as ignorant to say that masturbation makes nocturnal emissions cease as it is to say that if a guy stops masturbating or doesn't masturbate, then he'll have nocturnal emissions.) Many guys have nocturnal emissions *and* masturbate, while others who have tried to stop masturbating find that they don't have nocturnal emissions. And still other guys experience nocturnal emissions when they don't masturbate. There is no set cause and effect.

Other guys experience occasional nocturnal emissions or never experience them at all. This is more the norm among guys. Theirs can range from being a slow emission during their sleep to having an erotic dream that ends in orgasm. This type of nocturnal emission usually happens just before a guy wakes up, and it can be so arousing that it wakes him from his sleep. The former can leave a young adolescent guy thinking he's wet the bed. Many times a guy will confess he had a dream that he was going to the bathroom and found himself wet. In actuality he never passed urine but experienced a nocturnal emission.

One other disclaimer needs to be made here, this time regarding nocturnal emissions. We send a guy mixed messages about masturbation when we equate it with lust but say nocturnal emissions are acceptable. Consider this: Most anti-masturbation theorists seem to be all in favor of wet dreams. Their reasoning is that a wet dream can't be controlled, so God must be allowing it (or at least he'll be more tolerant of it). They write off a full erotic dream experience as *not* being sexual fantasy or lust. The trouble with this is that both forms of arousal stem from the same place—the mind. They accomplish the same result.[7]

This view is held by Arterburn and Stoeker in *Every Young Man's Battle*. They say nocturnal emissions kick in automatically as a natural response to normal sperm build-up. This simply isn't true.

They also don't bridge the dichotomy between conscious sexual thought (lust) of masturbation and unconscious sexual thought of nocturnal emission. They say,

GET A CLUE!

Often mothers will talk about their adolescent sons suddenly taking on a new responsibility around the house—changing their bed sheets and doing their own laundry. They don't know what's gotten into him—he's so responsible and conscientious! Maybe it's not what's gotten into him but what's coming out of him. Wet dreams can be embarrassing and will often force a guy to take charge of his own laundry. By the way—this is a good reason why parents need to teach their early-adolescent guys laundry skills and make them responsible to do their wash by design, rather than by default.

> You might wonder how such dreams can work toward purity since some of these semiconscious flights of fancy can get pretty hot and heavy! But don't forget that those hot and heavy aspects arise from what you've been feeding your mind each day. The same pure eyes and mind that keep you actively seeking release during the day will limit the impurity that your mind can use in your dreams at night. *These dreams will be dramatically purer in scope and content than you now realize.*[8] (emphasis mine)

That's where the authors leave the issue. They never explain how a nocturnal emission can be "dramatically purer in scope and content." And it's said with such authority that nobody questions it. So most guys believe themselves to be perverts because they have a dream involving intercourse with some attractive girl from their school and then have a nocturnal emission as a result. How could this be purer in scope? He won't relate it on a personal attraction scale? How could this be purer in content? He won't dream with detail? And what do you do with the guy who doesn't feed his libido but still has nocturnal emissions?

One guy told me about the turmoil he felt because he was having nocturnal emissions. He said he felt guilty, awkward, and ashamed when he saw the girl who appeared in his dream. This guy wasn't into porn. His family guarded the television and radio. How could his nocturnal emission be any purer in scope and content?

Once again we need to exercise caution when we dogmatically tell a guy that a nocturnal emission is God's way of allowing sexual release but masturbation is not. The only difference between the two is that masturbation is engaged in consciously. It seems ridiculous to overlook the similarities. And a guy could create a strong argument for masturbation, saying that having control over one's mind is more acceptable according to Scripture.

Emission must and does physiologically happen. The final way it occurs is through regular intercourse. We definitely have theological boundaries and scriptural support for this issue. While there is often more peer pressure put on guys than girls to lose their virginity and be sexually active, guys are still within the moral constraint to remain pure before marriage. And because it's more acutely defined than the acceptability of wet dreams and masturbation, it's less likely that a guy will engage in intercourse to achieve emission. This topic will be covered further in chapter 3.1.

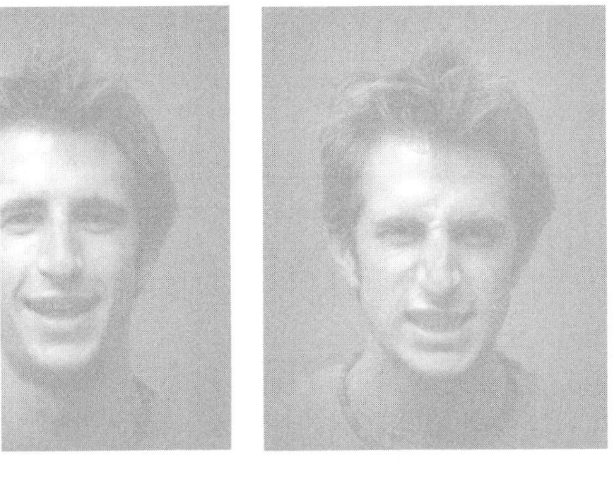

SECTION THREE

THE TEENAGE GUY'S SEXUALITY (SEXUAL IDENTITY DEVELOPMENT)

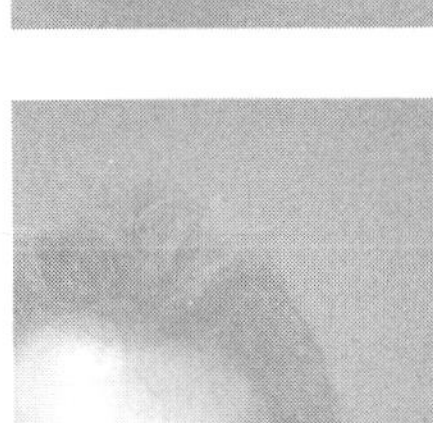
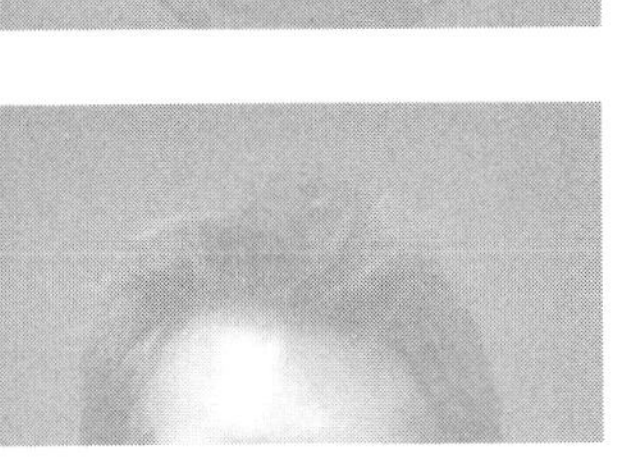
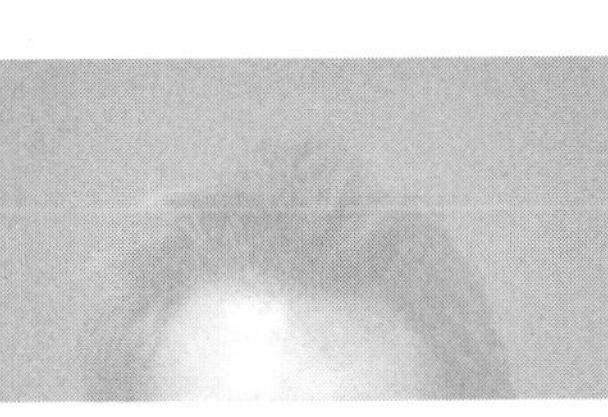

3.1 GUYS AND SEX

Guys are fascinated by, attracted to, and desirous of sex. Say the word *sex* around a group of guys, and they come alive, grunt, cheer, whoop, and holler as if sex were every man's battlefield or arena of conquest and adventure. But they react that way because they're conditioned to do so.

Guys receive mixed messages about their sexuality from the world around them. They hide behind myths that keep them in bondage about what's truly taking place in their bodies and what they're told—often erroneously—should take place. The Christian community also buys into many of these messages and then imposes additional myths and unnatural expectations on guys that constantly keep them bound in a sexual double jeopardy.

Let's sort through all of this.

TESTOSTERONE: SUPERHUMAN HORMONE OR POISON POTION?

We've given guys the impression that testosterone is like the elixir that Dr. Jekyll took before he turned into Mr. Hyde. It's viewed as the most radical, being-altering, wonder hormone of all time, with positive and negative effects. Feeble boys become manly men because of it. Sexual virility is defined by it. Real men drink a glass of it every morning for breakfast because, after all, there is more testosterone in a guy's bloodstream than...well, blood, of course!

Testosterone, it's said, will transform guys into dashing, sexually virile, potent superstars who single-handedly fight international wars while making

WHY ARE GUYS ALWAYS GRABBING THEMSELVES?

Without getting into the moral or socially acceptable realms of the issue, there are two reasons a guy does this. First and foremost, he's adjusting himself. Because a guy's genitalia are external to his body, there are a number of factors that force him to readjust. Walking, sitting, or any kind of movement can make things uncomfortable down there—even little boys learn they have to fix that spot. Sometimes a guy's boxers, briefs, or pants can be irritating if his genitals aren't situated correctly. The penis is highly sensitive; at times a guy's clothing can rub against him, creating an irritating sensation. The quick solution—grab it and fix it.

Another adjustment issue is the fact that a guy's scrotum is flexible, regulating the temperature of his testicles by either becoming more elastic (allowing the testicles to hang farther from his body) or becoming tighter (bringing the testicles closer to his body). This can be an unpleasant sensation, but a quick tug will fix the problem.

CONTINUED >

passionate love to beautiful women (at least four or five at a time).

Testosterone, it's also said, will transform guys into Jack the Ripper, a sexual super-deviant who lurks in the sexual shadows waiting to take advantage of, conquer, and prey on beautiful women (at least four or five at a time).

Either way you look at them, both of these views boost a young man's ego because they make a guy sexually "super." Men like to be thought of as sexually virile. Virility also reinforces the encoded messages that say men are powerful. Men *want* to be seen as sexual machines that are fueled by the wonder hormone.

Am I exaggerating? Consider this: most guys seem to believe the center of their being is just south of their belt line—and they cheer and yell when sex is mentioned because they're told they are testosterone-infused. Testosterone does have a dramatic effect on a guy's sexual development and desires, but we tend to give it deifying qualities.

This hormone physiologically changes boys into men, but with no more metamorphic power than estrogen changes girls into women. It also evenly regulates a healthy sex drive in a guy. (Rightfully, it does this more in males than it does in females because a guy's body produces more testosterone—but not so much that he becomes obsessed with sex.) Testosterone does have a powerful effect on a guy's body, but not to the extent that we elevate it.

There are two extremes in exalting the power of testosterone. One is that it turns a guy's sexual drive into something to be envied and indulged. I watched this play out not too long ago at a large hotel-conference center. That weekend a Big Ten college football game between rival schools was scheduled, and collegians filled the hotel the night before the game so they could attend this historic event. I love students,

CONTINUED >

A second reason a guy does this is bravado, pure and simple. Some guys (not all) see a full-on crotch grab as a salute to their male potency.

Now you female readers may be asking, "Okay, so why do guys grab *each other*?" Well, they really don't *grab* each other. They more or less flick, jab, or tap each other in an act of sparring, a test of their reflexes, or pure one-upmanship. Guys know this area of their bodies is the most vulnerable. A slight tap can put a man out of commission for a few minutes. So a guy can prove himself to be faster, stronger, and just more *manly* if he either intercepts the strike on the defensive, or if he makes the hit on the offensive.

Think of it as being the equivalent to what happens between male members of the same species in the animal kingdom. They're simply showing themselves to be the better and more virile male.

so a friend and I decided to have dinner in the lobby café and watch these kids come and go. Shortly after we got our food, a group of about eight guys took residency at the tables on either side of us. They'd also decided to watch the students—but they were there to watch the girls.

They called to the ones they knew, swooned over the ones they wanted to know, and applauded each other when any girl showed interest. These guys knew a lot of the girls, and many of the young women reciprocated their interest. (I should add that these guys weren't being sexually inappropriate, nor were they sexually harassing anyone. They never degraded the girls, nor made a single catcall.)

But one guy who was sitting closest to my chair started a conversation with me. He commented how men (referring to his band of brothers) just "gotta love being testosterone charged." To him, testosterone made these college guys strong, attractive, young, alive, virile, manly, uninhibited, engaging, desirous, with an irresistible aura. They'd experienced the elixir of virility, and gods were born. They'd bought into the deification of testosterone.

Society sends a message that guys have the right to play out their sexual bravado because of their testosterone levels. Subsequently, a guy has to present himself as more sexually driven than he really is because, after all, testosterone does that to a guy—doesn't it?

Testosterone as the Villain

Some Christians also buy into the testosterone deification theory. But we present it as super-sexually negative. We fear testosterone. We say it's so powerful that every man must battle it or it will unleash the out-of-control, sexual Mr. Hyde who lurks in the recesses of a young man's loins. We swing the pendulum the opposite direction, deifying testosterone as something to be feared, battled, and constantly repressed.

I've talked to hundreds of young guys in bondage to this notion. They're exhausted and spiritually defeated because they've been told that sexual drive, desire, or thoughts are all forms of lust. They've read books about dating that tell them not to; books about sexual purity that make sex anything but pure; and books about guys that give the impression that everything sexual within them is a dangerous, ravenous, demonic, overtaking battle that must be aggressively waged. These texts are built around the premise that a guy—who is created by God as a sexual being—should *only* be sexual when he's married. Until that time, he must battle the testosterone, or it will make him sexually impure. Guys come to believe that the slightest sexual tinge is the beginning of a cancerous spot that must quickly be eradicated. For a good number of Christian guys, all of their spiritual energy is consumed by eliminating sexual desire from their minds and bodies. This is nothing but a form of bondage. Guys are attempting the impossible—to be without testosterone.

Let's not deify testosterone as a vilifying force. This hormone upon which an adolescent guy depends for his physical and sexual development is the same hormone that's responsible for sex drives and desires that are designed, created, and sanctioned by God. In other words, they are *good*—because everything God creates is good (Genesis 1).

We need to teach guys how to *think* sexually pure (by this I mean they can think a lot about sex and still know that it's pure). That doesn't mean they have to ignore sexual desire or drive. It doesn't mean they'll never play out sexual experiences in their minds. (Sexual rehearsal is also a God-designed part of good sexuality. In fact, it's instinctual.) If we continue to give the impression that all sexual thought is lust and should be avoided, we become false teachers who cause these young guys to stumble in the name of a

faulty righteousness. We are warned that it would be better for us "to have a large millstone hung around [our] neck[s] and to be drowned in the depths of the sea" (Matthew 18:6).

This view is dangerously and recklessly proposed by Stephen Arterburn and Fred Stoeker in their best-selling book, *Every Young Man's Battle*. They propose that young men do all they can to eliminate their sex drive (or "Mr. Sex Drive," as they call it). They compare it to a sumo wrestler who needs to be knocked out of the ring. In their defense, they believe there is a God-given sex drive—calling it a *natural baseline*[2]—but they never define it, celebrate it, nor empower or encourage guys to explore it. They spend the majority of the time bashing sex drive and propagating a fear that it will wreck a guy's life. They advocate that a sex drive is a wicked thing that teenage guys feed. According to them, you can feed a lustful sex drive with everything from pornography and watching a girl's track meet to mental fantasies and watching movies such as *Dead Poets Society* (because it contains a scene of boys looking at a *Playboy* centerfold).[3]

I agree with the authors that there are God-mandated sexual boundaries that must be maintained for sexual purity. I also agree that sexual purity is a mind issue and there are deviant unacceptable sexual stimuli (such as pornography) that can pervert a sex drive. But *Every Young Man's Battle* throws out the baby with the bath water. A God-given sex drive can and should grow strong. It shouldn't be starved (by pushing out any sexual thought, desire, feelings, or the things that may incite them) or perverted.

While testosterone ignites a guy's libido, his sexual bravado is shaped by more than that. And other factors play into the development of a guy's sexual identity. I'll get to that in a second, but first I want to make sure the playing field regarding testosterone is leveled.

Not Good or Bad—It Just Is

Previously I described in some detail the physiological effects of testosterone. This hormone sets physical sexual maturation in motion. It also maintains sexual reproduction by keeping a guy sexually potent (i.e., his body is producing sperm and semen), regulating his sexual cycle of emission, and giving him a consistent, God-ordained sexual drive and desire. That means he'll have sexual thoughts, a sexual appetite, and sexual rehearsal (sometimes called "fantasy").

Thinking sexual thoughts originates from God's sexual design for guys. Therefore, according to Philippians 4:8 (NASB), they can think sexual thoughts that are true, honorable, right, lovely, of good repute, excellent, and even pure. To lead guys to believe anything other than this is *not* true, honorable, right, and so on.

How can this be? Perhaps we need to start with the premise that much of a guy's sexual thinking is purer than we believe because it's induced and regulated by a hormone that God put into his body. Keep reading; we'll discuss this further later on in this chapter. But for now, realize that we give testosterone more authority than it deserves.

IDENTITY AND MESSAGES OF VIRILITY

The media often capitalizes on myths about masculinity that send guys faulty or mixed messages. These myths are ego feeding, meaning we like them, and we believe them because they inflate our sense of self. As a teenage guy is formulating his masculine identity, he's bombarded with these myths that are never confronted nor put into right perspective. He's faced with a dilemma: either buy into it or feel abnormal. Most of the time a guy realizes these notions are not real *for him*, so he just plays along, puts on the mask of sexual bravado, and then perpetuates the myth as an adult. Male youth workers are notorious for this. We tend never to question the things we

hear that feed our sexual egos, and then we use them as authoritative support in a talk directed against healthy sexual development. Consider the following myths.

Myth #1: Guys have a sexual thought every four seconds. Wow! This either makes a guy a sexual god or a sexual pervert. I've heard this said before with such authority that I always want to ask the guy who says it if *he* has a sexual thought every four seconds. But I know that would backfire because answering affirmatively gives the impression of sexual virility. If the statement is said in the light of good sexual morals, the orator gets the added bonus of being a sexual stud *and* a super Christian by exercising *incredible godly discipline* every four seconds. (By the way, if I were to ask the question, or if I admitted that I *don't* have a sexual thought every four seconds, then I also expose myself as not being a "real man." Like most sexual myths, it becomes a catch-22 that perpetuates the lie.)

If a guy really had a sexual thought every four seconds, he wouldn't be capable of thinking rationally or reasoning soundly. Do the math: imagine you are engaged in an hour-long conversation with a normal teenage guy about, let's say, fantasy football. Are we really to believe that in the course of that hour, his attention will be diverted toward sexual things 900 times? That would definitely redefine *fantasy* football. I've never experienced that. And for the most part, guys can focus for long periods of time without hitting a sexual speed bump every four seconds.

If we apply the same mathematics to the natural waking hours in his day, this guy would have had 13,500 sexual thoughts before his bedtime. Doesn't leave much room for anything else, does it? But it does make a guy a sexual superstar. It also makes him abnormal if we propagate this myth as being truth. Guys think about sex often, but it's not the all-consuming subject on their minds. If I were to say that to a group of guys, then some wise guy would

jokingly say, "Well, it's the all-consuming subject on *my* mind!" And that guy would have proved my point exactly—EGO! The message is simple and distorted: guys must be sexual superstars!

Myth #2: Guys want sex all the time. When I was doing my post-doctoral rotation through the psychology department at the Sexual Dysfunction Center of Loyola University's Stritch Medical Center, I discovered that almost as many guys as women, if not more, refuse to have sex with their partners. We never see a male character on TV or in the movies saying, "Not tonight. I have a headache." If presented with the option for sex, a guy is always portrayed as being sexually ready, regardless of the circumstances or environment. Sitcoms play on this myth all the time. Just give the cue and a guy is running to the bedroom, undressing as he goes. This myth gives the impression that guys are sexual machines who would never let a sexual opportunity pass them by.

This myth makes guys look like mindless, undiscerning beings whose brains are in their pants. Think about some of the typical sex scenes from movies and television shows—sex occurs in the closet at a friend's wedding; in the back inventory room of a steel factory during working hours (while all the other workers are still on the job on the factory floor); even in the backseat of a car on the holding deck of a ship. I can name at least four or five recent movies that portray guys as sexual hounds who are ready to go at a moment's notice. Or they're sexually starved, so any morsel they can get they attack like a school of piranha. The media paints this picture well, reinforcing this myth all the more by portraying guys as wanting sex so much that they'll risk their integrity, their safety, and—if need be—their *lives* for that moment of pleasure.

Youth pastors reinforce this myth by telling guys they are sexual machines that can't be stopped once they get running. If I had a dollar for every time I've heard a guy's sexual desire compared to a locomo-

tive, a Sherman tank, a 427 cubic inch (7 liter), V8, 500HP engine with 475 pounds of torque, or some other piece of macho machinery, I'd be a wealthy man. Guys are led to believe that this fine-tuned, turbo-charged, sexual engine is ready to go at any—and *every*—moment.

So teenage guys are conditioned to believe that men are supposed to always be ready to engage in sexual situations. They see abstinence as something that only hinders the very thing they've been led to believe they need as much as they need oxygen. So for a guy who is sexually abstinent, it's as though he's holding his breath sexually. In his mind, some day (most likely on his wedding day) he will explode with a violent exhale and then have sex as often as he takes a breath.

I tell guys that sex, like everything else in life that is good, can be satisfying—meaning, when you have it available to you all the time, you find you don't need it as much as you once thought you did. One group of guys couldn't believe this was true because they'd rather believe they are sexual machines. So they put this premise to the test. They decided to ask their buddy who'd recently married. Surprisingly, he was honest with them. He confirmed that there are times he doesn't want sex. He also told them he was the first one who said "not tonight" in his marriage. Then he put it in perspective: "Now that I'm married, I know sex is a possibility anytime. So if I don't feel like it tonight, I know it will still be there tomorrow." Most guys respond with, "That will *never* happen to me!" because they've been led to believe they're sexually *more* than they really are.

This ego-inflating myth has two very destructive byproducts. First, it builds up sexual intimacy as the mother of all human experiences. Guys believe this will be the ultimate height of their human existence: fireworks will go off, angelic choirs will sing, and they'll have an out-of-body experience. (And because they are manly, they will naturally take their

partner with them.) In reality, some guys come away from their sexual experiences disillusioned. But the catch-22 plays in again—he can't talk about it because he may appear sexually incompetent. After all, guys want sex all the time, right? The truth is, sex is not the end-all of human experiences. And young married men have confessed to me that they like sex and think it's great, but they believed it was going to be something more than they experienced.

Second, this myth can lead to marital problems. I was meeting with a young (barely out of late adolescence) married guy who informed me that he was experiencing erectile dysfunction that prevented intercourse. Through proper therapeutic intervention, it came to light that he believed something was wrong with him because at times he wasn't interested in sex at all. If a guy is conditioned to buy into this myth about wanting sex all the time and then his experience runs counter to it, he believes there must be something wrong with him, his partner, or his marriage. To complicate matters, his wife also buys into the myth, so she believes there is something wrong with him, too. This can lead to sexual dysfunction.

By the way, the variation on this myth is that once the machine gets going, it doesn't stop. I hear guys talk about how they can't wait to have sex all the time—*four or five times a day*! Guys seriously believe their bodies and sexual stamina can sustain this. They believe they will wear their women out. Most times men don't correct this, or if they do, they say something such as, "You'll be lucky to get it at all," making it appear to be a female problem. The variation on the myth is ego inflating for manhood. To correct this urban legend would mean men aren't capable of the perpetual sexuality they've bought into. The catch-22 applies here, too: what sexually competent guy would say that it can't be done? The truth lies in a guy's refraction time (i.e., the time it takes after orgasm when a person's body can become sexually aroused again). While a woman's body can have

multiple orgasms (because God wired her to have a very short refractory time), a guy's body is built the opposite way. In truth, it's women who can have sex four or five times in a night, not men.

Myth #3: Guys are more sexually stimulated through their eyes. First of all, the primary sex organ is the brain. That's where sexual arousal begins.

Secondly, sexual arousal for a guy is very different than it is for a girl. This was already illustrated in our discussion about refractory time. The beginning stage of arousal is called the "excitement stage." This stage is very short for a man. He can become fully aroused and reach climax (the orgasmic stage of arousal) in a matter of minutes. The amount of time between arousal and orgasm in a guy's excitement stage is similar to a girl's refraction time in the resolution stage of arousal—meaning, he can get things going faster, but she can maintain it longer. A girl is different in the excitement stage because she has a much longer arousal time before she can reach climax.

Now we can debunk this myth. Guys are sexually stimulated quickly because their brains quickly process sexual information and direct their bodies into the stage of arousal. In addition, when a guy becomes sexually aroused, he has a defined physiological event—an erection. As soon as a guy's brain begins to process sexual information and trigger arousal, he can become fully erect in seconds. (Back to an earlier myth, imagine what would happen to a guy's body if his brain were processing sexual information every four seconds!)

The brain is an amazing sexual organ. It can trigger sexual arousal through all the senses, not just sight. Guys can be equally stimulated by odors—a girl's perfume and even her pheromones, those nonconscious odors that create arousal. Guys can be stimulated by sound. This is why guys are equally susceptible to phone-sex lines as they are to pornographic Web sites. Psychic stimulation, or stimula-

tion that starts in the brain, includes all of the ways in which the brain processes sexual stimuli: visual, auditory, tactile, olfactory, gustatory (taste), memory, logic, and imagination. So a guy is not more aroused by sight—he's just more easily aroused, period. And the visual process (think about it) is just the easiest way that sexual stimuli can be *marketed* to him.

It's dangerous to lead a guy to believe that he's more easily stimulated by sight because then he learns to guard the wrong organ. Instead of teaching guys to guard their minds, we teach them not to look. We forget that Satan also knows how a guy's body is wired. So while the guy "isn't looking," Satan can hit him from another direction. This is illustrated in Proverbs 7.

> My son, keep my words and store up my commands within you. Keep my commands and you will live; guard my teachings as the apple of your eye. Bind them on your fingers; write them on the tablet of your heart. Say to wisdom, "You are my sister," and call understanding your kinsman; they will keep you from the adulteress, from the wayward wife with her seductive words. At the window of my house I looked out through the lattice. I saw among the simple, I noticed among the young men, a youth who lacked judgment. He was going down the street near her corner, walking along in the direction of her house at twilight, as the day was fading, as the dark of night set in. Then out came a woman to meet him, dressed like a prostitute and with crafty intent. (She is loud and defiant, her feet never stay at home; now in the street, now in the squares, at every corner she lurks.) She took hold of him and kissed him and with a brazen face she said: "I have fellowship offerings at home; today I ful-

> filled my vows. So I came out to meet you; looked for you and have found you! I have covered my bed with colored linens from Egypt. I have perfumed my bed with myrrh, aloes and cinnamon. Come, let's drink deep of love till morning; let's enjoy ourselves with love! My husband is not at home; he has gone on a long journey. He took his purse filled with money and will not be home till full moon." With persuasive words she led him astray; she seduced him with her smooth talk. All at once he followed her like an ox going to the slaughter, like a deer stepping into a noose till an arrow pierces his liver, like a bird darting into a snare, little knowing it will cost him his life. Now then, my sons, listen to me; pay attention to what I say. Don't let your heart turn to her ways or stray into her paths. Many are the victims she has brought down; her slain are a mighty throng. Her house is a highway to the grave, leading down to the chambers of death.

This passage demonstrates the rapid downward spiral of a young man falling into sexual sin. It starts not with him looking *at* sexually charged material, but rather looking *for* sexual adventure. His feet take him to places where he shouldn't be. The spiral generates rapidly when he decides to engage in the sexual conquest. From that point on, everything from touch to smell to reason and rationalization becomes a factor in his demise.

Guys need to learn that sexual arousal is not wrong, and that the things they see *may* arouse them. The discipline of guarding one's mind involves understanding the process of arousal and setting boundaries about pursuing sexual adventure. [*Let me make another disclaimer here: I'm not saying guys shouldn't discipline their eyes. I strongly advo-*

cate that they should. *Yet we need to teach guys that arousal isn't the problem. It's the pursuit of sexual adventure that needs to be curbed.*]

The most common type of pornography is visual. Many guys who struggle with porn don't partake in it because guys are more visually stimulated. They do it because they love the sexual adventure. Most guys tell me the problem occurs when they're restless and bored at night, when they're winding down, and when they're feeling tired. These times illustrate the complex conditioning of a guy. His identity is wired for competition or adventure—for the hunt. In addition, he's wired sexually. Porn offers a gratification of both those dominant masculine needs.

Frank Hajcak and Patricia Garwood offer some insight on this issue in a journal article entitled, "Quick-Fix Sex: Pseudosexuality in Adolescents":

> We also know that some adolescents may have sex when the real needs they seek to satisfy may be to increase self-esteem, alleviate a sense of loneliness, meet societal expectations of what it means to be "masculine" or "feminine," express anger, or escape from boredom. During adolescence and throughout life, sex may be used as a way of expressing and satisfying nonsexual needs. Using sex in this way, however, may not meet such needs, and as a society we have a responsibility to teach our youth about this very human aspect of sexual expression.[4]

Sex used to meet non-sexually needs

Pornography has become a great issue with adolescent guys. At no other time in the history of our civilization has it been easier for guys to secure pornographic material than it is today. Online porn sites make it available anytime and anywhere. They also make it easy for a young guy to access it privately, consistently, and be exposed to more sexual situations and perversions than ever imagined. Guys can

even access porn on their cell phones. This easy accessibility has neutralized the taboo that used to exist in our society regarding porn. For high school guys, porn can rank high among their regular online activities. It's also become so acceptable among college guys that many will plan activities and conversations around it. This culture of porn includes rituals (like warning roommates not to enter the room while one is watching), pirating videos for friends, weekly features, and so on. What was once shaming has become a lofty, manly, bravado-inflating experience for late-adolescent guys. Some have even told me that their parents (both fathers and mothers) and even a grandmother purchased their porn subscriptions for them.

I was talking with a young guy who was struggling with his desire to look at porn. He'd tried everything to eliminate the problem: he moved the computer out of his bedroom, but still found ways to access the sites when his parents weren't aware. He loaded software onto the computer that would either block the Web sites or notify others that he was looking at them. But he found ways to end-run those deterrents as well. He confessed the problem to his accountability group, but they couldn't do anything about it. As we talked, he grieved over the fact that he was too visually aroused and he said he wished God could change that. I challenged that notion and redirected his thinking by pointing out that all of the attempted "road blocks" he'd put in place to eliminate the inappropriate behavior only made the hunt or adventure a greater challenge for him. He was, in fact, "winning" each time he found a way to look at porn.

As we talked he began to notice another pattern—he didn't seek it out as much when he was involved in the school play. Then his attention was diverted, and he had to guard his time because of rehearsals. He was often going over lines and scenes in his head, which also served to guard his mind. Basi-

GUYS AND PORNOGRAPHY

- Studies revealed that 75 percent of 18-to-24-year-olds (late-adolescent guys) visit online porn sites monthly, representing one-fourth of the visitors to all Internet porn sites.
- The next largest users of porn are men in their 20s and early 30s, 66 percent of whom report being regular users of porn.
- The porn industry uses soft-core pornographic images that introduce teenage guys to porn. This creates a desire and curiosity for more.
- Today's average teenage guy is likely to have seen thousands of explicit sexual images, ranging across the spectrum of sexualities and perversions.
- Twenty years ago 1 in 5 videos were categorized as "adult." Today more than 800 million pornographic videos are rented annually, constituting 20 percent of all video and DVD rentals.

CONTINUED >

cally, *he was pursuing a different form of adventure.* The same thing happens when a guy engages in a sport. At one time it was believed sports channeled testosterone because guys pursued sexual things less often while they were engaged in them. That isn't true; rather, it illustrates that the hunt is satisfied and the boredom is broken.

We need to help guys find adventure, break the boredom, and discipline their minds by actively replacing porn with healthy pursuits. This becomes a greater adventure when we draw a connection between the need for adventure and the need to be spiritually connected with God.

One way to do this is to challenge guys to craft, develop, and execute service projects. I know a group of guys who started working with an orphanage in Mexico. At first, they planned to do some simple repair work on the building. But they later realized there were needs for clothing, toys, supplies, and so on. So with the guidance of some loving older men, these guys put together a project. They used their talents and the times they could have spent engaged in looking at porn to raise the necessary funds. They wrote letters to businesses asking them to donate products. They trained for a marathon and recruited sponsors for every mile they planned to run. They created artwork for a show that would generate *more* funds, and on and on.

I know another small group of guys who decided to be even more adventurous. They determined to commit anonymous acts of kindness. They met a couple times a week, and in the stealth of the evening, they'd wash cars, rake leaves, shovel snow, deliver food, and leave encouraging notes on car windshields, mailboxes, and doorsteps. They developed a reputation in the community and even created a calling card to leave behind after each good deed. The amount of their involvement with porn decreased dramatically because they replaced it with another adventure—one of real value.

CONTINUED >

- Over 11,000 pornographic videos are produced annually, bringing in an estimated revenue of 5 to 10 billion dollars to the adult film industry each year.
- Pay-per-view porn comprises 80 percent of the hotel in-room entertainment revenue, and 70 percent of the total in-room revenue.
- Guys learn that according to the policy, anyone over the age of 12 can request (without parental permission) that a public library turn off the online filters from its public computers.[5]

So let's recap and bust this myth: Guys are not wired to be more visually stimulated than women. Instead they're wired to be aroused more quickly. The arousal itself isn't "wrong" because a guy's brain (his primary sex organ) is only doing what God created it to do. If we condition guys to avoid only the *visual* sexual stimuli, we set them up for greater defeat. Instead we need to help them understand that their brains need to engage in a different direction, strategizing and processing some kind of adventure that is godly. Remember the guy in Proverbs 7? He never would have been in a place of sexual sin if he'd wised up and pursued a different adventure altogether.

SEX ON THE BRAIN

We need to talk a bit more about a guy's brain and sexuality. Guys receive vague and typically negative messages about sexual thought that are bondage producing. This bondage puts guys in turmoil over who they are, who they think they should be, and who they want to be as men.

The truth is that a guy's sexuality is good, and it's a normal part of a guy's life. He is sexual from the time he is born, not just after he gets married. Throughout his life span, a guy's brain will think sexually. (By the way, sex is not only instinctual; it is also learned. That's why humans can enjoy it, redesign it, and perfect it all their lives.) Because we are sexual, our brains become the primary sex organ. Sexual thinking is a normal byproduct of how God created us to be sexually good.

When we coach guys regarding sexual purity and sexual thinking, we must make sure that we define what lust may *not* be. [*Time for another disclaimer: we can't really define lust, but we need to take into account that some forms of sexual thinking may or may not be lust.*] We have to be honest with guys and describe how they'll be prone to follow a sexual line of thinking, but it may not be considered lusting. Then we have to teach guys to rely on the power and leading of the Holy Spirit to direct them. There are three lines of sexual thinking that we must understand.

First, too much sexual thought doesn't constitute lust. I've heard many people put a commodity on sexual thinking, meaning that it's okay to have sexual thoughts as long as you don't have them too much—or as long as you don't entertain them. Christian guys grow up under the oppression that there is a "daily sexual thought quota," which, by the way, is never defined. As a result, a guy starts to believe that any sexual thought he has and enjoys is lusting.

Second, God created us to have unique sexual tastes. Guys are attracted to different physical, emotional, personality, and character traits in a partner. There is no cookie-cutter template. These tastes are developed through mind engagement—learning and encoding—or "sexual mapping." God allows a guy to grow sexually and to develop his own unique sexual tastes. To try to avoid having any sexual thoughts or curiosities runs counter to how God wires a teenage guy. Remember again that while this activity may play a role in a young man's lust, it may not—in and of itself—be lust.

The third sexual line of thinking is sexual fantasy. That phrase ruffles a lot of feathers in the Christian community. So let me say it another way: healthy sexual development requires sexual rehearsal and imagination. Imagination and rehearsal are a part of good fantasy:

> Part of what comes natural to us instinctually is the ability to create sexual rehearsal. Everyone daydreams about his or her honeymoon night, for example. We rehearse passionate kisses in our mind. We think about sex play that involves romantic interludes, exotic settings, even some

> elements of adventure. We may rehearse in our minds those sex roles and actions with people who we view as potential partners…Somehow we've gotten the idea that thinking through sexual situations, daydreaming of sex with a spouse someday, or envisioning passionate sexual circumstances is all lustful thinking.[6]

Guys can't read the Song of Solomon, define sexual purity, know sexual roles, or even understand sexuality in any form without sexual fantasy (imagination and rehearsal).

Adults need to lead teenage guys through these concepts. Young men need to understand that they aren't sexual perverts if they're thinking along these lines of sexual thought. They need to be taught to seek the Holy Spirit's direction as to when they're crossing the line and beginning to lust. They need to trust God, not the vague universalized mandates they hear, which run counter to their good, God-designed wiring.

OTHER SEXUAL MYTHS

Some youth workers perpetuate these myths; they can have negative and often damaging effects on a guy's sexual identity. You may even be buying into some of these myths and not realize it. You should explore the following myths on your own because I won't cover them in this book:

1. Habitual masturbation is a sexual addiction.
2. Sexual sin jeopardizes future relationships.
3. A guy's natural tendency is to objectify women.
4. Sexual sin, including lust, is the worst kind of sin.
5. "Sex" only happens with intercourse.
6. There really is a concept called "sexual compatibility."
7. Guys reach their sexual peak at age 18.

SEX AS A RITE OF PASSAGE

Part of healthy male sexual development involves the formation of a healthy masculine identity that resonates with a guy's created design (his physiological function) and is congruent to his sexual emotion, desires, and needs (his wiring). When we unknowingly perpetuate myths about masculine sexuality, we send faulty messages that make guys believe they're abnormal. The result: teenage guys either fight to conform to those myths (believing that it makes them more manly) or they hide in pain because it doesn't work for them. Either way, they experience an inner turmoil that may never be resolved.

The greatest sexual identity conflict occurs for Christian adolescent guys. All the cultural messages they receive about masculinity are pro-sex, while the messages they receive from the church are anti-sex.

The dilemma? He believes he isn't a real man because he has to keep his sexuality in check; he believes he isn't a real Christian because he has to keep his sexuality in check. To complicate this issue, the most overt rite of passage into manhood for a guy, in most cultures, is the loss of their virginity. The pressure and defeat for many Christian guys is too great to bear. They find themselves questioning their manhood and then living in defeat because they can't get their sexual desires under control. Many Christian guys cave in to the pressure because they need to make one of these two issues right.

Think about how this works. Single male youth workers are sometimes passed over for jobs because churches are suspicious of them. Guys have to pretend they are sexually experienced when they face a group of men. Married men pretend they've never had sexual struggles, or they pretend they've overcome those struggles since they got married. Now that they're sexually active and it's acceptable for them to have sex because they're married, they've resolved the conflict—and they perpetuate the bondage. In short, the only way for a guy to be a Christian man is to marry. The message is loud and clear.

I encounter many guys who confess they had sex before marriage. They did it because the pressure was too great—both sexually and on their identity. They felt forced to have a sexual encounter just so they could reassure themselves that they're real men. Many men don't feel they need to do this in order to prove their masculinity to anyone else. As a matter of fact, they rarely share it with anyone because they're ashamed.

We need to craft rites of passage that validate a guy as a man. Those rites need to focus on character, responsibility, and sex! *That's right—sex*. We need to affirm in guys that they're sexual beings with sexual power (not super power). They should understand that God created them to be sexual, regardless of their marital status. And since guys will always

function sexually, God has created certain boundaries (i.e., marriage) so sex will remain the way he intended it to be—good.

There should be many consistent and various rites of passage throughout a guy's adolescence that affirm his manliness. There needs to be frequent conversations taking place between younger guys and older men about sex. These talks must be open and raw, honest and unbridled so they'll satisfy a guy's curiosity and fascination about sex without inducing shame and guilt. They also need to be informational and spiritual, crafting a dream in a young man. They should create anticipation, not just demand repression. If guys know they are men and know their sexuality is good and celebrated, they'll be less likely to pursue intercourse before marriage in order to prove their masculinity or to battle an internal identity problem.

3.2 HOMOSEXUALITY

One of my good friends called me not too long ago. He's been doing youth ministry almost as long as I have, and occasionally we talk "shop" to make sure we're correctly reading kids, culture, and the church. He told me about a recent situation, one that he hadn't faced in youth ministry before. The parents of one of his senior high guys scheduled an appointment to talk to him on a weekday morning. My friend thought it was strange that they'd want to come at that time of the day. But he also knew it must be serious, since they'd both cleared their work schedules for the meeting.

Like any normal youth pastor, my friend's mind ran through the normal checklist: 1) What did I do? and 2) What didn't I do? He couldn't think of any reason for an urgent meeting. This family had been a part of the church for years. Their kids had grown up in the children's ministry and now their oldest son was a sophomore and active in the youth ministry. This was a great family with nothing but praise and support for the children's and youth ministries of their church.

The couple arrived at the church and walked back to my friend's office, but they hardly said a word. When they sat down, the father cleared his throat and began by saying this was probably the hardest thing he would ever have to say.

"We think our son is gay," he said.

The couple proceeded to tell my friend how they'd discovered gay pornography and pictures on their son's computer. They were broken, hurt, ashamed, and at a loss to know what to do.

My friend reacted with grace and wisdom. He warned the couple of jumping to conclusions. He promised to coach them through what could be a difficult chapter in their family's life. He also affirmed that he would continue to love, nurture, shepherd, and care for their son as he always had—and as he does with every teenage guy.

Countless youth workers experience what my friend did. Homosexuality is becoming the emergent issue in youth ministry. The media has already taken what it once saw as taboo and normalized it. Dating shows, reality TV, and sitcoms have presented homosexuality as an acceptable lifestyle, without realizing that doing so paints an unrealistic picture because it doesn't deal with the moral, psychological, and social tensions that are created in society, the church, families, and even in the life of the gay individual.

This puts youth pastors in a dilemma because the church is still afraid to address guys about masturbation, let alone homosexuality. Many youth workers are encountering gay and bisexual guys in their sphere of ministry. Some of these guys are questioning their sexuality; some are seeking help for the pain; and some are "out" or are "coming out," professing openly and accepting their sexual orientation.

Jake, a student I mentor, spent the summer working at camp with junior high and high school students. He told me how one of the middle-adolescent guys he'd befriended confessed to him that he was struggling with homosexuality and recalled the agony this teenager was going through. Jake quickly figured out that he'd just heard a confession that no other human had heard from this guy. He also knew he wouldn't be around to help the boy once he left the camp. "Maybe that's why he told me," Jake said.

In the middle of the conversation, Jake made a startling discovery. He'd always felt as though God was calling him to mentor and spiritually lead guys.

Jake said, "If I want to work with guys, then I'd better become equipped to deal with homosexuality. I realized that I've always worked with guys who are like me!"

Jake's words are an accurate assessment of the horizon and the challenge of effective youth ministry. We can't gauge our ministry to guys by our own experiences.

FOR CLARITY'S SAKE

This chapter isn't a position statement on homosexuality. I'm not going to debate the theological framework regarding this issue, nor will I debate the cause-and-effect theories that accompany it. Please don't try to assess what camp I'm in or read between the lines, assuming I have a theological agenda. This chapter is about guys and their struggles. I trust that if you're reading this book, you care about teenage guys as much as I do. If so, then equip yourself by reading as much as you can about homosexuality. Learn about all sides of the issue with the understanding that guys are caught in the crossfire of a battle on rightness. While groups clamor to present their personal understanding of biblical truth, countless teenage guys face this issue in silent pain, walking away from a warring church and society into the embrace of homosexual communities.

GETTING ON THE SAME PAGE

While they may engage in the same activities, embrace the same masculine mask of bravado, and even force themselves into heterosexual relationships, homosexual teenage guys still feel as though something deep within them is different.

Some confess knowing they were homosexual long before puberty occurred (because they had strong romantic feelings for someone of the same gender), while others struggle with their internal de-

sires, feelings, and resolve about their homosexuality into their early adult years.

This is no different from what heterosexual guys experience. I've talked with many guys who said they knew they were sexually attracted to girls in elementary school, while others didn't even know girls existed until they were about 17 years old.

Likewise, sexual identity follows the same path for a homosexual guy as it does for a heterosexual guy. There is never a point of choice when a heterosexual guy "chooses" to be a heterosexual, nor does that day ever occur for a homosexual. Sexual *orientation* is not chosen, but sexual *behavior* is a conscious choice of engagement.

[*Disclaimer: Because orientation is not chosen, it doesn't make the theology or morality of any view of homosexuality more acceptable. If we really want to understand a teenage guy who struggles with this issue, then we need to be clear on this point. No theory, research, or experience shows that orientation is chosen.*]

During my teenage years, I don't recall waking up all excited one morning and thinking, "Today will be the day I choose to be a heterosexual!" I just recall that at some point, internal feelings of attraction, desire, and even lust for girls started to formulate. They even played out in my unconscious dreams. But choice? I must have been sick that day. The same is true for the homosexual guy who, in the midst of all the pressure (heterosexual pressure) to prove himself manly and sexually potent, feels incredibly abnormal. In the light of all this pressure, what young adolescent guy would *choose* homosexuality?

The 1992 film *Doing Time on Maple Drive* portrays this well. It's about an American family trying to work through some dysfunction while presenting an image to the world that all is well. Each of the three siblings is dealing with an issue. The youngest teenage son—the shining star of the family—is in turmoil over his internal battle with homosexuality. In an effort to hide it and stop his pain, he attempts suicide by wrecking his car. But he recovers. When he comes out to his family, they cannot accept it, and his mother thinks he has chosen to be gay. His response: "Mom I didn't choose to be gay. Do you think I'd choose to be this different from everyone else; that I'd choose to make you and dad this upset—and what about AIDS? Suppose somebody *wanted* to be gay, would they want to be gay now?" This teenage guy's impassioned plea puts the internal dilemma into perspective.

Guys don't choose heterosexuality or homosexuality. The peer pressure to conform to masculine heterosexual scripts is burdensome. That pressure would make the choice easy, if there were a choice to be made. And if a guy *did* want to choose homosexuality, then he would have to fight continuously to adopt a non-dominant identity, all while surrounded by messages, behaviors, negative reinforcements, pain, and rejection regarding an identity he hasn't yet formulated. The amount of peer pressure regarding issues much smaller than this one can cause guys to succumb and to conform. So the issue of homosexuality just screams "uphill battle" with lots of pain and distress in the process.

UNDERSTAND THE DILEMMA

While doing research for this book, I found a few Web sites dedicated to helping gay teenagers with their struggle. Some were pro-homosexuality, while others were not. Nonetheless, as I read through some of the postings by teenage guys, a pattern emerged. These guys were evidencing what researchers have been telling us: Guys who struggle with homosexuality feel isolated, alone, afraid, helpless, incompetent, ashamed, and have a sense of self-abasement. These feelings run counter to the mask of masculinity that a homosexual guy must wear.

Homosexual teenage guys appear to be heterosexual while they struggle with homosexual feelings, urges, and identity. Many times they will act out heterosexual, masculine scripts by dating girls, participating in sexual conversations as a heterosexual, and avoiding behaviors that may be misunderstood as homosexual. They go to the extreme—putting on the machismo and buying into the bravado—all in an attempt to throw off suspicion and perhaps to feel some sense of normalcy.

This behavior is known as *passing*. Passing makes it safe for a guy who is struggling with his sexual identity. Teenage guys and the world of men can be cruel to a guy who doesn't fit into the mold of masculinity. Many effeminate *heterosexual* guys have experienced the brutality of bullying through verbal beatings and even occasional physical abuse because they deviated from the culturally embedded prototype of manhood. Some heterosexual non-effeminate guys even guard their behaviors (such as the way they show affection to each other; they won't show emotion; they even refuse to engage in some activities that aren't deemed manly) out of fear of being called a "fag." This form of *homophobia* prevents guys from being themselves.

While a homosexual guy may not be effeminate, his homosexuality deviates so far from the prototype that he'd be a target for other guys who need to validate their manhood with cruel aggression. This aggression can result in something as mild as a wounded ego to something as unbelievable as death (lest we forget the tragic beating and death of Matthew Shepard in October 1998 by two heterosexual guys).

Studies have shown that 80 percent of the homosexual teenagers surveyed were verbally bullied, 43 percent had objects thrown at them, 17 percent were assaulted physically, and 10 percent were assaulted with a weapon. So passing makes life safer, while complicating the inner turmoil of a gay teenager who already believes he's abnormal.

One guy, on his online Web posting, said that on a daily basis he has to pretend to be someone he isn't. He commented that he felt as though he was—"just a poser." So the struggle of living a lie and being fake just compounds his guilt and mars his identity even more.

I've heard many Christian heterosexual teenage guys talk about the guilt they feel over pretending to be sexually experienced, or how they've fallen sexually because of the pressure they feel to portray themselves as sexual studs. Many anguish over living a lie just so they won't be rejected as men. But they can still retreat to the knowledge that someday they *will* be sexually active in an acceptable way. Gay teenage guys feel the same anguish, but without the retreat. Instead, they have the added burden of knowing they will always be outside the norm. They flounder in an attempt to internalize a masculine sexual identity that is barbed no matter how they try to wear it. Often this guy's only alternatives are to embrace his homosexual tendencies and face the rejection (which may be less painful than the internal turmoil because he can find solace in an accepting homosexual community) or live in quiet pain.

COMING OUT

Coming out means telling others that you're homosexual. This is a very dangerous thing for teenage guys because it's a radical deviation from the script. That's why gay teenage males are hailed as brave and courageous when they come out. By the way, when a teenage guy approaches a youth worker seeking spiritual guidance on this issue, he's experiencing a coming out of sorts. It takes as much courage (if not more) for him to talk about it with a church leader. Fear of rejection is what often prevents Christian homosexual guys from disclosing their struggle.

Therefore the church should react to the *individual*, not the issue. I've watched many youth workers take the information they've received from guys and, in the name of trying to bring about reconciliation, they take it to other church leaders and the guys' parents. Basically they "out" them without permission while expecting the safety of pastor-student confidentiality to continue. In the end, the leaders' attempts to "help" these students actually bring more pain, shame, and humiliation into the guys' lives.

One of my students befriended a guy named Adam while working in a street ministry in Los Angeles. When I met Adam, he was 18 years old and a new street kid. He came to L.A. from the suburbs of Dallas—down in the heart of the Bible belt. He told me he had two younger siblings, his family was middle-class suburban, and he was raised in an evangelical church. Adam seemed bright, and he didn't look like a delinquent. But as I probed for more of Adam's story, he finally broke. Adam told me he was a homosexual. He'd kept it a secret through his early teenage years, and he never acted on his homosexual urges—in fact he did everything he could to avoid them. Finally, out of desperation, he decided to talk to his youth pastor. Instead of being supportive, this man decided Adam should no longer serve in any leadership positions in the youth ministry. So Adam was removed from his role as a member of the worship band. This began a string of humiliating, painful events that exceeded Adam's control.

Naturally, Adam's parents (along with everyone else) wanted to know why he was asked to step down, and Adam was forced to disclose his struggle to them. Adam told me he knew this hurt his parents deeply, and he'd never wanted that to happen. They sought help from the same church that continued to shame and humiliate Adam. The church called it "humility" (in their perception Adam was being humbled by God), but in reality it was "humiliation" as more and more people began to reject him. Through the designs of the church's counseling, Adam (16 at the time) was given two years to change his ways.

To make a long story short, when Adam turned 18, his parents could no longer condone his homosexual orientation, so they kicked him out of the house. They believed this to be the wise and biblical response, and their church supported their decision. In short, Adam found himself living on the streets of L.A. without a job, adult guidance, or a place to live.

Some studies have shown that Adam's experience is not unusual for gay teenagers. The Los Angeles County Task Force on Runaway and Homeless Youth reports that approximately 25 to 35 percent of their youth are homosexual; similarly, the Seattle Commission of Children and Youth reports 40 percent of their homeless youth population is gay.[2] These kids, having been kicked out of their homes, are called "throwaway teens." Many of the guys who are throwaways end up engaging in "survival sex"—selling themselves to get money for food and shelter.

ACTS OF DESPERATION

It's difficult for many to agree on a definition of *homosexuality* because many heterosexual teenagers experience a homosexual encounter (or encounters) while exploring sexuality.

I know that statement raised many eyebrows, so let's unpack it.

Up front, let's acknowledge that the church fears sexuality and sexual issues. Her silence on many sexual issues screams negative value and disdain. What's more, many in the church may have experienced homosexual encounters during early adolescence while exploring sexuality with same-gendered friends. This is not uncommon. Many guys fear they are homosexual or could become homosexual because of this behavior. Many men carry the guilt of these experiences in the recesses of their minds, be-

WAKE-UP CALL!

Youth workers are on the front lines with teenage guys. Many times a guy will confide in a youth worker before he'll tell anyone else about the things he's going through. Many guys who struggle with homosexuality often disclose this issue to close female confidants. So if you're working with guys, you may find yourself in that position.

Consider these stats:

- Parents are seldom the first people an adolescent tells about his same-sex attraction.
- Mothers are usually told before fathers, possibly because of the distance that teenage guys feel in their relationships with their dads.
- Mothers are more likely than fathers to know about their son's same-gender attraction.
- The person to whom an adolescent guy may disclose his homosexuality or bisexual identity is most likely a close friend.[3]

lieving there is a dark seed of homosexuality within them. Thus they remain silent because they're afraid they'll be stripped of their cloak of heterosexual manhood. They believe a sexual encounter mandates sexual orientation.

One 15-year-old guy confessed he thought he was gay because he masturbated. His logic was that if he loved touching a penis that much—even though it was his own and he was engaged in heterosexual fantasy at the time—he must be gay. Does sexual behavior define orientation?

Some would say a person is a homosexual if he engages in homosexual behavior. Some would identify a guy as homosexual if he were sexually attracted to another guy. Others may say that homosexuality includes attraction *and* sexual behavior. Still others may say that homosexuality involves attraction, sexual behavior, and identifying oneself as homosexual.[4]

The church seems to have a reductionist view of this issue, opting to resolve the problem by using the common phrase, "Hate the sin, and love the sinner." But when the definition of homosexuality and homosexual sin or behavior is so vague, that phrase is not easily applied. A dilemma is created because the line between the sin and the sinner is often blurred. And more consistently, the sinner is hated because the church views homosexual sin as the mother of all sexual sins. The hostile climate prevents guys from seeking out support, information, help, and care. As a result, the despair that's generated within the soul of a homosexual guy increases, and all the more if he's a Christian.

The depression, hopelessness, rejection, and fear that accompany homosexuality may lead a guy to resort to suicide. Recent random sample studies show that the suicide rate among gay teenagers is anywhere from two to 14 times higher than it is among heterosexual teenagers.[5] Therefore, we're more likely to believe that a homosexual teenager is most at risk of a successful suicide attempt. A study of homosexual teenagers in Australia revealed that they were also more likely to commit suicide than heterosexual teenagers. And if we compound that information with the current data we have on guys and violence, we can conclude that homosexual guys are two to five times more likely to reattempt suicide.[6] The message we're getting from homosexual guys in Western cultures is that they'd rather be dead than gay.

DESTRUCTIVE BEHAVIOR

Suicide is not usually the primary option. Many guys will turn to destructive measures as a masculine form of coping with pain. I've already mentioned guys' violent and aggressive nature. As an acceptable masculine emotion, anger becomes the common option for a teenage guy, regardless of his sexual orientation. But anger turned inward is often self-destructive.

A guy struggling with homosexuality is faced with the predicament that his masculine identity is being called into question. Feeling trapped and compromised, he may start the process of a "slow suicide" rather than killing himself instantly. The first and most common self-destructive behavior is substance abuse. "Sexual minority youth (those who identified themselves as gay/lesbian/or bisexual and/or who had any same-sex sexual contact) had higher rates of drug use than their peers, including higher lifetime rates of using marijuana (70 percent versus 49 percent), cocaine (29 percent versus nine percent), methamphetamines (30 percent versus seven percent), and injected drugs (18 percent versus two percent)."[7] One study found that approximately one-third of the adolescent homosexual guys who participated in the survey reported some form of intentional, self-destructive act, with 21 percent of those requiring medical care or hospitalization afterward.[8]

Am I Gay?
Some teenage guys fear they might be gay for the following reasons:

1. Guys often compare their anatomy to their friends' by looking while they're changing clothes or showering. Some guys believe they may become gay just because they look.

2. Some guys don't date or don't even have a desire to date. They face incredible pressure from a society (and especially the church) that is always trying to hook them up. Singleness and celibacy are not honored. Consider how people become suspicious about the sexual orientation of a single older male.

3. Some guys fear they are gay if they enjoy the love and affection generated between male friends. Their alternative—don't love.

Another form of self-destruction is self-mutilation, which includes piercing, cutting, branding, and tattooing. While this is also known as "body modification" and could be considered fashionable, many guys choose it as a physically painful remedy to escape their emotional pain. These behaviors may also be used to make a statement of rebellion or self-abasement, induce fear and intimidate others, or identify a guy as "macho" or "homosexual."[9] When these activities are taken to the extreme, more than a fashion statement is being made. The extremes often include multiple piercings horizontally or vertically through the glans or head of the penis; piercing through the urethral opening of the penis (known as a "Prince Albert" after a British royal who had this procedure done); piercing the shaft of the penis, the frenulum, and the scrotum; penile subincision (cutting the underside of the penis lengthwise and into the urethra); and genital tattooing, among other things. Risk-taking behaviors and increased sexual activity are also more often associated with teenagers who engage in self-mutilating behaviors than with those who don't.[10]

HELPING A HOMOSEXUAL TEENAGE GUY

It must begin long before anyone even encounters them. It starts with youth workers, parents, teachers, counselors, pastors, and mentors determining to create safe environments. Guys need to know they can talk about things with confidence, that the information won't be "leaked" to anyone, and they won't be judged. They need to know you'll take to your grave the things that are said to you in confidence.

The only way to make the environment safe is to educate and engage church leadership, families, school administrators, and others in conversations about how to be safe and what to do when a guy does disclose. Instruct parents about the line of action you'll take if their son discloses. Make sure they know you'll coach him to talk with his parents, but if he doesn't choose to do so, you'll keep the issue between just the two of you. This will allow him the opportunity to struggle with adult input instead of keeping the matter to himself and self-destructing later.

You may also have to get past your own desire to be needed in order to become a safe place for a guy to share. Remember my friend at the beginning of the chapter? He made it a safe place for the parents, too. He coached the father to talk to his son. He also told the parents he wasn't going to say anything to their teenage son until the son said something to him. He kept things as they were—investing in the guy without hesitation, as it should be.

Make it safe by educating everyone regarding the abuse and harassment that homosexual teenagers face. Take a zero-tolerance stance against derogatory remarks and jokes aimed at homosexuals. Build a loving community—one that doesn't label people. Make sure that the more effeminate guys or those who are weaker aren't labeled or judged. Don't allow adults or students to jump to conclusions about a guy's sexual identity. Labeling can sometimes lead to a guy's reactive attempt to prove everyone wrong—often with tragic results.

A safe place is also established when people actually *listen*. Learn to avoid a knee-jerk reaction when a guy discloses that he struggles with homosexuality or when a guy starts attending your youth ministry and he's out to everyone. If you haven't encountered this yet, it won't be long before you do. Be prepared. Be quick to listen and slow to speak. That means don't try to fix things right away. Effective listening also involves empathy. More than anything else, a struggling guy needs to know that you understand his struggle. So listen between the lines.

Mobilize resources. Coach the guy to deal with the issues that accompany his struggle, such as depression, insecurities and fears, and confusion. Commit to walk alongside him. Help him to learn that

HOMOSEXUAL BACKLASH

One of the most overlooked areas of ministry is to the families of homosexuals. The most obvious recipients are the parents whose dreams, desires, and hopes for their sons are now dashed. The pain of not being grandparents, of watching their sons struggle, and of wondering if they did something wrong will haunt parents. Effective ministry to homosexual guys also means ministry to their parents.

Another not-so-obvious backlash is when guys discover a parent is gay. Many guys feel the hurt of this and bury it. They may lash out, rebel, or become self- destructive. If the gay parent is the father, many guys fear they might be gay, too. They may also be confused about masculinity since their fathers may have been their icon of manhood.

Help a guy navigate through this. He may need to cry and rage through it. The rage part will be easiest, but the crying part may never come (he doesn't want to be perceived as being gay just because he's crying).

he's more than a "sexual identity," and that life isn't reduced to sexuality. Show him that he can have healthy relationships, be successful in his endeavors, and be used by God.

METROSEXUAL?

Straight guys who pamper themselves with the finer things in life are often jokingly called *metrosexual*. Like a woman, a metrosexual guy can be interested in skin and hair care, manicures, pedicures, and get his hair highlighted. He likes to go shopping *and* play football. He enjoys the ballet *and* camping. He's soft and rugged. He may be a bit of a renaissance guy, with knowledge of the arts, culinary skills, and gardening. And those who hold to a more traditional masculine code may believe he's gay. Many teenage guys are free to explore these things (once thought to be birthed out of the feminine side of a man) without fear of being labeled gay. But a guy who does may still be bucking the "Boy Code." (We'll cover this concept in the next chapter.)

THE REST OF THE STORY

My friend (from the story at the beginning of this chapter) advised the boy's parents not to act rashly or hysterically. He let them cry through the issues and heard their pain of dashed hopes and dreams, their feelings of guilt and humiliation, and their anticipated hurt for what their son was going through and would probably continue to go through.

With coaching, the father decided to take his son rock climbing the following Saturday. They had done this before so it wasn't unusual, but it was always special. He and his son climbed to the top of a lookout and sat there enjoying God's handiwork. The father expressed his undying love and adoration for his son, and then he confronted him. He mentioned they'd found gay porn on his computer, and he asked the boy to explain. His son hung his head in shame and got quiet. The father put his arm around his son and reassured him there wasn't anything he couldn't talk about, nor was there anything that would compromise his love for his son. The boy confessed his struggle with homosexuality.

About two weeks later, the teenage guy came to see my friend—his youth pastor. The guy said he knew his parents had come to talk to him. My friend pulled the guy close and hugged him, reassuring him that he was loved and that they'd all walk through this struggle together.

As I wrote this chapter, I called my friend for an update on this family's situation. He said his student had resolved that homosexual behavior is a sin. My friend said he'd talked with him just a few days earlier, and the young man had concluded that he would have to remain celibate for the rest of his life. He also

knew he was more than his sexuality and looked forward to a productive life. He'd seen that other men (who weren't homosexual) never married, yet they remained sexually pure. They were incredible role models and offered hope for a guy who was struggling to make sense out of the messages that form sexual identity.

SECTION FOUR

THE TEENAGE GUY'S EMOTIONS (EMOTIONAL DEVELOPMENT)

4.1 EMOTIONAL MYTHS THAT INFLUENCE GUYS

Seth is a typical 16-year-old guy. He's active at school and in his youth group. His life is packed full of activities, ranging from varsity soccer to a relationship with Ashley, his girlfriend of six months. He's a very good student, and he works hard to keep his grades at a 3.7 GPA.

Seth surrounds himself with quality friends, and he has a tight "band of brothers" (his small group). While these relationships are great, Seth appears to be distancing himself from his family and his friends. His parents' assessment is that Seth is growing up and he needs more space.

Seth found the space he craves in his bedroom, where he has a great sound system, TV, and his own computer. His parents often comment that when Seth comes home from school and soccer practice, he typically showers and then goes straight to his room to do homework, only coming out occasionally to grab some food. While this behavior pattern sometimes bothers them, they've accepted that this is just part of the process of Seth's autonomy and a result of his busy schedule.

Seth's parents approached me to ask if their son is normal. As his youth pastor, I'd noticed he seemed far away at times. But whenever I asked him if things were all right, Seth often responded affirmatively. When pressed, he'd say he was "just tired," but otherwise "things were great." While things did look normal on the outside, I could sense something was brewing on the inside.

Every autumn our church hosts a family camp at a retreat center on a beautiful wooded lake in Wisconsin. The turning of the leaves is brilliant, and the air is brisk and refreshing. Seth and his family are regulars at this retreat. One afternoon while I was walking near the lake, I noticed Seth sitting on the shore and tossing rocks into the water. I approached him.

"Hey, how's it going?" I asked.

"Great! It's so cool out here," he replied.

I asked Seth if I could join him, and he welcomed the company. We sat quietly and looked at the ripples Seth made by dropping rocks into the water. I knew this was my opportunity to probe into Seth's emotional state.

"Seth, maybe I'm reading this wrong, but I've noticed you seem distant lately. And I miss you," I said quietly. There was a long silence. When I glanced at Seth, I saw he was fighting back tears. I put my arm around his shoulders and said, "Hey buddy, what's going on inside of you?" With that, he burst into tears.

Seth was on an emotional roller coaster that often took him to a place of isolation and loneliness. The regular pressures of his life felt overwhelming at times, but Seth felt he had to hold it all together and keep things "under control." He was a product of what William Pollack calls the "Boy Code."[1] He was hiding behind the cultural mask of masculinity.

Like most guys, Seth was trying to navigate through his emotional development with a faulty, inaccurate compass. He was buying into the many myths that exist about men and their emotions. So what he believed about masculine emotion was in direct opposition to what he was experiencing internally. This gap between Seth's beliefs and his emotional reality created a constant, unbearable conflict. Like many guys, Seth believed his only alternatives were to retreat, avoid, or explode in a fit of rage.

EMOTIONAL DEVELOPMENT

Before we can fully understand the uniqueness of male adolescent emotion, we must examine the landscape of adolescent emotional development. G. Stanley Hall (the "father of adolescent development," as noted in chapter 1.1) aptly deemed this life stage "storm and stress."[3] Hall was aware that an adolescent went through traumatic developmental changes, and his assessment led him to ascribe an emotional label for this age, capturing the emotional turmoil of adolescence.

Adolescents, like all human beings, are created with a full range of emotions. A developmental theorist believes that emotional development parallels and is influenced by our other developmental processes. For example, research shows us that physiological developmental changes give rise to emotional shifts in the adolescent, citing the direct effect of hormones[4] and the indirect effect of physical changes.[5] As a teenager's identity develops, the adolescent also begins to develop a sense of individuation. The relinquishment of family dependencies and the search for autonomy give rise to many positive and negative emotions.

As the mind of an adolescent guy develops, he has the ability to label abstract emotions—even his moods. Additionally, an adolescent's perceptions of gender identity may interfere with his ability to express emotion. Some developmental theorists believe that the range of intense emotions (e.g., love, empathy, fulfillment, anger, shame, guilt, and so on) play a significant role in the moral and spiritual development of the adolescent.[6]

Given these insights, we can begin to see a pattern that's thrust upon the emotional development of an adolescent guy. Follow the logic: His body is rapidly changing, releasing hormones that alter and affect mood. He can't quite verbalize what he experiences because he doesn't know how to conceptualize

BASIC TENETS OF THE BOY CODE

1. **Be the "Sturdy Oak"**: Men should be in control of their emotions. This is evidenced by showing little or no emotion because emotional expression is a sign of weakness. Stoicism, rugged individualism, and independence become the marks of stability.
2. **"Give 'Em Hell"**: Men should operate in the profile of "masculine bravado." This tenet assumes men are wired to be superheroes. Thus, "boys will be boys," and that means they'll engage in risky, aggressive, high-energy, often violent, macho behavior.
3. **Be the "Big Wheel"**: Men need to keep a sense of power, dominance, and an achieved status. Behind this desire is the underlying drive to avoid shame at all costs. Men are taught to wear the "mask of coolness," which implies that everything is great and under control, even when it isn't. Nothing should ruffle a real man.

it yet. Then on top of that, Western society and the Christian community impose cultural expectations on him that counter his internal emotional experiences. He learns quickly to operate within a very limited range of emotions. This is defined negatively. So he quickly learns to draw a line whenever he's experiencing negative emotions, which doesn't allow him to show any vulnerability, feel anything he cannot control, or demonstrate any physical expression of those emotions. In other words, our boys grow up to be men with *restricted emotionality*.[7]

Healthy emotional development can occur when we help guys understand that there are many myths that have shaped their emotional formation.

MYTHS ABOUT EMOTIONS

Myth #1—Emotions reflect your morality. Often we give guys the impression that there is morality attached to certain feelings. For example, some Christians hold to the premise that if an individual's spiritual life is right, then they'll feel emotionally positive. I once heard a pastor sermonize that if you are depressed, then it's because you "don't have your life together with the Lord." He continued to explain that people who have their lives together—when God is the center and the source of life—*never* get depressed. This myth equates spiritual vitality with emotional contentment.

When guys hear this, they're faced with a dual dilemma. First, our culture tells them that expressing any negative emotion besides anger (and its derivative forms) is a sign of masculine weakness. Second, the church tells them that expressing those negative emotions signifies a spiritual problem.

The truth is that God created us with a full range of emotions, and everything God created is good. Sometimes we forget we're created in the image and *likeness* of God. And Satan's tactic has always been to mar the likeness of God reflected in us. But

4. **"No Sissy Stuff":** Pollack cites this as the most traumatizing and dangerous injunction of the Boy Code, labeling it the *gender straightjacket.* This tenet prohibits guys from expressing any emotion or engaging in any activity that may be seen as "feminine." Thus warmth, empathy, compassion, need, sorrow, and so on, are constantly being repressed.[2]

MALE YOUTH WORKER ALERT

As you read about Jesus' life and ministry, you become aware that he publicly demonstrates a wide range of emotions, some of which may be uncomfortable for us today. Do you really want to be like Jesus and feel the things he feels? Will you model this for the adolescent men in your ministry?

throughout Scripture, we can see that God is emotional. So our ability to experience a full range of emotions serves as evidence that we *are* created in his likeness.

Teenage guys are also wired to feel these things, and they do. But when we send messages that say expressing your emotions is bad, we put adolescent guys (who are in hormonal-emotional overload as it is) in a position either to deny or to bury any emotion. Like Seth, they're constantly attempting to restrain what often feels like an emotional locomotive barreling down a track.

For some, this struggle for restraint often escalates into an eruption of anger. While anger isn't considered morally acceptable, it's certainly understood as an emotion that doesn't reflect weakness. Guys save face by being unacceptable and strong rather than unacceptable and weak. Our boys become men and carry the baggage of emotional denial with them into adulthood.

While guys need to learn that they will experience every emotion—and that those emotions are okay to feel and express—they must also learn that the actions that follow those emotions have moral consequences. Scripture says, "Be angry, and yet do not sin" (Ephesians 4:26, NASB). The emotion isn't wrong, but acting violently as a result of it is.

Myth #2—Emotions are gender specific. Throughout their lives, guys receive messages that say there are "guy" emotions and there are "girl" emotions. This is usually demonstrated through statements such as, "Boys don't cry," and "Suck it up and be a man!" This imprinting on the emotional hearts of young men causes them to live in repression. They can never unleash their hearts for fear of being too emotional or "girly."

I try to make my students aware of this myth. I often tell them that part of our ministry of reconciliation is freeing guys from the bondage of this emotion-gender myth.

One of my seminary students approached me one time and said, "Doc, you'd be really proud of me."

"Why?"

He proceeded to tell me that his sister had just had a baby girl. She also had a three-year-old son, and he was sitting in the hospital waiting room with the extended family when it was announced that he now had a little sister. But instead of being excited about the news, the little boy burst into tears. The little guy was angry because he wanted a little brother so badly. The crying and sobbing helped release his anger.

My student said, "I just held him and said, 'Go ahead and cry, buddy. You can be sad about this. You just cry and cry all you want, and I'll just hold onto you.'" Then he told me that his dad (the boy's grandfather) kept saying, "Don't cry. You're the big brother—and big boys don't cry!"

He finished his story by saying, "You would have been so proud of me because I turned to my dad and said, 'Dad, it's okay for boys to cry. Let the kid cry.'"

Guys are bombarded with this myth from an early age. They need men in their lives who will model emotional freedom and help them reframe their perspectives. They need to erase old mental tapes and experience a sense of normalcy without having to fight an internal battle against the voice that says they're emotionally feminine just because their hearts betray them. They need to have men fight the cultural landscape by running counterculture to these messages.

While our culture is softening on this issue, it still sends strong messages that say men are less emotional than women. Let me illustrate this for you. There are days when my wife comes home after a

EXPRESSING EMOTION

Guys need to learn to talk about what they're feeling. You can help the guys in your sphere of influence if you ask them to help *you* feel what they're feeling. By painting a verbal word picture, they become more emotionally expressive.

Here's an example: A teenage guy once told me he was going through a difficult time in his life. When I asked him to tell me what he was feeling, he said, "I don't know." So I asked him to try describing what he was feeling in two ways. First, I asked, "If what you're feeling were a physical feeling, what would it feel like—maybe a headache or a sore throat...?" The guy replied, "It would feel like someone hit me in the stomach really hard."

I then asked him, "If you had to paint a picture of what you're feeling, what colors, shapes, and other things would you use?" He went on to say that it would be a black painting of him standing in a storm of blue and black rain. This guy was feeling despair. While he couldn't put a label on his feelings, he could certainly create a vivid picture for me to empathize with him and coach him to be more emotionally literate.

very frustrating day at work. She walks in the door and slams her purse onto the table. Then she walks over to the kitchen sink and starts doing something.

I say, "Hi, honey. Are you okay?"

"No. I've just had a really hard day," she says through her tears.

Let's replay that scenario but in a masculine gender.

Now *I* come home from work after having an equally frustrating day. My wife asks me what's wrong. Crying, I say, "I had a really bad day."

WRONG!

While we experience the same emotions, the translation of those emotions is different. I play it out in silence, stewing, with short-tempered jabs, and maybe even outbursts of anger. Those are "guy emotional responses" or translated—guy emotions. The way we express our emotions also becomes gender specific. Thus guys learn to eliminate *sad*, *hurt*, *discouraged*, and so on from their emotional repertoire.

The truth that busts this myth is that God created us to be complete, balanced, and with a full range of emotions. While we may be culturally conditioned to respond a certain way, God lets us feel all things as he does.

We see this evidenced in Jesus' life and ministry. Many times Jesus is moved by compassion and weeps publicly. On one occasion he's frustrated that the people of Jerusalem don't understand his mission. They refuse to believe or cannot comprehend that he is *Messiah*. Jesus weeps openly because he feels compassion for the people; he feels the pain of rejection; he feels the discouragement of not getting through to them. Jesus demonstrates a balanced expression of emotions. It's appropriate for the emotions he's experiencing, and he's experiencing a full range of them.

While we challenge our teenage guys to be like Jesus, we send messages that run counter to his heart. If we want to be like Jesus, then it isn't going to evidence itself in our actions alone—it also comes out through our emotions. Jesus will make us feel his heart. Guys who want to be like Jesus are going to feel things they never felt before. And when they do, they should feel them *and* express them.

I issued a challenge to my students: Ask Jesus to let you see people the way he sees them. I told them the challenge was dangerous because if they asked God to do this, then he would. A few weeks later, one of the guys—a six-foot-two, 240-pound football player—caught me between classes.

He said, "Doc, I'm really angry with you, and we have to talk." I swallowed hard and asked what the problem was. As we stepped into my office, he told me how he had taken up my challenge. At lunch that day, he'd been sitting alone in the cafeteria when a freshman girl came over and asked if she could sit at his table. He obliged, and they sat silently for a few moments. Compelled to be like Jesus, this burly guy introduced himself and started a conversation. (While he was sharing his story with me, he started to tear up.) He told me this girl was very lonely, and she was struggling through a lot of painful issues.

Then, in his most manly voice, he said, "And I'm mad at you for that challenge because I burst into tears in the cafeteria—right in front of her. I'm such a girl since I took the challenge." He was so moved with compassion, he couldn't control his emotions. His emotions and emotional expressions were NOT confined to gender. He was being Jesus to this girl, and Jesus would have cried, too.

Myth #3—A person is either a thinker or a feeler. This myth categorizes people as either emotional or rational. The line is already drawn in a society that values reason over emotion. Many times this myth is modified by the gender-specific emotions myth that

conditions men to believe that girls are the feelers and guys are the thinkers. Guys are taught to view emotion as weakness; therefore they learn that being rational supersedes emotion. In fact we believe the illusion that these two "types" are actually polar opposites—reason or thinking is at one end of the scale, and feeling or affect is down at the other end. This pits reason against emotion. But who said reason and emotion are opposites? They're really not.

Ask a guy how he feels about a situation, and he'll use the word *feel* in his response, but he's actually telling you his thought processes. You'll hear something like, "I feel like this is a bad thing." "I feel we should do something exciting." "I feel as if I made a mistake." These aren't feelings; they're thoughts. A feeling can be expressed in a single word, "I feel—excited, hurt, happy, sad, peaceful, overwhelmed," and so on.

What entrenches this myth is another modification that says guys can't or don't make emotional decisions. This is destructive to the emotional lives of teenage guys.

Here's the truth: A person is neither a thinker nor a feeler. The truth is that God creates guys to be *balanced*, and both reason and emotion are essential for a balanced, healthy life. They're not opposites on a continuum. Guys need to understand that they can be fully engaged logically and fully engaged emotionally. Does that mean they should make decisions based on emotion? Yes, they should make decisions based on emotion—and also reason.

Guys must learn that they need to think things through *and* trust their emotions. Balanced living uses both the heart and the mind fully. Even throughout Scripture we can see that God addresses the hearts and minds of his people. He transforms and heals both. He restores and renews both. He develops and works through both. When we push boys to be driven only by their reason and logic, we create imbalanced men.

Myth #4—There are times when I don't feel anything. Emotion affects perception. Feelings help us gauge our circumstances and discern conversations. Basically our emotions are like a gyroscope that keeps us functioning normally. But guys have moments or large gaps when they cannot feel anything.

I've found myself in countless conversations where a guy will tell me about a situation when he was "devastated" or "torn apart" or "crushed." But when I ask him what he's feeling while he tells me these things, he says, "Nothing."

Guys are trained to detach from their feelings. They can learn to use emotional language without connecting to the emotion. Thus, there are times when they don't feel anything. To be honest, death is the only time when we don't feel *anything*. By virtue of being human, we are always feeling something.

God created us alive, and we are always processing. Here's how the process works (it's a little equation that's used often in counseling circles):

Thought + Feeling = A Behavior

When we act on something, it's because we think *and* feel. Our minds and hearts are constantly processing. This is indicative of being fully alive.

Myth #5—Time alone with God heals all wounds. This myth is the masculine favorite because it keeps guys in seclusion and isolation. He never has to face his woundedness; he just has to self-medicate until he can either detach so he doesn't feel anything or think things through so he can disengage his heart from his mind (shades of the other myths).

Christian men spiritualize this myth by making their woundedness a "me and God" thing. While God can and does meet us in our aloneness, he has chosen a wonderful vehicle through which he brings

YOUTH WORKER TIP

Sometimes a guy may not be in a place where he can cognitively identify his emotions. This may elicit a "nothing" response when you ask him what he's feeling. Guys need their emotional vocabulary expanded, and they also need role models to show them how corresponding behavior and emotions work. For example, a male youth worker should tell his students how *he* feels when he's in a certain situation or experiencing a set of circumstances like the ones they're currently going through. This helps guys fight detachment and teaches them to identify and name their emotions.

healing—the Holy Spirit who superintends his power through his people. God works through community, and Christ has united us in his body. Guys are taught to believe this theological truth, but to deny its power by buying into another ideology—rugged individualism. This is what births the "me and God" majority heresy.

I had a student come to my office after going through a very difficult and painful breakup with his girlfriend. He explained the story calmly, but he told me he was devastated. I mentioned that he didn't look or sound devastated, although I had a hunch it was eating him alive. His response—he just needed to drive for a while and have some time alone with God. I agreed that time alone with God was good, but I asked what he wanted God to do for him. He said he wanted God to heal his heart. When I asked him to describe how that would look, he said he wished God would just sit next to him and assure him that he was going to be all right. Without hesitation, I sat down next to him and put my arm around his shoulders. I reminded him of how much God loves him and that nothing could separate him from God's love. He fell apart in my arms.

The truth that busts this myth is that God created us to need him. God does heal all wounds, and he uses his people to accomplish that task. Guys are taught that if they have an emotional need, then they're weak. Once again this plays into the fact that we teach guys a strongman Christianity. We spiritualize our pride in the form of individualism.

Look at creation. God creates and then he pronounces it *good*—without hesitation. Yet he says there is one thing that is *not good*—Adam was alone. This doesn't make sense. Adam wasn't really alone. He was with God. Adam and God, a majority! As a matter of fact, Adam walked with and talked face-to-face with God. You can't get less alone or more "me and God" than that. Yet God says this isn't good.

So God created a wife for Adam. This action sets into motion the beginning of God's design through which he would meet us. God creates relationships. Next he creates family. After that he creates community, soon followed by a chosen nation. Eventually he ushers a Messiah into the picture. And then he uses Christ's disciples to create the body—the church. God still operates through that body. It has always been his design to work through his *people*. But we train guys (who will one day become men) to believe they're the exception to that plan.

God wants young men to experience his touch, his love, his rest, his embrace, and his heart. He allows that to happen tangibly as the church steps in to be his hands, arms, wisdom, and love to each other. Being emotionally alone only makes God a distant concept. Being emotional with his people allows God to bring validation to our experiences. Guys need to feel God. We need to show them what he feels like.

4.2 EMOTIONALLY ABANDONED GUYS

BEING A FATHER TO THE FATHERLESS

One of the girls in our youth ministry introduced me to Jason. She told him she thought it might be a good idea for him to talk with me. Jason seemed to be a typical all-American kid. He was a junior at the local high school where he got good grades, he was involved in school leadership, and he'd just secured a starting spot as the quarterback on the varsity football team. Jason was a good-looking, relationally engaging guy. But he was a little nervous when he started our conversation.

"I'm trying to find a place to stay," he began. "My dad kicked me out of the house a week ago, and I've been staying with different friends." Jason acknowledged that he thought this was a temporary thing and that his dad would eventually let him return home, but he wasn't sure how long it would take. Every evening he faced living on the street unless he mobilized resources and found a place to stay. He was totally on his own, yet he still managed to get to school every day and on time, to complete his homework, and to be at football practice until 7 p.m. I could tell he was in agony over his home situation. He was alone.

Jason's mother walked out on her marriage and family when he was about seven, leaving Jason and his younger sister with his father. Jason's dad immediately married a woman who had very little time for Jason, although she connected with his sister. As the years went on, Jason's dad became less interested in him and more influenced by his wife's dislike for the now-teenage boy living in her home.

Jason got attention by overachieving. While he gained the recognition he craved from school authorities, his dad labeled his achievements a "con job." His stepmom was convinced that a teenage guy couldn't be as good as Jason seemed to be, so he must be cheating and lying. The tension escalated into shouting matches that only further entrenched his parents' opinions and gave his stepmom more ammunition to fabricate the theory that she might be in danger if Jason ever got angry.

Jason was at the end of his rope. Everything he did was viewed with contempt by his dad and stepmom. There was nothing he could do to satisfy or please them. Jason wanted so desperately to connect with his father. But his dad's loyalty to his wife—and her utter contempt for Jason—blinded him. Short of his little sister, Jason felt as though he had no family. He felt the pain of emotional abandonment.

I knew Jason needed to experience the love of a *heavenly Father*, but I recall wondering how that would ever happen, given the scars and woundedness this teenager carried. "God, how can I lead him to a loving, ever-present, never-abandoning, gracious, healing, compassionate Father when his concept of a father, or any parent for that matter, is so twisted?"

You probably have a student like Jason in your youth ministry. High national divorce rates, economic instability that forces parents to be absent physically and emotionally, parental incompetence, and family dysfunction will ensure that more guys experience emotional abandonment and aloneness. What complicates the issue is that teenage guys are conditioned to prove themselves. They learn not to ask for help because that would make them appear weak or "less than masculine."

Like Jason, they display the bravado of independence and only seek help for an immediate problem. They would never disclose the internal agony they face. Sometimes a guy can be surrounded by men and still feel abandoned because he believes he must be a lone ranger. He may get messages from his father or other close males that he should be tough and relationally independent. He'll usually feel a compulsion or a competition to prove his masculinity, and that can put him in a lonely and unsupported place.[1]

The cultural mores that generate a guy's need to prove himself as a male are largely shaped by the discrepancy that exists between traits associated with being young (such as dependence, fear, and anxiety) and traits that are associated with being male (such as strength, courage, competence, and independence).[2] His father may not be present—physically or emotionally—to help him navigate through this difficult transition. Or he may isolate himself, creating a self-induced abandonment for fear of being viewed as a wimp—or worse, not finding favor with other men. This lone-ranger mentality, whether induced by abandonment or isolation, must be combated in order to produce relationally healthy, emotionally stable men. Other men need to parent young guys through this turmoil.

PRACTICAL THEOLOGY

Effective youth ministry is built around the principle that youth workers are representatives of Christ. We call this incarnational ministry. In Ephesians 5:1 the apostle Paul tells us we are to imitate Christ. We become the visible and tangible expression of Christ as his ambassadors. Paul uses a similar phrase in 1 Corinthians 4:14-16. He reminds the believers in Corinth that they may have many teachers in Christ, but not many spiritual *fathers* in Christ. Paul "became [their] father through the gospel" (v. 15). He then exhorts them to be imitators of him. The progression is simple: I imitate Christ by *parenting* guys, who then imitate me. This is a scary thought if you've never had a good parenting model yourself. It's also scary if you've never been a parent. What should you do if you don't know how to parent hurting guys?

There are a few helpful tips that will get you on the right track.

1. Redefine success in ministry. James 1:27 defines successful ministry by the way we attend to widows and orphans. Emotionally abandoned teenage guys also belong in this orphan category. Many times guys who are kicked out of their homes (like Jason) are called *throwaway kids*. It's difficult to get statistics about them because they're never reported missing. They are, in fact, orphaned because they have no primary caregivers.

While a guy may not see himself as needing adult help, he certainly isn't developmentally equipped to be alone. Our commitment to orphaned guys will require all of our attention for a lifetime. When God gives a child to a parent, that parent is charged to nurture the child until the child is autonomous. To care for orphaned guys or to be a surrogate parent (especially a surrogate father) to a hurting guy is no simple task. It is difficult, time-consuming work. Resolve that you may not see the fruit of your labor for a long time.

So often our youth ministries perpetuate abandonment because we look for quick, measurable results. We pay minimal attention to abandoned, parentless guys because we buy into the bravado by helping them with immediate solutions and not taking the time to break through to the heart.

Decide that you will *invest* in hurting guys. Realize that this is a slow, methodical process that won't be completed until the young man is a stable, autonomous, God-honoring adult. Paul knew this process was long and required more than delivering the gospel. He says, "Having so fond an affection for you,

we were well-pleased to impart to you not only the gospel of God but also *our own lives*, because you had become very dear to us" (1 Thessalonians 2:8, NASB; emphasis mine).

2. Establish trust. Guys who have been abandoned have a difficult time trusting. Their lives have been riddled with false promises and dashed hopes. When we encounter guys like this, we are moved to minister to them. But our compassion can make us promise things we can't deliver. Broken promises only reinforce a pattern of emotional abandonment. Without follow through, our good intentions only confirm that this guy isn't valuable.

I've done this before, and I've had guys confront me on this issue. If trust is going to be established, then we have to make sure we watch what we say. Don't promise to do something, be somewhere, or meet some need that you cannot follow through on. Trust takes time and initiative. The adult youth worker, not the teenage guy, must take the initiative to keep contact. Make calls, initiate meetings, and send e-mails when you think about or pray for him—*without* promising to do any of that ahead of time.

3. Build a family around a guy. Youth groups and the church can often become a surrogate family for guys with abandonment issues. It's during this time that the labor of building a loving community yields fruit.

Jason got pulled right into our youth group. He felt the genuine and real love of that community. He witnessed my genuine love as it played out in my relationships with my staff and the other students. He also saw his peers trust in those loving encounters.

This was so foreign to his personal experience that he wanted more of it.

He also got a chance to see good role models in other men. Jason's first response was to distrust and question, but as he encountered other men who would care for him as I did, my motives were no longer suspect.

A youth group can also serve as an *extended* family. More and more the recruitment of parents and older adults ministers effectively to hurting guys. They get a chance to experience healthy multigenerational relationships. Empty nesters are the greatest untapped people-resource in the church for doing ministry with hurting guys. These couples in their late 40s to early 50s have raised children. Yet they still have a lot of energy, wisdom, and time to give to a guy. An adult male who has a track record of being a loving father becomes the strongest connecting point to a hurting guy, even more than a youth worker who is closer to his age.

Recently I had a conversation with some friends whose children grew up in my youth ministry. They'd raised two sons, both of whom were now out of college and into their careers. When their boys left for school, they moved to another state and got involved in a new church. That church needed volunteer youth workers. So they fearfully considered the prospect of working with teenagers, but prayerfully decided they would try it. Needless to say, God has taken their parental instincts and used them to minister to abandoned, parentless guys. It was a natural fit for them. They're impacting guys for Christ, and they love every minute of it.

4. Be available. Parentless guys need someone to rely on. They will test your genuineness by being overbearing and sometimes demanding. They may want to control your time, test your authority, demonstrate their power by being strong-willed and defiant, and give you attitude. Teenage guys quickly learn what buttons they can push to see if you'll leave. They figure that if you're just going to walk out on them, they might as well find it out early. And because it's a guy thing to be in control—they'll control when that's going to happen, if it happens at all. You have

to remain patient and available. Availability doesn't mean you are without boundaries, though.

I was talking to a young man who had come through a very tough adolescence. His father passed away years prior, leaving him to navigate adolescence without a strong male figure in his life. This led him into all forms of rebellion and grief, which he directed at his mother. As we talked, he said he felt as if his teenage years were out of control. At the time, he never talked about anything he was going through and he still had difficulty doing so. I asked him about his youth ministry experience at that age. He commented that he would go to church just to make his mom happy, but he didn't want to be there. He'd walk into the church service after it started and sit in the back.

His family had attended this church forever, so the people in the congregation knew him well and were friendly toward him, engaging him in conversation, albeit in a surface-y, shallow way. He also said they knew all the garbage he was into because his mother remained very connected to the church. But nobody confronted him or took the time to "pursue him." My friend told me he wanted so much for a man in that church to tell him that he saw the stupid mistakes he was making. He wished some older man would have "set him straight," even though he knew his behavior was delinquent and destructive.

I asked him how he would have responded if someone had done that. His answer was textbook: he would have been angry, strutted his stuff by telling the guy where to go, and then he would have run. And if the guy really meant business, then he would have modeled strength by pursuing him.

Boundaries become a form of security for a guy who feels the insecurity of abandonment. They help him to establish some sense of normalcy. The pursuit would have demonstrated availability. Guys with abandonment issues often either overachieve, conforming to the rigid standards of the institutions around them, or they become delinquent, finding camaraderie in a band of misfits or a gang. Nonetheless the first line of defense is availability to pursue a guy and form a relationship so that boundaries can be established.

My friend told me he still has a difficult time letting people in because he's afraid that after they get to know him (and see all the junk from his past and the ways he still screws up), they'll leave. Now in his late-adolescent years, he still struggles with abandonment issues. He realizes he either pushes people away or runs when he makes mistakes. As a young adult, he now controls the abandonment process by leaving people before they have a chance to leave him. He's done this to girlfriends, close buddies, and even mentors. He will never know the fullness of God's grace, forgiveness, and mercy unless he is pursued.

So for my friend, I established a boundary on our relationship. I agreed not to be his judge and not to think less of him if he screws up. He had to agree to tell me when he's struggling and not to run when he feels down on himself.

5. Don't compromise authority at the expense of rapport. Many youth workers fear they will compromise their relationship with a student if they lay down the law. This is false and destructive, especially to a parentless guy who needs some sense of stability in his life. Emotionally abandoned guys are desperate for security. They don't know where the lines are, so they need the security that comes with the authority of a parent.

Don't look the other way when a guy does something or says something inappropriate. When a youth worker is perceived by a teenage guy to be a *peer*, that youth worker will never be perceived as an authoritative *role model*. If you are just like his friends, you won't be trusted or viewed as being able (or

credible) to give any kind of authoritative direction to a hurting guy that he isn't already receiving from his insufficient network. Abandoned guys don't just need to vent, they need stable advice and direction. Loving parents want their children to know and to do what is right. Establish a loving authoritative relationship that keeps the doors of communication open. This creates an environment that balances authority and rapport.

One evening after youth group, I overheard a conversation between Jason and some students who were complaining about their parents' "strict" curfew rules. When Jason was asked about his curfew, he said, "I don't have one." The other students proceeded to tell him how lucky he was and how great that would be. Jason interrupted by saying he *wasn't* the lucky one. He told them he wished his dad "cared enough" to make him come in at night. Jason soberly commented, "My dad doesn't ever know where I am, who I'm with, or what I do—and I wish he did."

Effective youth ministry demands that we model. If we compromise the authority that God gives us in the life of a teenage guy, we will neglect the security he needs.

6. Establish a mindset of ownership. Many youth workers have an opportunity to be a spiritual or surrogate parent to a teenage guy. God may be entrusting that guy to your spiritual care and direction, as he did Timothy to Paul, who called Timothy a dear son (2 Timothy 1:2) and a true son in the faith (1 Timothy 1:2). Paul also says this of the Corinthians. In 1 Corinthians 4:14-16, he refers to them as beloved children; and while they may have many "tutors" in Christ, Paul says, "For in Christ Jesus I became your *father* through the gospel. Therefore *I exhort you, be imitators of me*" (NASB; emphasis mine). We imitate Paul's ministry by parenting hurting guys.

We need to develop a sense of ownership with abandoned teenage guys. We need to see them as we would see our own children. Let me give you some quick thoughts on ownership:

a.) Affirm his value. That teenage guy is so valuable to God that he cost the life of God's Son. While none of us are *worthy* of that, we certainly are not *worthless*. Treat teenage guys with respect and honor.

b.) Don't be afraid to verbalize your care and love. You must tell hurting guys that they are loved. Tell them how valuable they are. Let them know when they're doing good things, and lovingly tell them when they're not. There is healing and power in spoken words (Proverbs 16:24). It's especially critical that men declare their love to teenage guys. Our culture is homophobic and self-reliant, both of which make men intimidated to declare their love. Men don't want to appear gay or weak, so we don't tell other guys we love them. All guys—but especially emotionally abandoned guys—need to see men model healthy emotional attachments. A declared love begins the process. Many guys grow up never knowing that anyone loves them because they never hear it said.

c.) Recognize their potential. Look for anything and everything that's positive about him. Help him cultivate his talents, gifts, and abilities. Give him a realistic dream of what he can accomplish by telling him you can see him coaching Little League some day, or being effective in a business setting, or creating beautiful works as an artist, and so on. Be a coach and a cheerleader. By the way, don't just recognize a guy's outward abilities; recognize his inner qualities as well. Notice and tell him when he's relationally engaging, compassionate, patient, or thoughtful. Let him know that those qualities are the measure of a man.

d.) Listen to him. Be intense about hearing what he has to say. Ask clarifying questions. Always check the affect or emotions of the conversation, as well as the content. Ask him what he feels about the things he's talking about. This will help you connect with the heart and soul of the guy. It will also affirm that you understand him.

e.) Don't be afraid to use meaningful touch. We live in a litigation-happy society that has impaired our ability to be Christ's arms to guys. We need to combat this by building healthy, intimate, parenting relationships with guys and reinforce them with appropriate parent-reflective touch. In other words, as the relationship deepens, show the appropriate affection that a loving parent would show. Meaningful touch is shamefully missing from the life of emotionally abandoned teenage guys.

I was once having a conversation with a guy who began to open up about some hurt in his life. While he was talking, he became angry and things started to escalate. So I put my hand on his shoulder, and he immediately stopped talking, lowered his head, and started to weep. After a few minutes, he said, "No one ever touches me." Jesus would have done the same. We are allowed by Almighty God to be his arms, heart, and love to guys in a more tangible way. Jesus doesn't always give advice; sometimes he just holds a guy to let him know he is secure, valued, and unconditionally loved.

f.) Share a dream for his spiritual life. Tell him how God rescues abandoned teenag-

> ers by giving him a vision of Joseph and Daniel, two teenage guys in Scripture who were abandoned yet succeeded because they were plugged into God. Let him know that God desires an intimate relationship with him, and then be the conduit through which God can accomplish that in his life. Help him to see, know, and experience that in Christ "old things have passed away…all things have become new" (2 Corinthians 5:17, NKJV).

Parenting hurting, abandoned guys implies great, uncompromised ownership built on insurmountable value and unfathomable love.

After about a year of building a relationship with Jason and modeling a loving father for him, I had the opportunity of watching him develop some quality emotional attachments—with others and with God. He finished strong during his senior year and went to college, healed and new.

Now Jason lives in another state. He's a college graduate and into his career. But he called one night to thank me for being the only real dad he'd ever known. As Jason shared his heart, I realized that God had done a great thing in his life, and I had the privilege of going along on that ride.

4.3 ANGER, DEPRESSION, AND SUICIDE

In order to fully understand depression and suicide as it relates to teenage guys, you must first grasp some pervasive dynamics that affect a guy's emotional identity development, creating a *triple jeopardy effect*. Two of these three dynamics are ingrained in Western-cultured guys, and the third in Western-cultured *Christian* guys. And it happens from the time they are born.

THE TRIPLE JEOPARDY EFFECT

Dynamic #1: Lack of Emotion Equals Strength

Eddy was a 19-year-old college sophomore. His dad had been battling a fatal disease for a long time. His dad wanted life to remain as normal as possible for his children, so Eddy went to school knowing full well that at any moment he could get a phone call with the devastating news.

The family had anticipated and planned for his father's death for more than a year. On the night Eddy's dad passed away, Eddy called me to let me know he was going home and wouldn't be in class. I arranged to meet with him before his plane left, and I asked him how he was doing.

"I knew this was coming for a long time," he said. "So I feel as prepared as possible." What impacted me most was not Eddy's candor and discerning perspective but his plan of action. He said it was going to be hard for him to see his mom and sisters because he had to be strong for them. When I asked him what that meant, he said he couldn't show that it was rip-

ping him up inside. He was afraid he would cry too much. Eddy believed that being emotionless demonstrated control, and control made him strong. He was afraid of the sadness because he saw it as weakness. Eddy had learned well that if he was sad, then he couldn't be strong for his family. So he believed he had to suck up his feelings for their sakes. If this is ingrained in guys regarding loss and death, then the stakes are even higher if he experiences some form of depression.

Terrence Real, in his book *I Don't Want to Talk About It*, notes that women are allowed to openly express their depression and sadness. He identifies this as *overt depression*. Guys, on the other hand, are not allowed to do this, thus they experience *covert depression*. Real says; "Because of the stigma attached to depression, men often allow their pain to burrow deeper and further from view."[1]

Covert depression keeps a guy from being seen as weak or womanly. Beginning in childhood, a guy feels pressure from society to bury his negative emotions, such as sadness and depression. Real recognizes this as well. He identifies that this is the result of the social construct that a guy bends and conforms to.[2] The first jeopardizing dynamic is the buy-in that a guy is strong if his emotional level is controlled to a minimum or not displayed at all.

Dynamic #2: Derivatives of Anger Are Acceptable Emotions

Okay, so you push this guy to tell you what he feels, and he begins to see the point. He realizes he can't get away with telling you what he thinks, so he says losing the football game made him feel—frustrated. Western culture creates an emotional line of demarcation for guys. That line is anger and its various forms. If a guy is going to feel anything negative, he quickly reduces it to some form of anger, such as frustration, aggravation, confusion (or mind anger), and upset.

THINK ABOUT IT…

The National Longitudinal Study of Adolescent Health found that teenage guys who were exposed to or engaged in street violence and adolescent violence experienced less depression than guys who weren't violent. Could this reinforce the notion that the coping strategy for depression in guys is aggression and violence?[3]

Here's how it plays out: a guy is in a conversation and someone says something derogatory about him; he gets angry. If a guy has an argument with his girlfriend and you press him to identify his emotion, then he'll say he's frustrated. If he experiences getting cut from the team, then he feels confused. While these are valid emotions, they are secondary ones. That means a guy feels something else first (a primary emotion), but quickly replaces it with anger or some form of it. Guys are trained to reel in their emotion to a place that's acceptable for them as men. That place is a cadre of various forms of anger.

If he were honest about his primary feelings in these situations, a guy would say he first felt embarrassed by the derogatory comment, but then quickly opted to a more acceptable secondary emotion of anger. He may have felt afraid or insecure about losing his girlfriend, but it's more masculine to be frustrated. He probably battled feelings of sadness, disappointment, inferiority, and defeat after being cut from the team, but he learned fast to reduce that to a much more manageable emotion of confusion.

Guys learn that anger and its variations, although sometimes socially inappropriate, are generally acceptable masculine emotional responses. While anger is negative, it is also powerful, intimidating, commanding, forceful, and strong. It releases the bravado in a guy, so naturally it becomes the masculine emotion of choice. Thus, guys don't cry; they hit things. They don't feel embarrassed; they retaliate.

When it comes to negative feelings, a guy draws a line that is marked by anger. Intense negative feelings that cross that line become quickly reduced or pulled back into the comfort zone of negative feelings (see fig. 5). This is the second great jeopardizing dynamic. If he begins to feel extremely depressed, then he will mask that primary emotion with anger. The more intense the negative feeling, the more he holds the line so as to maintain some sense of masculine power and emotional control. This is commonly

known as a *masked depression*. The depression is not detected because the guy is so angry, oppositional, or even violent (in order to cover the real emotion). If this sadness gets too out-of-control for a guy, his attempt to hold the anger line can turn into rage, evidencing itself in self-mutilation and even suicide—the ultimate form of self-directed anger.

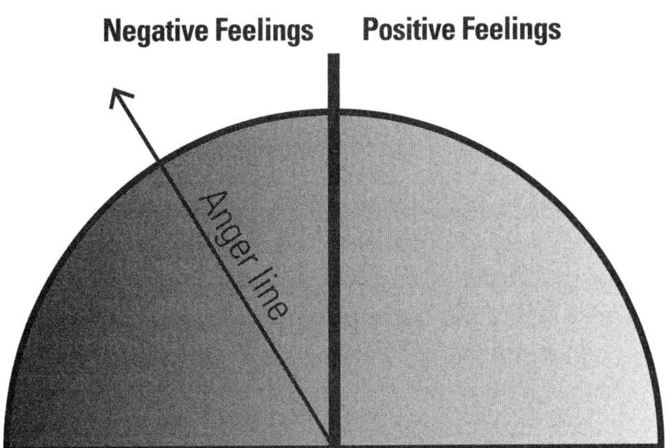

Figure 5

Dynamic #3: Depression Is Evidence of Spiritual Deficiency

I attended a Sunday morning worship service at a very large church. The pastor preached on depression. His basic premise was that depression could be prevented and cured if the sufferer's relationship with God was more intact. He based this on the idea that God is the giver of abundant life; therefore, if God is at the center of one's life, then that person should be depression free.

The message is clear: spiritual vitality prevents and cures depression. It's equally clear, although unstated, that anyone experiencing depression has some spiritual problem that facilitates this. This pastor's viewpoint is common. Many Christians believe mental health issues are rooted in spiritual deficiencies.

I've often said I want to be in heaven to hear this pastor explain his view to Elijah. (Elijah came through great spiritual victory at Mount Carmel. Yet after this, he experiences a deep depression and even suicidal desires. Elijah wants to die. But there was no spiritual deficiency in Elijah's life at this point.) Just as this pastor finishes, I would invite Jeremiah, the weeping prophet, into the conversation.

But for Christian guys, depression is another sign of weakness. If he's experiencing depression, then he's weak as a man and weak as a *spiritual* man. This creates the triple-jeopardy effect I referred to at the beginning of this chapter. Depression and sadness back him into a corner. He can easily lose hope and not find the necessary resolve to overcome his depression.

Guys are bombarded with this jeopardizing trifecta throughout their lives. When dealing with guys and depression and suicide, it's important to understand that these dynamics must also be battled in helping a guy get through the dark times.

DEPRESSION

While teenage guys approach depression differently than their female counterparts, all adolescents experience depression. It's as common as a cold. And like the common cold, there are many theories and scads of research that have been done to discover what causes depression—but nothing conclusive has been found. Most therapists would agree that depression in adolescents is induced in two ways. The first is physiological; the second is situational. Yet they go hand in hand.

Depression is manifested in many forms. A severe depression, known as *major depression*, is usually treated with anti-depressant medication. Another manifestation, often more common in adolescence, is *dysthymic disorder* or *dysthymia*. This isn't severe, but it's a pervasive sense of negativity and sadness that comes and goes. It's what's commonly referred to as "feeling blue." The last is *bipolar disorder*, at one time called *manic-depressive disorder*. This involves severe lows of depression followed by episodes of mania or severe highs—two polar (bi-polar) extremes.

Another type of depression is *situational depression*. It involves more of the brain processes that I describe in chapter 5.1. Scott was a teenage guy in my youth group who had a very promising football career. As a freshman he played on the varsity squad. He was being watched and recruited by colleges by the end of his sophomore year. As a junior, Scott suffered an injury that ended his sports career trajectory. Every time he played, he was in pain. Soon his doctors told him that if he wanted to walk or play with his future children, then he shouldn't play football anymore. All of Scott's plans and dreams were dashed. And his ticket to a good college was taken away because all the scholarship offers dried up. He'd built an identity around something that wasn't permanent, so that identity was lost as well.

Scott plunged into a depression as a result of his situation, and it became so severe that he even contemplated suicide. Scott's story is not so unusual. Many adolescent guys encounter situations where they experience loss, death, broken relationships, family conflict and divorce, or chronic illness, among other things. These negative life situations serve as facilitators for depression. And sociological situations may also bring about depression, such as poverty, discrimination, bullying, terrorism, and so on.

Symptoms of Teenage Depression in Guys

While symptoms of depression are common among teenage guys and girls, they're often observed differently. Remember, a teenage guy's way of dealing with depression is colored by the three dynamics that were mentioned at the beginning of this chapter. Here are some of the symptoms you should watch for.

Withdrawal and isolation. These are the most common. Since depression involves feelings of sadness, anxiety, hopelessness, and melancholy—and they're all outside the radar of perceived masculine strength—a guy will isolate himself so they won't be discovered. If a guy you know begins spending unusual amounts of time alone in his room; if he comes to school or youth group and avoids his friends or sits by himself; if he isolates himself by withdrawing inwardly (not engaging, avoiding conversations, and so on); or if he runs away, these may all be methods of avoidance, and they could be symptomatic of his depression.

Anger. Remember, a guy may deal with sadness and hurt by lashing out. This symptom is played out in various forms, from being verbally short with someone to physical fighting. It may appear as though he's becoming more rebellious by defying authority, pushing the boundaries, and so on. His anger can also be seen in risky behaviors such as cutting class, driving recklessly, engaging in physically dangerous stunts, experimentation with or use of illegal substances, and sexual promiscuity.

Guys may also try to avoid the inward pain of depression by creating outward physical pain. This evidences itself in self-mutilation—cutting, branding (hot metal is applied to the skin to leave a wound that scars a pattern), tattooing, and piercing.

Now let's get something out on the table right away: Just because a guy gets a tattoo or has his nipples pierced doesn't mean he's depressed. But if this behavior is outside the norm for him, and if

it becomes excessive, then there may be something more to his actions than a mere fashion statement. Many guys who've had multiple tattoos, piercings, and body cuts (e.g., having their tongue slit at the tip or their penis pierced) talk about how the physical pain creates a rush that takes their mind off the emotional pain.

Craig was a 17-year-old gymnast who began to isolate and withdraw. His family became very concerned about him because this was outside his usual personality. I had a good relationship with Craig, so I arranged to meet with him regularly. One summer afternoon, Craig met me wearing a long-sleeved shirt (out of the ordinary for the season and for Craig). I became suspicious because guys may use clothing to hide needle marks from drug use or the scars from cutting themselves. I confronted Craig and asked him to pull up his sleeves. Craig had begun cutting patterns into his arms with a sharp piece of broken glass. The pressures of his sport, along with his inability to meet those demands, were making him depressed. He couldn't talk about it because it only affirmed his weakness and the already growing ineptness he was feeling. He said the physical pain from cutting was a relief because it diverted the mental anguish. The initial pain releases endorphins into a guy's system, which slightly elevates his mood and creates a bit of a head rush. Then the extended pain of healing takes attention away from the emotional depression. It's easier to nurse physical wounds than emotional ones.

After Craig was discovered, he began to cut his lower abdomen and thighs, where nobody else would see. Craig was one step away from suicide. His parents got him into treatment immediately because his severe depression was masked with incredible anger.

Apathy, lethargy, and loss of interest. This is played out in multiple ways. For example, if a guy is an artist but he doesn't have a desire to paint anymore. His grades may suffer because he doesn't care

about homework. Sometimes it even comes out in routine behaviors such as hygiene. He may become too lethargic to shower, shave, brush his teeth, and so on.

Lethargy can be evidenced in attitude. This is the flatline effect. It's where a guy isn't fazed by anything, meaning he isn't moved by tragedy, nor is he excited by something really great. Ultimately he may experience something known as *anadonia* or the loss of any pleasure. Anything that brings the slightest bit of good feeling—such as going to a movie, listening to music, or seeing his favorite pet—doesn't do it. Loss of interest overlaps at this point with lethargy.

One distinct way that loss of interest is manifested is in concentration. A guy who's depressed may have difficulty concentrating and remembering simple things that occurred five minutes ago. Loss of interest is also evidenced by loss of appetite. Guys are more prone to avoid eating when they experience depression, although the opposite does occur. Teenage guys devour large amounts of food mainly because their bodies need it and also because this is a point of pleasure for guys. If they suffer loss of interest and pleasure, then their appetite will diminish.

Another way a guy evidences lack of interest and pleasure is in a diminished sexual desire. Guys with severe depression will often comment about not having any sex drive or sexual interest. This is often measured by diminished masturbation in most guys. Remember that while diminished activity may be more common, the opposite can also occur. Some guys say they masturbate *more* when they feel depressed. They often cite this as an attempt to bring some pleasure back into their lives.

In any case, any extremes from the normal patterns of life may be symptomatic of depression.

Headaches, back pain, stomach and bowel issues, and fatigue. He may experience irregular sleep pat-

terns resulting in oversleeping and frequent napping. Depending on how the depression affects his appetite, you may notice physical changes in a guy's weight, resulting in either rapid weight loss or gain. If he starts using substances to medicate his depression, you may notice physical symptoms of drug and alcohol use, such as glassy eyes, a runny or chapped nose, emaciation, skin pigment changes, and so on.

Preoccupation with death and dying. This symptom links depression to suicide and suicide ideation. Depression in adolescent guys can be fatal.

SUICIDE

Do a quick search online, and you'll find statistics on adolescent suicide from nations around the world. The United Nations reports that approximately four million suicide attempts take the lives of more than 90,000 adolescents each year.[4] The overwhelming common denominator is that guys are more likely to succeed at taking their life than females. Teenage guys in the United States are four times more likely to commit suicide than teenage girls.[5] Guys are more violent and use more violent means. In the United States, guys use firearms as the primary method of carrying out suicide; suffocation by hanging is the secondary leading method. Guys tend to respond more in anger, which makes their attempts much more compulsive, potent, and sure.

According to the United States Census Bureau's *Statistical Abstracts of the United States: 2004-2005*, suicide among adolescents has increased almost 300 percent since 1950. *It has become the third leading cause of death among adolescents in the United States, preceded only by homicide and accidental death.*[6] It's even been speculated that many of the accidental deaths could potentially be suicides as well. If that were the case, then suicide would be the second leading cause of death among American adolescents.

WHY DO TEENAGE GUYS ATTEMPT AND COMMIT SUICIDE?

1. Pressures of adolescence: This age span can be rough on some guys. The attempt to change, wrestle through identity development, and find some semblance of normalcy along with the competition and pressure to be a competent, successful man can leave a guy feeling hopeless and weak. Suicide can become an escape option.

2. Outgrowth of depression: We have already discussed depression. Suicide is the ultimate resolve to some guys caught in the grip of severe depression.

3. Feelings of being unwanted, devalued, and unloved: While girls tend to be more relationally secure than guys, guys still need connectedness for survival. If a guy feels as though he's not a valued part of his community, he may turn his anger on himself.

4. Feelings of loss and despair: It's critical to remember that loss for a teenage guy can include loss of hopes, aspirations, and dreams. Since much of his world defines him by his skills, this loss can be devastating.

5. Physical and sexual abuse: Many guys would rather die than admit to being abused, especially sexually. Most of the time, the profile of the *abuser* is male, not the profile of the *victim*. It's estimated that one in seven or eight guys is sexually abused. Guys who are abused struggle with identity issues, power and competency issues, and gender issues. Suicide can become an option to silence the internal conflict resulting from a guy's abuse.

6. Improper view of life and death: I've talked with guys who are so angry that their suicidal ideation leads them to see suicide as an attempt to get even, to hurt someone, or to get attention. Adolescent guys may not see the permanence of suicide, which is why it must be talked about in raw, real, and

blunt terms. This brings a proper perspective back to death and life.

What Are the Warning Signs?

There are always warning signs. Youth workers need to become experts at reading and interpreting the signs.

Verbal cues. Guys may not talk much about what they're feeling, but they will give verbal cues as to suicide ideation. He may speak in terms of being better off dead, which can be said as self-abasement or as a joke. Suicidal and homicidal threats or wishes may also be expressed in outbursts of anger. A youth worker's radar should home in on comments like that. A guy may speak in terms of wondering what it would be like if he were never born (the *It's a Wonderful Life* syndrome). Verbal cues may also come in the form of morbid conversations—fascinations and obsessions with death, killing, or dying. He may make morbid comments that exclude himself from the landscape of the future. Or those same morbid comments may include phrases like, "If something were to happen to me…" or "When I'm dead and gone..."

Behavioral cues. As previously mentioned, changes in hygiene habits and eating and sleeping patterns, isolation, extremely reckless and risky behaviors, use and experimentation with substances, and self-mutilation become more pronounced as depression gets more severe.

A guy may attempt to get his affairs in order as he entertains suicidal ideations. These behaviors include giving away prized possessions, such as baseball cards, trophies, pictures, and so on. He may also start backing out of his commitments, such as quitting a team or a job, canceling appointments, or not making new appointments. Other similar behavioral cues have a "last will and testament" feel. They may include making arrangements with a friend to take

care of his dog or younger siblings if something were to happen to him; planning a funeral (checking into the cost of cremation, writing eulogies, and so on). I've encountered guys who wanted to check out funeral homes and visit cemeteries. They presented this curiosity in a light manner so as to throw off any suspicion as to their true intentions. Many times a guy will become morbidly sentimental by writing notes of gratitude to friends or making a music CD of all his favorite songs for a friend to remember him by—"just in case something were to happen to him."

Another strong behavioral cue is a prior suicide attempt. Guys who survive a suicide attempt have already formulated a plan or strategy. He has rehearsed acquiring the means to accomplish his plan. He's already worked through the fear, intimidation, and immobility of following through with his plan—having been there and done that before. He may now have a new sense of follow through. This may give him a new determination to complete his task. He may also believe that the help he's getting is not remedying the situation, so it can only entrench or reinforce his desire to make another attempt and follow through with his original solutions.[7]

Descriptive clues. These are the personality, character, and attributes a teenage guy exhibits in his daily lifestyle, which may also put him at risk for suicide. For example, if a guy tends to be compulsive, that descriptive cue puts him at risk for suicide when coupled with an already severe depression. His compulsion may lead him to make rash decisions regarding suicide.

Lacking problem-solving skills is another descriptive cue. If a teenage guy has trouble making wise, logical, rational decisions, his judgment regarding life may be jeopardized.

Another descriptive cue is seeking attention. A guy who seeks attention may fantasize about every-

one coming to his funeral, crying, and reminiscing about his life. This is self-centered and simple attention seeking. It can also be deadly when coupled with severe depression.

If a guy is prone to stubbornness or has tunnel vision, the risk rate elevates. If this guy makes a decision about suicide, then often there is no turning back. He may not seek out help. If this descriptor is evident in a guy whom you know is battling depression, then it's best to ask direct questions about his thoughts and future.

A guy who is quick-tempered, easily set off, or has violent outbursts of rage is extremely at risk. So is the guy who is overly introspective, secretive, withdrawn, and over-guarded.

Situational clues. We've already talked about many of the situational clues that serve as warning signs for suicide. They're the same situations that gave rise to depression in a guy's life. Chronic disease, loss, life stresses and pressures, trauma, and many others can set off suicidal ideation. A youth worker must always listen and remain very aware of the situations of an adolescent guy's life.

One situational clue we must talk about is cluster suicides. This phenomenon occurs in a community of adolescents when one kid dies or commits suicide. It's best described as a ripple effect that gives teenagers, guys especially, the impetus (whether it's in the form of courage, permission, empowerment, actualization, or sheer despair) to follow suit. This is why crisis counselors are immediately brought into death situations when a teenager is involved. A teenage guy may see the shock, sadness, and trauma that suicide has on his peers and community and begin to desire that same response for himself.

Another situational cue that must be taken into account is a family history of suicide. While suicide is not hereditary, family history carries the same phe-

nomenology as cluster suicides. A past suicide can model a way of escape, as well as demonstrate positive and negative effects on families, friends, and communities.

YOUTH WORKER TIP

In his book *Hear My Story: Understanding the Cries of Troubled Youth*, Dean Borgmann writes, "Suicide is not chosen; it happens when pain exceeds the resources for coping with pain. Whether we fully agree with this statement or not, it helpfully reminds us we are not trying to talk someone out of their pain—or worse, denying the existence of the pain. We may suggest that others have gotten through their dark nights, and we can talk (or read) about how they did it."[8]

How Can a Youth Worker Help a Guy through This?

1. Be available and listen. This doesn't mean you don't create personal boundaries (such as allowing a guy to call you all night), but a guy needs to know that you genuinely care and value him. Listening conveys that.

2. Stay calm. In an escalating situation, you need to stay calm. Quick solutions are often not good ones.

3. Verbalize your thoughts. Ask questions in a straightforward, direct manner. For example: "Are you thinking about killing yourself?" These kinds of blunt questions don't put thoughts into a guy's head; they unmask his intentions. If you aren't direct, then a guy can easily deceive you and himself.

4. Speak in terms of finality. A guy isn't thinking straight when he's caught in suicidal ideation. He romanticizes death. Because of this I tend to avoid using the word *suicide*. It sounds too surreal. Instead I always use the phrase "killing yourself." There is a stark, cold finality to that phrase that robs a guy of the romance. Romeo and Juliet killed themselves. It was a great romantic story, but in the end the two kids were still dead.

5. Don't be silent; suicide is not confidential. Realize that you are responsible for the knowledge you receive from any minor. You need to let guys know that if harm is going to come to him or to anyone else, then you are required by law to report it. In almost every state, people who work with minors are liable for the information they have.

6. Mobilize resources. Many times a guy just needs to be with someone during a crisis. People are the best

resource. If a guy is suicidal, then the best advice and preventative measure you can take is to have parents and loved ones be with him. And always refer the guy to a trained counselor. Coach his family, if possible, to get him into therapy immediately.

Some Things You Shouldn't Do

1. Don't underestimate a guy's sincerity or resourcefulness. Crisis to a teenage guy is different than crisis to an adult. We have worked through coping strategies and have developed better problem-solving skills. Don't downplay a guy's problem and despair, no matter how simple the solution could be or how insignificant you believe the issue is. Also realize that guys have a very high accomplished suicide rate; four times higher than their female peers. A guy can easily commit suicide.

2. Don't try "shock treatment." Joking around or flippantly affirming that he should go ahead and do something stupid can only give a guy the permission he needs to follow through. If a guy says he'd be better off dead, don't even jokingly agree with him. Your joke may be taken as affirmation of his perceived lack of value and worth. Be aware that other guys may also be struggling. So while the guy you joke with may understand that you're teasing, the others may hear a different message. Remember, he may joke around to mask his real feelings and hide perceived weakness.

3. Don't assume time heals all wounds. The most common mistake a youth worker can make is to assume that a guy will grow out of this dark phase. While he may, a guy may also lack the patience, vision, and hope to see it through. Time does not heal wounds—God does, and he uses his people as a vehicle through which he works. There are no lone rangers.

4. Don't make false promises. Sometimes God doesn't deliver people from a depressive situation in

the way or time frame they expect. Don't put words in God's mouth. In addition, realize that you don't have to disclose all the facts to a guy, either. For example: If a guy is contemplating suicide because he's been diagnosed with a chronic problem, don't tell him God will make him well. He may not! On the other hand, if he asks about the disease, don't tell him about your friend who died from it. You don't want to give false hope, but you don't want to rob him of hope, either.

5. Don't give pat answers or clichés. "Don't worry, be happy!" "Things will work themselves out." Even Bible verses such as "God works all things together for good to those who love him." They minimize the issue. A guy needs you to be genuinely concerned. He needs you to be real.

4.4 AGGRESSION AND VIOLENCE

My telephone rang about 11:30 one evening. The voice on the other end belonged to a former student of mine who was now a youth pastor at the church down the street from where I lived. He was pretty shaken up. They'd just had their weekly youth Bible study, and after the meeting, kids were hanging out on the church grounds. Apparently two of the guys in the parking lot had a problem with each other. Words were exchanged; tempers flared; and in a fit of rage, one guy pulled out a knife and plunged it into the other guy's shoulder.

"This isn't supposed to happen at church," my friend said.

While we want to make sure the church is a safe place for guys to work through their mental, emotional, and spiritual struggles, it also needs to be a physically safe place for students. Students should be well-monitored, and we also should understand the makeup of guys in our society today.

In the last decade of the twentieth century, youth workers encountered a new and sobering concern. Kids were killing kids or committing acts of *adolescentcide*.[1] In April 1999 the world was shocked to hear that two teenage guys, ages 18 and 17, walked into Columbine High School in Littleton, Colorado, and killed 13 people before killing themselves. This was the worst of the school killings that preceded it. During the 1997-1998 school year, violent teenage guys from all over the United States left 14 dead and over 50 wounded in their wake. A 14-year-old in West

Paducah, Kentucky, killed three; an 11-year-old and a 13-year-old in Jonesboro, Arkansas, killed five; a 15-year-old in Springfield, Oregon, killed four; a 16-year-old in Bethel, Arkansas, killed two; and a 15-year-old in Conyers, Georgia, opened fire on his classmates, wounding six. Since 1987 the School Violence Watch Network has recorded a timeline of more than 68 incidents of violent crimes and deaths in schools—all committed by teenage guys.[2]

In the United States, there has been a rise in violent crimes committed by adolescents over the last 10 years. American teenagers are twice as likely to become victims of violent crimes as adults. And homicide is the leading cause of death among adolescent African and Hispanic American males.[3] It's the third leading cause of death among all teenagers.[4]

Many teenagers are afraid to go to school because of the potential for violence there. There's a wide scope of violent acts that can either strike adolescents or be inflicted by adolescents, including fights, bullying, physical or sexual assault—with (usually) or without a weapon—robbery, suicide, and homicide. From 1999 to 2000, an estimated 1.5 million violent incidents occurred in public elementary and secondary schools.[5] Thus schools have resorted to hiring security officers, initiating searches and dress codes, and installing metal detectors to curb gang violence and other dangerous activities.

More recently teenage guys have been involved in a new form of violence labeled *juvenile mass murders.* These violent acts resemble a drive-by shooting, but they're not gang related. And while gang violence *is* an ongoing problem that must be addressed, it's only mentioned here as an example of one type of violence that affects adolescents and as a point of comparison for the issue of juvenile mass murder.

Juvenile mass murder occurs when a socially and psychologically maladjusted adolescent opens fire on a crowd of unsuspecting adolescents. With the exception of one account, in every recorded incident the killer is an adolescent guy.[6] Often the victims have little or no relationship to the killer, nor are they associated with the plight of the killer. The chosen venue of the juvenile mass murderer is usually one where teenagers congregate, such as a schoolyard, cafeteria, or at school events (e.g., a dance). Anywhere adolescents tend to hang out can become a venue for a juvenile mass murder. Businesses that cater to teenagers, concerts and theaters, and church youth ministries may not be exempt.

While juvenile mass murderers typically target other teenagers, no one is safe. Adult caretakers, authority figures, or rescuers (i.e., anyone who tries to help the victims during the incident) will often become victims as well. The killer calculates the time and place, utilizing the element of surprise. Shots are fired, but students mistakenly believe it's only fireworks or caps being used in some kind of prank. This notion is quickly dispelled as curiosity gives way to terror, panic, chaos, fear, and trauma. The entire incident only takes a matter of minutes, but it leaves many people dead or wounded.

Usually there is a precipitating event that triggers the teenage guy to murder someone. It's the "straw that breaks the camel's back" or the one thing that pushes the adolescent killer over the edge. But as we will examine later, there is also an underlying disturbance in the adolescent's psyche or social structure. This guy's mind seeks out a permanent and deadly solution to his problems. Unfortunately, his victims become the unwilling and unsuspecting recipients of his rage.

Forensic psychologists have discovered that many of these teenage guys who act out in a violent rage were often victims of bullying or abuse themselves. A downward spiral of "cause and effect" is woven into this discovery. First, a bully mercilessly picks on a young man. (Keep in mind that the bully is just another guy trying to prove something to the rest

of his peers through deviant behavior.) Second, the bullied guy is so hurt by the experience that he loses all hope of recovery. Many times his masculinity is wounded to the point where he believes the only way he can recover his manhood and regain respect is to do something desperate. Third, he believes *everyone* is laughing, belittling, and victimizing him. This "psych ache," as Edwin Schneidman calls it, becomes insurmountably unbearable.[7] Fourth, he fantasizes about wiping out all of his enemies in a single act of revenge for the disrespect, humiliation, and merciless shame he has suffered. In addition, he believes his vengeful act will also serve to show others that he is strong—a force to be feared and reckoned with. It's his belief that this strong, masculine identity can only be acquired by taking away the identities of others who are popular, unique, superior, better off, and accepted, yet also hurtful, cruel, rude, and disrespectful.[8] Fifth, a deep anger builds inside of him until it reaches the breaking point of rage. And finally, his rage is triggered by what seems to be a mild incidental act (e.g., a teacher confronts him in class, a rude comment is made in the hall, and so on), and the guy explodes in a homicidal frenzy. He plays out his rampage of revenge and retribution, sometimes culminating in the ultimate act of hopelessness—namely suicide.

RAISING CAIN

The first murder recorded in Scripture is that of Abel by his brother Cain. We get a glimpse into the *male* human condition by reading the narrative. Cain's sacrifice is found lacking in God's eyes. His immediate response is anger, which grows out of the wound of shame, rejection, and sadness. God immediately offers Cain grace and healing. He says, "Why are you angry? Why is your face downcast? If you do what is right, will you not be accepted? But if you do not do what is right, sin is crouching at your door; it desires to have you, but you must master it" (Genesis 4:6-7).

Judging from God's response, we learn he has built within men a predisposition to have dominion over things—including sin. Cain is challenged to master his sin. But the problem is that the nature of man is also affected by that same sin. Cain's father passed that sin from generation to generation. So Cain ignores the counsel of the Lord. He allows his woundedness to turn into a jealousy that can only be satiated by rage. Instead of controlling and dominating his sin, he redirects it to control and dominate the situation using all the aggression that was needed to overcome the sin problem. Cain becomes violent to the point of death.

As a result of this act of aggression, Cain is cursed to be a "restless wanderer on the earth" (v. 12), a punishment that is more than he can bear. This wandering, while literal for Cain, is also representative. It illustrates his self-imposed detachment from God and community. Cain's natural instinct was to resolve the pain appropriately, but he chose to nurture his pain into rage. This led to a psychological alienation, to which God turns him over—literally. Could it be that this curse on Cain is passed on to mankind, just like the sin curse of his father Adam?

Like Cain, guys have an internal mechanism that often causes them to isolate themselves and then respond in aggressive defense whenever they feel threatened, vulnerable, or emotionally wounded. In *Raising Cain: Protecting the Emotional Life of Boys,* authors Dan Kindlon and Michael Thompson suggest that guys are primed to see the world as a threatening place and to respond to that threat with aggression. They say:

> Because they are caught in the trap of trying to satisfy the impossible requirements of the traditional masculine self-image, boys are sensitive to any perceived disre-

> spect. Furthermore, their experience in the culture of cruelty leaves them expecting hostility in their interactions with others. Last, boys, because of their emotional illiteracy, are bad at reading emotional cues in social situations. As a result, they're more likely to interpret neutral situations as threatening.[9]

In just about every culture, guys have to prove their masculinity to other males. This creates a fight for status and acceptance. This fight may come in the form of "demonstrating their prowess in stereotypically masculine traits and pursuits, such as toughness and interpersonal dominance, sporting ability and physical skill, heterosexual sexual achievement and popularity, and humor and bantering."[10] Many times this fight becomes physically aggressive, and the conditioning to gain and hold on to masculine status can become harmful.

Guys cross the line all the time. It starts with bigger and older guys picking on younger guys. This may turn into seemingly innocent bantering and practical joking. At some time, most every guy has been the butt of a joke that's designed to humiliate or embarrass him. Jokes range from trying to make a poor guy wet the bed by putting his hand in water to elaborate scenarios designed to humiliate him in front of the opposite sex. Vying for masculine power is a process that's often refined in the locker room. Jokes are made about physical size—from a guy's stature to his genitalia. Pranks that are designed to test a guy's physical strength, such as putting Icy Hot® in his jock strap, run wild. Acts of physical aggression (such as roughhousing, snapping towels, and, more cruelly, urinating on weaker or unsuspecting guys in the shower) are also demonstrated here.

Many fathers, even Christian fathers, give their sons permission to fight back. In truth, we don't want our sons to be weak "sissy boys," so we've learned a theology of violence that denotes times when it's acceptable and unacceptable to physically fight, emotionally attack, and even wage war. We don't really understand the difference between "being empowered" and "wielding power." Power and violence go hand in hand in a guy's world.

I encountered a pastor who had a reputation for being cruel at times. He would intimidate and control people like some kind of spiritual bully. When I confronted him on this matter, he dismissed it as spiritually acceptable in the name of *truth telling,* motivating people to be about kingdom work, and confrontation of sin. While his explanation demonstrated shades of empowerment (the working of God's power through someone), his actions were just the exertion of his own raw power over people. He also noted that his style of leadership was that of an army general. He needed to be direct, demanding, forceful, and strong.

Unfortunately this type of masculine power mongering achieves results because people fear it and other men desire to have it. The results are interpreted as spiritual success, generating what I call a *Christian Strongman Syndrome*. This behavior runs rampant in Christian circles, and it only further confuses teenage guys, reinforcing an aggressive spirit in them.

Now it may be good to note here that masculine aggression is not necessarily a bad thing. What is bad is that, like Cain and the above-mentioned pastor, guys have the curse of getting the trajectory off course. Aggression becomes a destructive force when a guy learns to use people and value things rather than using things and valuing people. Guys receive numerous messages that say people are expendable objects to overpower. This idea is constantly played out for them in the media, especially on reality TV shows.

Competition

Right from the start, I'll acknowledge that competition is healthy, and it can produce honorable charac-

ter in guys. But we don't teach them how to quit or how to recognize when it's time to surrender. (Just typing those words makes me feel less than masculine!)

Real men don't surrender. Real men don't lose! Teenage guys learn it's disgraceful and feeble not to rise to the occasion when they've been challenged. Even if he knows full well that he's going to get beaten up, a guy often will engage in enough trash talk to circumvent the challenge. As one guy told me, the motto for guys in this era is: "I don't get even; I just get ahead." This competitive edge can often become destructive when it's unbridled, and bridling it runs counter to the masculine identity that's internalized in guys.

YOUTH MINISTRY TIP

At one point in time, competition was a drawing factor in youth ministry. Elaborate competitions are appealing to guys. But youth workers today need to be aware that competition can alienate some students and negatively reinforce the aggressive identities that are forming in teenage guys. While I wouldn't avoid competition altogether, youth workers should be highly sensitive to this issue and its effect on mainstream, as well as marginalized, guys.

Media

Competition and violence have become the steady diet of entertainment for a teenage guy. The heroes in movies are tough and rugged men who are quick to fight and kill and less likely to find peaceful solutions to the problems they encounter. Judging from the genre of movies from the last decade, many heroes don't even have to be good guys (e.g., *Payback, Boondock Saints, Fight Club, Blue Streak, American Outlaws, The Transporter,* and so on).

After reviewing 30 years of research on media violence and how it affects children, four national health organizations—American Medical Association (AMA), American Academy of Pediatrics (AAP), American Psychological Association (APA), and American Academy of Child and Adolescent Psychiatry (AACAP)—concluded that there is a direct link between violence in the media and violent children. This doesn't mean that violent media affects every viewer the same way (i.e., not every viewer of violence becomes violent). But it does substantiate the fact that violent media influenced minors who committed violent acts.

Guys can easily enter the world of violence and competition through cyber-gaming and the Internet. The popularity of violent cyber-games (such as *Doom* and *Halo*) among adolescents illustrates a guy's desire to wed violence and competition in a game. Some research claims that such a rehearsal of killing and massacre only desensitizes guys toward death. This is done by playing into the aggression that already exists in teenage guys and encouraging other things, such as a lack of personal investment in problem solving, use of instinct rather than thought, and the destructive elimination of the threat as a viable solution.[11]

In *Hear My Story*, Dean Borgman notes that violent cyber games affect guys. And while he doesn't condone them, he doesn't condemn them, either. Borgman realizes that male aggressiveness combined with a society's glorification of violence (in its historical conquests of war) creates an inescapable combination of influence on a guy. Violent virtual reality games may be a *necessary* escape, provided the teenager doesn't blur the realms of reality. Borgman says:

> In many cases video games that leave us aghast may serve as virtual release for rage that might otherwise be killing real people. This is not to justify or excuse gory and degrading media violence, but boys need significant activity and someone who cares, rather than mere prohibitions against games that serve as outlets for their rage.[12]

He's right; the absolute best solution is for caring men to come alongside teenage guys. They must model appropriate outlets for aggression, teach them to manage their anger, and coach them in effective problem solving.

EMOTIONAL AND PSYCHOLOGICAL PROBLEMS

Obviously, teenage guys who act out in violent, criminal ways have problems, from mental disorders to poor home environments. The cases reveal that some of the guys involved in these crimes have had serious depression and were even being treated for it. Some were from good homes. But almost all of them lacked adequate supervision, allowing them the opportunity to mobilize resources, such as securing firearms or learning about explosives and then constructing a pipe bomb using instructions off the Internet. Some of these guys come from impoverished communities, while others are very affluent.

Despite all of these factors, most violent acts that are perpetrated by guys can be stopped. Youth workers fill a front-line position to battle this problem in a preventative way.

Preventing Guys from Committing Violent Crimes

1. Listen for verbal cues. In every incidence that escalates to violence, there are verbal cues that could serve as warning signs. Guys who say they will act violently, plot acts of vengeance, constantly put other students down, or become verbally abusive are candidates for later violence.

It's important to note here that youth workers have a "duty to warn" if a guy plots violent acts. That means that police, parents, and schools should be notified. This is serious and should not be treated lightly or as a confidential issue. Youth workers should also teach and empower other students to report should another student disclose plots of violence.

Guys who are violent have something to prove. They're desperately trying to regain personal power, so they need someone to know their plan. In the recorded incidences of fatal violent acts committed by guys, almost all of them verbally revealed their ag-

gressive and angry intentions. But most people just dismissed it as a *guy thing*.

2. Read warning signs and recognize if a guy is a prime candidate for violence. Some of these signs are:

- Outbursts of anger
- Easily set off by seemingly minor issues
- Victimized by bullying, shunned by other students, or not given appropriate attention
- Often teased, insulted, verbally abused, or manhandled
- Low self-esteem
- History of abuse
- Obsession with violence, deviance, weapons, or death
- Tends to isolate and spends prolonged periods of time alone
- Cruelty to animals
- Overly sensitive and very insecure
- Tendency to blame others or feels as if justice is always misappropriated
- Dabbles in the occult, pro-Nazi, or hate group practices and ideologies

3. Model. Show students that you're a disciple of Jesus Christ by your love (John 13:35). Help to heal a guy's hurting soul. Be vitally interested in, spend time with, and demonstrate that you recognize the value of a guy who believes he doesn't cut it on the masculinity scale. Do everything you can to create a compassionate community: Challenge students to reach out to those who are bullied or not accepted. Create an environment that has zero tolerance for bullying. Correct those students who put down or tear

down others. Realize that the student bully may also be feeling as though he is or has been victimized.

4. Monitor. Be aware of which guys in your youth ministry spend a lot of time alone. Guys whose parents are absent much of the time, who pull away from the body of students, who don't have good peer relationships, and so on, should be monitored. Provide opportunities for these guys to talk through their issues. Effective use of free time during retreats could be a place where connections are made.

5. Mentor. Know the guys in your ministry. There are times when youth workers would be wise to recruit one adult male to care for one teenage guy. This mentoring relationship could serve as an anger- or violence-prevention measure, as well as a healing endeavor. We will discuss mentoring later in the book.

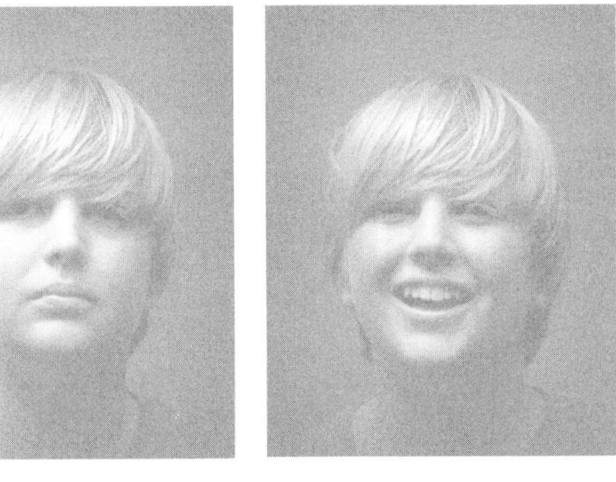

SECTION FIVE

THE TEENAGE GUY'S MIND (INTELLECTUAL DEVELOPMENT)

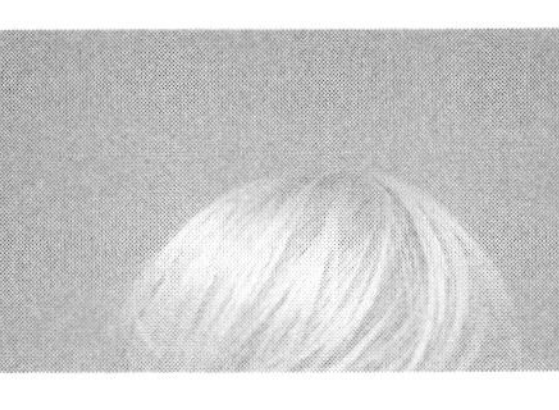
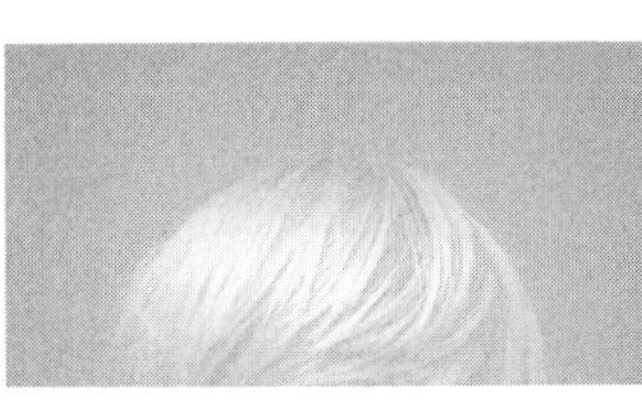

5.1
A GUY'S BRAIN

A friend who was monitoring the progress of this book asked me what chapter I was about to write.

"A guy's brain development," I responded.

He thought for a moment and said, "That should be a short chapter."

The stereotype is that the only things a guy thinks about are girls, sleep, food, playing games, and… girls. While guys may typically express themselves in only these critical areas of their lives, they certainly don't compose the entire scope of their thought capacity.

A guy's brain is complex. It's developing just like the rest of his body during puberty and adolescence. This growth has great implications on his reasoning skills, how he processes information, the development of his passions and desires, and his ability to communicate.

In addition, a guy's brain develops differently than a girl's brain. This accounts for many of the differences we see between men and women. It's also God's way of helping us gain a more complete perspective because men don't perceive things the same way women do, and vice versa. This can—and often does—produce conflict, as well as completeness. The structure and function of the brain accounts for some of these gender differences.

BRAIN GROWTH

When a guy is still an infant and moving into the toddler stage, the prefrontal cortex (the area of the brain right behind the forehead) begins to grow. This is evidenced by the production of brain cells, called *neurons*, and *synapses*—the gaps between cells that fire electrical currents regulating mood, reasoning, organization and planning, judgment, self-control, impulse inhibition, some memory, and critical thought. An overproduction of these cells means the brain is producing more *gray matter*. This brain growth during the infant to toddler stage allows the boy to learn more.

It was once believed that the brain growth process stopped around the time a child went to kindergarten, meaning the architecture or hardwiring of the brain was completely in place by that time. Beyond that, maturation occurred, which resulted in the brain being sculpted or programmed.

But Dr. Jay Giedd, of the National Mental Health Institute, studied preadolescent and adolescent brains using harmless MRI (Magnetic Resonance Imaging) procedures. And he found that a second growth spurt occurs in the brain right before puberty. That means the brain continues to develop during adolescence and right up until a guy is in his early 20s. Neuroscientists now know that brain growth during adolescence affects its structure and functioning. But because this second growth process begins at puberty, and because guys start puberty later than girls, it puts a guy's cognitive development behind females.

The overproduction of brain cells and synapses causes the adolescent brain to begin a "pruning process" in which it cuts back on some of the gray matter, allowing the functioning circuits to flourish. Frequently used neurons remain while those that aren't used very often wither away—something Giedd refers to as a "use it or lose it" process.[1] Like many people, you may believe that teenage guys lose more than they use—not true. Keep reading.

Gray Matter Versus White Matter

The good connections (the ones that are used) are bolstered with a white, fatty matter called *myelin*, which acts as an insulator and keeps the brain's electrical activity stable. This myelination process isn't complete until late adolescence.[2] So while a guy's brain grows larger than a girl's brain, she has more gray matter, and his brain is more myelinated or has more white matter. Some may joke that this makes a guy a "fat head," when in reality it does account for some differences in brain function and thinking.

Gray matter is the part of the brain that allows us to think; white matter allows us to transfer information over larger areas of the brain. While there is no conclusive evidence for this, some believe testosterone and estrogen are responsible for these physiological brain developments and the resulting differences in gender thought processes.[3]

It's Time to Try Something New

Most hypotheses about the "use it or lose it" theory say that teenage guys who play video games and sit in front of the television for hours upon end only reinforce certain functions and areas of their brains. But this endless activity is actually cutting a function pattern in their brains by reinforcing the paths that virtual gaming requires, such as hand-eye coordination, quick judgment, fast memory retention and recall, and immediate problem-solving skills. While these results may be considered positive, gaming and TV watching can also yield some potentially negative ones. For example, they don't exercise those brain functions that involve seeing a bigger or more inclusive picture of reality, long-term reasoning, critical thought, or communication.

Regardless, the "use it or lose it" theory calls for parents, educators, and youth workers to challenge teenage guys to experience a variety of activities that will exercise *all* areas of their brain. Guys may avoid some of these experiences because they believe the activity isn't manly enough, such as child care, cooking, singing, and so on. Yet these types of activities will stimulate areas of the brain that would otherwise lie dormant.

Some cognitive therapists who've worked with patients evidencing minimal brain dysfunction have noted changes in concentration, problem solving, and mood when guys are challenged to regularly engage in a series of prescribed physical exercises. A teenage guy should also be challenged to engage in other brain-related activities, such as regular reading, writing, and problem solving. These higher thinking skills are more difficult for a teenage guy because his brain hemispheres don't allow him to do the same cross talk that a girl's brain does. (This will be explained in more detail later on in this chapter.) So reading, for example, comes easier for girls, while guys have to be coaxed more often to crack a book.

The Battle of the Sexes

These developmental differences between the genders create the appearance that girls are smarter than guys. Girls' brains just have an earlier upstart, which gives them an edge over guys in the beginning. The common notion is that guys remain behind girls intellectually, generating stereotypical expectations, responses, and labels that "dumb down" the guys. In reality the differences between a guy's brain and a girl's brain have no bearing on the individual's intellectual capacity. Therefore it's important to ask a guy for his ideas and opinions about situations and to question how he arrived at certain solutions. He needs to exercise logic as his brain develops.

It's also important to understand that the brain "learns"—with amazing flair and adaptability—the skills and processes needed to accomplish great things. This means girls aren't limited to these certain brain functions and guys to others, which was once believed true. Because a guy has a larger brain than a

girl, it was thought that he was better equipped to utilize more advanced thinking skills. The truth is guys have difficulty with certain brain functions that come more easily for girls, and vice versa. Despite this, the brain learns to overcome, and ultimately it will yield fully functioning, critically thinking beings.

Safety Issues

While anatomical changes occur in the brain during adolescence, functioning may not be as quick to transform. The prefrontal cortex of a guy's brain first begins to develop during puberty. This part is responsible for discernment and judgment, something teenage guys often lack. The immaturity of his brain development may interfere with a guy's ability to accurately judge safety and the long-term effects, consequences, and implications of the risks he takes. Many times guys find themselves in hot water because they didn't think before they did or said something.

Ruben Gur, a noted neuroscientist, believes this also affects some of the criminal activities that guys engage in, stating:

> The cortical regions that are last to mature, particularly those in prefrontal areas, are involved in behavioral facets germane to many aspects of criminal culpability. Perhaps most relevant is the involvement of these brain regions in the control of aggression and other impulses, the process of planning for long-range goals, organization of sequential behavior, consideration of alternatives and consequences, the process of abstraction and mental flexibility, and aspects of memory including "working memory." More recent evidence implicates the frontal lobes in processing aspects of morality and moral judgment. If the neural substrates of these behaviors have not reached maturity before

adulthood, it's unreasonable to expect the behaviors themselves to reflect mature thought processes.[4]

Gray matter is believed to be the part of the brain that allows us to think. Because of this difference, teenage girls may be better than teenage guys at making judgment calls. But there's still hope for guys; they'll soon catch up.

COMMUNICATION AND BRAIN DIFFERENCE

A guy's corpus callosum (the fibrous bundle of nerves that connects the hemispheres of the brain) is not as dense or as large as a girl's. As a result, a guy's brain doesn't engage in the active brain hemisphere cross communication that a girl's brain does. This is why guys don't process emotive data as quickly as girls do. Many times a mother will become concerned by her son's reaction (or lack of reaction) to emotionally charged situations. She sees his response as heartless, failing to understand that his brain doesn't process data the same way her brain does. Guys do read the emotional genre of a situation rather easily and quickly. But they tend to, first and foremost, analyze the situation for a solution, rather than for an emotive response.

Studies have also indicated that when a guy is engaged in active-listening skills, the neurons in one hemisphere of his brain are triggered—but the neurons in *both* hemispheres of a girl's brain engaged in the same situation are triggered.[5] The hemisphere cross talk and activity that's so easy for a girl's brain allow her to have a better grasp on the interpretation of language, reading facial expressions, and verbal communication.[6] A guy's brain doesn't go there as quickly. This can account for why a guy uses fewer words when he communicates.

You may have encountered this situation: you ask a guy about his day, and he tells you it was "fine." While not very descriptive or elaborate, his answer

GENDER DIFFERENCES

A teenage guy will pay more for auto insurance than a teenage girl does because guys typically get more traffic tickets and cause more accidents. And that's because they also tend to take more adventurous and unusual risks. Many factors play into this:

1) Brain development is different; a guy's prefrontal cortex doesn't mature as fast as a girl's, making him more susceptible to adventure-seeking behaviors and slower to calculate the risk involved with many of his behaviors.

2) His body is on adrenaline overload, and testosterone affects aggressive behavior somewhat. So the risk gives him a rush.

3) Risk plays into the cultural "bravado" to be courageous, daring, aggressive, competent, competitive, conquering, and so on.

The combination of all these things contributes to the high level of risk-taking activity among teenage guys—and their higher auto insurance rates.

encapsulates all of the brain processes that considered the question and determined that his day was fine. Thus, his brain processed the information about his day thoroughly, quickly, and sufficiently before accurately communicating his response. Yet, if you ask a girl how her day was, you'll get a conversation. She talks through the *brain* process, verbally recalling the events, feelings, and highlights that made it "fine." This is why women often need to "think out loud," while men need to "mull things over" in their minds. The conclusion is the same; the process is different.

Women develop verbal and emotive skills more quickly than guys. They also tend to use about five times the number of words that a guy uses in one week. When problem solving, girls process and communicate the emotions of a situation. Guys, on the other hand, are more likely to verbalize the content or facts, not the affectual dynamic of an event. A guy's brain is programmed to analyze; a girl's to process.[7]

YOUTH WORKER TIP

Have you ever noticed that many guys aren't good on the phone? You call them; they don't say much. You may feel as though you're doing all the talking, and were it not for an occasional grunt, you'd wonder if the guy had already hung up. On the other hand, call a girl and she'll carry on a conversation for hours. The difference is due to the way their brains work. Guys communicate with fewer words than girls do. So don't get frustrated with your phone calls to guys. Just keep it short and sweet.

Penny for Your Thoughts?

Craig, one of my students, cornered me in a hallway at the university. He needed advice regarding a communication problem with his girlfriend. Two things emerged from our conversation. First, he was exhausted because she "over talked." He told me he was exasperated because he couldn't get off the phone with her. So even though he loved her very much, he was reaching the end of his patience.

Second, he was frustrated with her because when he'd tell her his day was "fine," she just kept pushing him for more information. He didn't know what she wanted to hear or how to answer her differently. His frustration centered around what part of "fine" she didn't understand and how much more could be added to that word. After all, his day *was* "fine." So then, out of irritation, he would add, "great," "wonderful," "peachy!" And she'd end up feeling hurt and devalued, while he'd be angry and overanalyze the situation.

Craig's problem is common. It doesn't indicate that guys lack emotional depth, nor does it mean that girls lack analytical skill. It just points to the fact that their brain processes take different routes. Both sexes need to hear each other, recognize their differences in the process, and learn to accommodate.

Now put that together with the "pruning process" (described at the beginning of this chapter) and we can conclude that an immature adolescent brain processes and functions immaturely. As a guy's brain is developing, he may need to be *coached* on how to see things from another person's perspective. Craig could certainly learn a different way to process; all guys can. The more a guy's brain exercises these functions, the more likely it is that they'll stay with him in his later years.

Teach Them a Better Way

There are a few critical tips to be followed when coaching a guy to engage in more hemisphere cross talk. First, ask open-ended questions—a question that cannot be answered with a single word. Instead of asking how his day was, ask him what the best part of the day was and why it was the best. *What* and *why* questions tend to be more open-ended. You may also try to evoke a thoughtful response without even asking a question. Make a statement such as, "Tell me something positive that happened to you today."

Second, ask him to describe what he feels about situations. Let's apply that to the ongoing conversation regarding his day. You could ask, "If you had to categorize this day by your emotions, what would be the most dominant one?" Keep him processing emotively by asking him to describe his feelings. Say something like, "What would your feelings look like if they were a painting, or a car, or a ballgame?" He might tell you that it's overcast and every time he steps

up to the plate, he strikes out. An exercise like this calls on his capacity to expand his brain functions.

TOO MANY HITS TO THE HEAD?

A stereotypical label of "dumb jock" is often given to a guy who plays football. It comes from an ill-founded notion that football players take too many shots to the head, thus impairing their thought processes. This is a myth. BUT the machismo among teenage guys that leads them to go out and drink after every game may do more damage than taking a hit during the game. Research shows that ongoing alcohol use by a teenager can impair brain functioning. And because the brain is still growing during adolescence, the implications of alcohol use on a teenage brain can have serious, long-term effects.[8]

SPATIAL FUNCTION

A guy's brain tends to engage spatial relationships better than a girl's brain does. This makes spatial tasks, such as building or fitting things together, more rewarding for him. Assembling and disassembling things, calling on mechanical skills, manipulating tangible material, and the mental rotation of objects or ideas are all easier for guys. This is one reason why playing sports is fulfilling. A guy can gauge distances; devise and reverse play strategies; pass, throw, and intercept objects—and all because of his spatial abilities. It may also account for why men are often better at thinking in conceptual patterns and forming links between abstract relationships.

A guy has an ability to "get in the zone" or focus on a task by tuning out all other stimuli. As I mentioned earlier, he can do this because his brain tends to trigger electrical activity on either one side of the brain or the other, whereas a girl's brain triggers this same activity in both hemispheres simultaneously. This explains why a guy can walk right past you and never acknowledge that you're there, or you can speak to him and he won't hear a word you're saying. He just was in the zone. Guys need to be made aware of this because it sometimes gives other people the impression that they are extremely self-centered and self-absorbed.

When he's on task, a guy may become aggravated by interruptions because they require his brain to shift in a different direction. A teenage guy who is asked a question while he's watching television or who is asked to give a helping hand while he's in the middle of playing a video game can get very annoyed. The interruption breaks his concentration; but more pointedly, it changes the processing direction of his brain.

OTHER "GUY BRAIN" FUNCTIONS

There are a few more minor differences between a guy's brain and a girl's brain that should be noted. Often an awareness of these things can give a parent, youth worker, or mentor an edge when understanding a guy. For example, since guys tend to stay focused on tasks, one might assume they have a relatively long attention span. These are not one and the same. Actually, guys have a shorter attention span than girls. Many times guys get a lot of grief for not paying attention.

But while his attention span is shorter, his focus may be more intense. This means he really *does* know what you said to him while he was channel surfing. There is no evidence that shows any connection between a guy's attention span and proclivity toward Attention Deficit/Hyperactivity Disorder (ADHD) in guys, but it's interesting to note that two to three times as many guys are diagnosed with ADHD.[9]

Guys also tend to absorb less proximal or sensory data than girls do.[10] This may account for why a guy doesn't see a room as being as dirty as his mom does, or why he doesn't recognize when his girlfriend is wearing a new lipstick color, or why he doesn't hear a teacher calling on him in class. Yet a guy often does better with visual problems and interpreting visual information.[11]

Another difference lies with the development of the cerebral cortex of the male fetus' brain. Guys' brains have a higher number of nerve cells that require maintenance in a developing fetus. Early damage to the developing male brain could result in higher losses of needed neurons, leading researchers to note that guys are more prone to learning disabilities or mental retardation than girls.[12]

A girl's brain tends to be better at language and verbal skills than a guy's brain, as we have already established. But research also shows that language

and communication processing problems occur more often in guys than in girls. For example, developmental language disorders are greater in guys.[13] Guys have higher incidences of dyslexia.[14] A dyslexic guy also uses about five times the brain area as a normal child while performing simple language tasks, indicating that there are chemical differences in the brain function of a dyslexic guy.[15] Guys are more prone to Asperger syndrome.[16] And autism is four times more common in guys than girls.[17]

God designed our brains to be fully functioning, but guys and girls think differently—their brains follow different paths as they learn, process information, and communicate. Many times this becomes a point of conflict in relationships, but we should celebrate the differences instead. As my little Italian grandmother always said (with her strong Italian accent), "Ifa two people always agree, one isa not necessary."

5.2 FROM CONCRETE TO IDEALISM

Sometimes an early-adolescent guy will say something so incredibly profound that it will catch you off guard—then with the same breath he'll say something so outrageously moronic that you believe he needs an intellectual booster chair just to get into the "normal zone."

A junior high guy's thought processes are definitely otherworldly. But it doesn't get better. As he matures into middle adolescence, he gains more confidence and a better grasp of the conceptual. Now he knows everything, and in his mind *you* need the intellectual booster chair!

When he enters late adolescence, he hits a more rational, logical stride. This would be great if he didn't idealize everything. Now everything becomes black-and-white with no gray. Now every conversation is a debate! Welcome to the dark chasm of the teenage guy's mind. Other than from infancy to the toddler years, never is intellectual change so pronouncedly marked as during adolescence. A guy's thought processes and intellectual capacity will change dramatically as he navigates through three very distinct stages.

STAGE #1—CONCRETE

This movement puts a junior high guy in the intellectual twilight zone. As a child he could only understand things in the context of the concrete. Beginning at about age eight he'll start to change, developing the ability to reason. During the time of pre-puberty

(until he's 11 or 12), he'll be in a cognitive developmental stage that Jean Piaget, a Swiss developmental psychologist, called the "concrete operational thought stage." Piaget used the word *operations* to describe reason and logic skills. A guy in this stage will have a difficult time with abstracts because his logic and reasoning skills are at a concrete level. He'll only understand abstracts and concepts in the light of the concrete.

For example, I was invited to a public school to talk to a large group of sixth and seventh graders. In the middle of my dialogue I decided to test Piaget's theory. I asked, "How many of you *love* TV?" Almost every hand in the room was raised. Then I asked, "How many of you *love* having fun?" Once again, many hands went up in affirmation. I proceeded to ask how many *love* animals. The response wasn't as great as it was for love to have fun. My last question was how many *love* their parents. Again, many hands went up.

Now I was ready to get to the heart of the issue. With all these junior highers sitting around me, I asked them to explain the difference between their love for animals and their love for their parents. They couldn't do it. While they understood the concept of love, they couldn't fully grasp the abstract. They could understand love (abstract) as long as it was connected to a concrete example. After a moment of silence, one guy in the class blurted out, "The difference between loving animals and loving our parents is that we love animals more!" The whole class got a laugh out of that, but he illustrated the point nonetheless. Logical thinking replaces intuitive thought as long as the concept is applied to a concrete example.[1] In this case the concrete notion of volume (loving more) was the guy's line of logic.

A guy in this concrete operations stage will begin to organize his thoughts more coherently and exercise his reason and logic skills. This means he'll argue just to argue. Early adolescent guys are obnoxious.

Even when they know that something is the way it is, they will still argue with you for hours.

We got brand-new, white marker boards mounted on the walls of our Sunday school rooms at church. So I thought it would be cool to use these boards during the first Sunday school time after they were installed. I was teaching a class of my junior high guys, and during the lesson I invited a few guys to come up and draw a cartoon illustration on the new marker boards. But I said, "Come up and draw on the new blackboards."

"Pastor Steve, they're white boards."

"Okay, come up and write on the white boards."

"Well, really they're marker boards."

"Okay, come up and write on the marker boards."

"Well, really you could still call them blackboards or you could call them chalkboards, if you used chalk." Forty minutes later they're still arguing, and I'm ready to strangle them! Been there?

In reality junior high guys *have* to argue with you. If you say snow is white, they're going to argue with you even though they *know* that snow is white. Why do they do that? Because they are demon possessed? (Well, no, not all of them.) Actually, it's because they're going through intellectual gymnastics. They have to. They're caught between concrete and abstract. They're developing higher reasoning skills. So they're going to go back and forth and back and forth through a line of logic that they process verbally.

Basically teenagers are just beginning to work through the thought processes and functions that an adult works through in a matter of seconds. And they continue to do this through age 14 or 15 **(see fig. 6)**. Parents, youth workers, teachers, and mentors need to allow a guy to perform these mental gymnastics

yet still control the obnoxiousness and annoyance of it by *separating issues*. Acknowledge that the guy is really thinking (issue number one), but tell him he's pushing the game too far (issue number two), which makes him socially annoying. Focusing on the correlating issue of annoyance can bring a guy back into the zone. It can also become very concrete if there is a boundary and a consequence created for when he continues to annoy.

INTELLECTUAL DEVELOPMENT

11-12	14-15	17-18	23-24

Concrete Thinker

Figure 6

A guy's brain is starting to operate at a higher cognitive level. His mind is beginning to process more data, and he's functioning at a higher rate. His mind *centration* (i.e., his ability to concentrate on one central thing) shifts. Now he begins to process many ideas, tasks, inputs, and so on. With all of this going on inside a guy's brain, something is bound to give—his memory. Guys tend to forget things. If you tell a junior high guy to run to his room and change his shirt, he'll oblige and run off. After about 15 minutes, he hasn't come back, and you're wondering if he's fallen into some dark abyss. A few minutes later he comes waltzing in wearing the same shirt. You confront him; he says he forgot. How could he have forgotten something in such a short time?

So you give the guy the benefit of the doubt and tell him to go back to his room and change. He

starts out again. But if you were to get up and quietly follow him after a few minutes, you'd find an interesting phenomenon occurring. He walks into his room, which looks like a war zone, and starts digging through the piles of clothes and debris. He's looking for a special shirt he has in mind to wear. As he looks, he comes across a piece of candy—so he indulges. It's a little old, which makes it difficult to unwrap, but he manages to complete the task. As he devours the candy, he goes back to the digging. He finds the remote control for his stereo, which he lost about a month ago. Overjoyed, he needs to see if it still works. So he pops in a CD. Cool, it works! He takes a moment to find the right song and adjust the volume. So now he has tunes. He returns to the floor and comes across a note from that cute girl he's always teasing. He lies down on the bed and reads the note.

Now you do the math: he's eating a great piece of candy, listening to his favorite band, kicking back on his bed, and thinking about the woman of his dreams, yet only five minutes have passed since you told him to change his shirt. By this point, he has no idea why he went into his room in the first place. His mind can't multitask well, so his attention is diverted from one thing to the next until the central task is forgotten.

Many parents and teachers interpret this to be Attention Deficit Disorder. They describe what they've observed to their pediatrician (who probably isn't qualified to make a decision regarding mental health issues, but is qualified to prescribe medications). The pediatrician prescribes Ritalin for a problem that is more pronounced during adolescence because of a developmental shift, not because of a disorder. This is why nearly every teenage guy is diagnosed as having ADHD. However, forgetfulness and lapses in concentration at this stage of development are part of the process his mind goes through while he's learning to multitask intellectually.

This constant cognitive shifting doesn't make an early adolescent guy feel very secure. He experiences times when he feels as though his brain is clicking on all cylinders. Other times he can't quite get it in gear. This has positive and negative effects on his ability to carry on a conversation as well. He may find he has something very profound to say, but by the time it leaves his mouth, it wasn't exactly what he'd formulated in his head. This problem, along with the fact that he doesn't verbally process as well as his female counterpart, makes him say very little when he's called on to give an answer. He may even know the correct answer to a question, but he would rather keep his mouth shut for fear he won't say it well.

WATCH YOUR WORDS!

Early adolescent guys tend to be in another world intellectually. Often they will respond or do something and then not recall the intellectual process that led there. People who work with early teenage guys can easily become frustrated and exclaim, "What were you thinking?" The truth is—he wasn't. And even if he was, he doesn't have the capability to analyze the cognitive process and then verbalize it. Instead he'll just feel like an idiot. That kind of comment can erode a guy's esteem, especially when he's trying to become a competent man.

STAGE #2—ABSTRACT

A middle-adolescent guy has had a bit more time to exercise a linear direction of reasoning. He's mastered some logic skills and has even begun to grasp abstracts. The cognitive tasks he found to be difficult during the concrete stage are not as difficult for him now. This gives him more confidence in his ability. He has a feeling of having intellectually arrived. He sees he's no longer an idiot, and he can even logically think through more complex issues, albeit in an idealistic and simplistic way. He feels a certain power from his ability to reason, which leads him to believe he knows almost everything and maybe someday you'll catch up to him. The slogan, "Hire a teenager while he still knows everything," evidences this phenomenon.

Mark Twain explained it this way: "When I was a boy of 14, my father was so ignorant I could hardly stand to have the old man around. But when I got to be 21, I was astonished at how much the old man had learned in seven years." Twain recognized that at age 14 he was in a formal operational stage of cognitive development. Twain also recognized that adolescent cognitive development, along with the other areas of development, made it difficult to live with teenagers.

This led him to also say, "When a boy turns 12, you should put him in a barrel, nail the lid down, and feed him through a knot hole…when he turns 16, plug the hole."

The formal operational stage begins at about age 12 and continues through middle adolescence (see fig. 7). It's important to note that these stages don't just start and stop, but rather they blur together as a guy navigates through them.

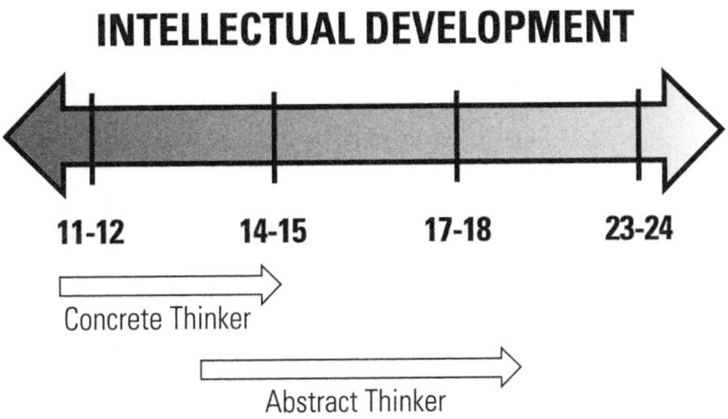

Figure 7

The new sense of power and freedom that a middle-adolescent guy experiences comes from his new mastery of logic skills. Here's an example of how it works. I asked my college underclassmen to respond quickly to this scenario: "You are now the parent of a 16-year-old guy. He asks you if he can have the car, some money, and stay out with his friends until 3 a.m. Respond." Immediately, the majority of the class says "NO." They're right—I'd respond the same way.

Most of the students in this class were past the cognitive stage of a 16-year-old. Therefore, they were able to process the situation quickly and come

to an immediate conclusion. When I debriefed the exercise by asking why they said no, they said things like, "I have no idea who the friends are," "What could you possibly be doing at 3 a.m.?" "Chances of getting in trouble at that hour are greater than if it were earlier," "It's not good to begin bad habits like staying out late," "As a parent I'd worry, and the kid doesn't realize that others are affected by his actions." All of these things occurred in their minds in a matter of seconds. They heard the scenario (let's call it "point A"), and they arrived immediately at a decision ("point E"). But they processed all the notions of risk, wisdom, variability, safety, influence, time management, health, and crisis prevention in a matter of seconds (points B, C, and D). Their minds subconsciously flashed through the other points because their logic skills have become more acute. Like other adult thinkers, they drew upon their past experiences, the resources of their knowledge, an acquired wisdom, and their maturity to reach an immediate decision.

This is not so with a 16-year-old guy. While he has mastered a more fluid movement between points A to B to C (and while he's even capable of moving from point A to C and bypassing B), he still isn't thinking at the same level as a more critical thinker. So when a middle-adolescent guy is told he can't stay out until 3 a.m., he believes he has already thought through the entire scenario. When you bring up an issue (point D) from your line of logic, it may not even show up on his radar. So naturally he gives you that "Are you an idiot?" look because, to him, he's rational and you're—from Mars (or Venus).

It becomes important during this stage of cognitive development to be patient and explain as best you can *how* you arrived at your decision. Guys are learning to learn at this stage of the game. Learning about learning is called *metacognition*. He'll notice flaws and inconsistencies in his and other people's thinking. He may begin to distinguish between pos-

sibility and probability; between the real, the abstract, and the hypothetical. He masters *hypothetical-deductive thinking*—understanding that there could be multiple solutions to a problem and then weighing the implications for each. He can also understand and appreciate satire, analogies, metaphors, parables, and the dreaded sarcasm. This means he can be cynical, prone to exaggerate, and manipulative, understanding the difference between the spirit of the law and the letter of the law.

Let's play out a situation that illustrates this. Remember, a middle-adolescent guy is becoming aware of how thinking works. In addition, he's been conditioned by the "Boy Code" to compete, be competent, and remain rational. In other words, he has a natural bent to find the loopholes in any argument or set of rules.

My wife and I got legal custody of a 16-year-old guy, Steve, shortly after we were married. We became instant parents. One of the things we quickly learned is just how often senior high guys look for the loophole in the rules. We had a curfew rule of 10:30 p.m. on a school night and midnight on the weekend. The first night after we talked about curfew, Steve came in on time. So I wanted to be a good dad, and I praised him for that. The second time, he's in right at midnight. He's doing a good job.

The third night he's five minutes late. When he comes through the door, I confront him. He immediately responds with, "It's only five minutes—that's not late." Now I'm faced with a cognitive standoff. In my adult mind, there are broader issues at stake here, such as responsibility, trust, boundaries, respect, integrity, and obedience. Is being five minutes late a big deal? Not in the mind of a teenage guy. But in an adult mind, five minutes is a big deal because the teenage guy is still developing life-long disciplines. Adults can see from points A to E with the understanding that this is about more than just being late. Teenagers only see from points A to B.

So Steve says, "I'm not late."

I want to work him through the cognitive process by pushing the boundaries of the abstract for him. I ask, "Steve, if five minutes isn't considered 'late,' then at what point does *late* become late?"

He thinks for a moment and says, "Well, I guess late would be one minute past midnight."

I say, "Uh-uh, nope, guess again."

He says, "Thirty sec—"

"Wrong answer! Try again."

"Okay, one second."

"Nope, that's still one second *late*!"

He says, "Well, you can't even measure it then. I guess I just have to be here at or before midnight." We then talked through why that boundary meant more than just a nitpicky rule of successive moments.

Now he knows the boundaries well because he attempted to define them in the concrete (letter of the law), but we also defined the abstract (spirit of the law). This puts the ball in Steve's court, so he makes his next move to figure out the loophole.

A few nights later he comes in late again. When I confront him, he looks at his watch and shows me that by his watch, he's on time. He's rationalizing shifting standards. He knows it will be difficult for me to challenge his motives—something so subjective. So in order to win this battle, we go by the clock on the kitchen wall—Kitchen Standard Time. Can he find another loophole?

Steve learned that if he came in the back door or the patio door away from the living areas of the house, it would be impossible for me to know if he was in on time. He would quickly take off his shoes—and sometimes his shirt—to give the appearance that he'd been in for hours already, but I just didn't know it. He was learning that some things are subjective and are difficult to challenge—his word against my experience. I needed to help Steve see that there was an issue of trust, and it was now being violated.

These games went on and on, and they exhausted me because I wondered if Steve was seeing the bigger picture while he was exercising higher forms of reasoning and logic (a positive thing). I finally decided to put an end to it by making it more concrete, yet without diminishing Steve's desire to have some sense of control—as evidenced by our competition. We set an alarm and agreed that Steve had to turn the alarm off when he came in at night. If the alarm went off, then he was late and suffered the consequences. We now moved from Kitchen Standard Time to Alarm Clock Time. He could no longer play mind games by manipulating the situation or my trust. This worked really well, and it ended up being fun for both of us. Every night that first weekend, Steve came in 10 minutes early and shut off the alarm (his way of proving he wasn't playing mind games!).

The second weekend, he wasn't 10 minutes early anymore. He got there one minute before and killed the alarm. The third weekend, I could see him running up the driveway with all of his might and pushing open the door. I deliberately stood in the way, just to make things a bit more interesting, but he got around me. He ran up the stairs, hit that alarm just in time, screamed, "Yes!" and did a little touchdown dance. He then proceeded to throw his victory in my face. Having beaten the clock, he felt strong and in control.

There were other times when I stood next to that alarm clock and pleaded, "Ring! Ring! C'mon RING!" because I wanted to win, too! And when it did, I threw it in his face! We discovered how to learn a new discipline in a fun way.

Abstract-thinking guys are still exercising higher logic skills. Whereas they still argue things out, their arguments take on a different tone, shifting from argument to debate. They enjoy the intellectual banter of hearing other sides, raising competing issues, and finding the flaws. This may lead a guy to raise critical questions regarding morals, values, and ethics, so these debates should be encouraged. (I'll share more about that in the last chapter where we'll examine faith formation and moral development.) Too often we fear this intellectual inquisition, and we want to tell guys *what* to think rather than mentoring them so they learn *how* to think.

This concept is brilliantly illustrated in the classic movie *Dead Poets Society*. The middle-adolescent guys in the film are experiencing new vistas when they're encouraged to be thinkers. By asking questions, debating issues, and attempting to understand all things, life becomes richer, deeper, and fuller for each guy. The movie also shows the tension and fear of those (parents, teachers, school administrators) who still want to tell these young men what they should think. These adults are afraid that questioning, analyzing, challenging, and discovering new ideas and thought will lead to destruction. But this potential is evident even when a guy is told exactly what to think.

We need to encourage guys to be thinkers as an act of worship—loving God with their minds. As they move into late adolescence and idealistic thinking, they develop the capacity to think critically and think theologically.

STAGE #3—IDEAL

Somewhere around age 17 or 18, another shift will occur. A guy will begin to move into a stage I call "idealistic thinking" (see fig. 8). Late-adolescent guys tend to think concepts through to their purest or most ideal form. Have you ever noticed how many

political uprisings start on college campuses? This is because late adolescence brings idealism to thought processes. A guy in this developmental stage thinks through every aspect of an ideology and processes out the impurity.

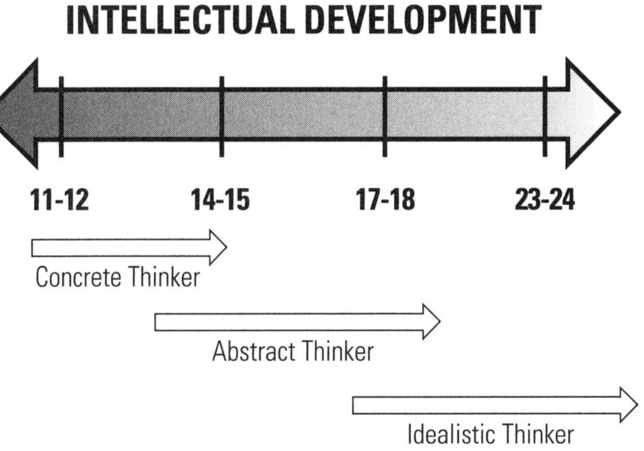

Figure 8

Parents will often offer their gratitude to mentoring professors for investing in their son, but then in the next breath they'll mention how they taught many of these same life lessons in their home. They don't understand why it suddenly became so real and vibrant in their son's life when his professor said the same things they'd been teaching him. I explain that their son has come to the cognitive stage where he hears these teachings differently, and he starts to idealize them. He starts to romance them. He starts to grasp them in their conceptual stages. The abstract thinking guy has worked through the reason and logic skills enough to really understand and idealize the complexity of the abstract.

For most guys who are in this idealistic-thinking stage, there is only black-and-white; there is no gray. Compromise is a bad thing; there is no middle ground. Idealism can become judgmental to a fault.

It can be bent on finding the discrepancies and then rationalizing conclusions in a self-serving manner. He'll find fault with authorities, claim to understand and yet misinterpret another's motives, and think in extremes to the point of cynicism. He sees irony in everything, yet he has great desires to engage others. This idealistic thinking fuels his passion. He believes he can conquer the world because he sees the real problems. So he wants to help others see it, too. While this is vibrant and refreshing, it can also be annoying because it's a crisp perspective with a certain amount of naïveté.

I've had idealistic thinkers pick apart the hypocrisy in the church. The ability to see the hypocrisy is a positive of idealism. But when played out fully, that same guy will refuse to go to church because of the hypocrisy. When confronted with this issue, he'll respond with something like, "Well, at least I'm being honest about it!" Idealism draws self-serving conclusions with delusional, faulty rationality.

Therefore mentoring becomes a critical way to help a guy navigate through this stage. He longs for and is open to having a mentor who can challenge his idealism in the context of a sterile environment by pushing him to think beyond the ideal. A mentor must help a late-adolescent guy *discover* truth by leading him to it, not merely telling him the truth. Guys need to work out the practical application of the things they discover.

A mentor can also facilitate discovery, practice, and the value of middle ground by exaggerating the tensions between two ideals, such as justice and mercy, liberty and constraint, peace and power. With the help of a God-honoring mentor, an idealistic guy stands at the threshold of wisdom ready to become a wise man.

5.3 LEARNING PROBLEMS

I stopped Scott as he walked into church one Sunday morning. "Are you going on the retreat next weekend?" I asked.

"No," he replied. "I'm grounded."

"What did you do now?" I asked.

"It's not what I did, it's what I *didn't* do—my homework." Scott continued to tell me that his grades were really bad on his latest report card. Scott is a bright guy; he just isn't motivated to get the work done.

Maybe you have a guy like Scott in your youth group. His grades are below average, and they certainly don't reflect his potential. Teachers constantly tell him that he doesn't "apply" himself. Scott gets bored with school. He hates homework and puts it off or just doesn't do it. He's been tested for learning disabilities, but there are no signs of a brain dysfunction. Scott just doesn't care about school. His apathy is killing his grade point average, his college future, and now his social life.

On the other hand, there is Kevin. How many times has this occurred: You plan a great talk or lesson, and you're really excited about it. Three minutes after you start your delivery, Kevin starts to disrupt things. He's the class clown who performs week after week. You confront, you warn, you contact his parents, you may have even threatened not to allow him to come back to any group-learning situation. These things may work for a while, but Kevin returns and the cycle starts all over again.

What you're interpreting as a behavior problem may actually be a learning or brain functioning problem. Kevin may be exhibiting one of any number of learning disabilities, while Scott may just be experiencing apathy toward school.

A guy with a learning disability (LD) has a difficult time—or may take a longer time—with brain functioning or processing skills. This guy may have a problem grasping or taking in information. He might not be able to use or retrieve information in a timely or sequential manner. That same guy might evidence long- and short-term memory problems, or he may have a difficult time expressing what he knows both verbally and in written form. This can often lead a guy to become frustrated. As a result, he may act out inappropriately.

A guy who has a learning disability may be unable to concentrate or understand what you're saying, or he may be frustrated with his inability to understand. This leads to disruption. Often he may not believe or even realize that he's behaving this way. He may lack the logic skills that make something such as disrupting a class so easy for a non-LD student to see.

Early on, a person with a learning disability understands that he may have to compensate for the extra attention he receives for not understanding the question when he's called on during class or for not completing an assignment when everyone else has it done. He doesn't want anyone to know that he doesn't understand what a teacher is talking about, so he creates some sort of smoke screen to divert the attention away from his deficiency. After all, a guy is culturally conditioned to never show signs of being vulnerable, weak, or in this case—incompetent. These smoke screens can range from charm to humor to bad behavior. It can even be masked as apathy. That's why Scott may seem to have an overt learning problem, while Kevin's learning disability may go undetected.

Overcompensating or masking the deficiency is a defensive measure on the part of a teenage guy with a learning disability. Often he's just protecting a fragile self-esteem. The LD student may be working very hard to achieve, but the outcome is always poor. He may often present himself being very bright but not working to his potential. As a result, he's misunderstood, pushed harder, punished for behaviors that he may not be able to control or didn't believe were problematic, and sometimes put down by family, friends, and peers. While the pushing and negative consequences may work for Scott, they can erode Kevin's sense of value. They may also lead to anxiety, depression, anger, and even suicide.

Learning disabilities can often be misdiagnosed, overdiagnosed, or may go undiagnosed. There is a wide range of learning disabilities, but I'll cover a few of them:

Attention Deficit/Hyperactivity Disorder: This evidences itself primarily with concentration problems. A guy with ADHD has difficulty staying on task or completing assignments and projects; can often daydream; is easily distracted; acts impulsively; has difficulty following directives; cannot keep things organized; misplaces or loses things; can demonstrate apparently rude behaviors, such as interrupting conversations, walking in between people who are carrying on a conversation, butting in lines, and so on.

ADHD is often accompanied by hyperactivity, but it doesn't always have a hyperactive component. The hyperactivity is marked by constant energy; fidgeting; aggressive behaviors; or being overly stimulated by music, lights, and noise. Many professionals believe this disorder is overdiagnosed or misdiagnosed, which means a number of teenage guys who wear the ADHD label don't really have it. Those who do can be treated with medications such as Cylert or Ritalin, with cognitive behavioral therapies, and with some modifications in diet and nutrition.

Dyslexia: A student with this disorder has a difficult time reading and writing, and they often struggle to follow directions as well. While there are various types of dyslexia, the most common is visual dyslexia. The student with this type of dyslexia will often confuse, reverse, or get letters, numbers, and symbols out of sequence. He may have difficulty reading because it's difficult for his eyes and mind to skip from one line to the next on a page. The same student may have problems copying lecture notes presented in a classroom. Other forms of dyslexia may include problems with coordination, the inability to tell left from right, and the inability to comprehend simple directions.

Other Learning Disabilities: The range is great, including developmental, reading, writing, math, speech and language, and motor skills disorders.

DETECTING A LEARNING PROBLEM

Learning disabilities are difficult to diagnose in adolescent guys. Many educators pick up on the warning signs more quickly than parents and youth workers do. Nevertheless, anyone who works with teenage guys should be familiar with these warning signs:

- He seems brighter than his grades reflect.
- He has difficulty concentrating and focusing.
- He has social and behavioral problems.
- He can't stay on task and he lacks organizational skills.
- He has difficulty with problem solving and basic logic skills.
- He shows verbal frustration with his inability to keep up in class.

- He becomes frustrated when he knows what he wants to say but can't verbalize it or has difficulty expressing himself.
- He complains that he reads and writes more slowly than his peers.
- He has difficulty memorizing and remembering directions.
- He begins to talk about himself as being stupid, worthless, and so on.
- He shows signs of depression and anxiety.
- He demonstrates avoidance behaviors, such as getting sick in order to miss school, skipping classes, and so on.
- He becomes aggressive, takes unnecessary risks, or becomes prone to outbursts of anger.

MINISTRY AND MENTORING TIPS

1. Create a study environment for students. Many youth ministries are creating programs to help students with their study skills. One such way is to have a "Homework and Hang Out" night. Students come primarily to do homework together and then to hang out. If you keep them on task, then they often help each other. This creates a semi-formal peer tutoring network, study groups, and a greater sense of community in your youth ministry. And this kind of study environment often helps a student like Scott to be more motivated, simply because he's surrounded by peers who are motivated. Start out by hosting this gathering one night a week for all students. For some youth ministries, this type of program is so successful that it develops into a regular after-school center.

2. Teach basic study skills. A student may need to learn basic study skills. Recruit a teacher who can

offer a workshop on study habits, and offer it during one of your Homework and Hang Out nights.

3. Create a resource network. Recruit male teachers and other adult men from your congregation who are willing to tutor guys who are having problems. Ask them to volunteer their time and skills not only as tutors, but also as mentors. Learning becomes the port of entry into many teachable moments that can shape a guy's life forever.

4. Watch for warning signs. Encourage parents to bring their observations to the attention of school officials. Encourage them to have their children evaluated.

5. Avoid humiliating or putting an LD guy in a humiliating situation. Don't put him on the spot in a Sunday school class or call on him to read out loud.

6. Encourage the student in his strengths. An LD guy is not mentally retarded, nor is he non-functioning. This guy can and will excel in many other areas. Play to his strengths and praise his good works.

7. Battle the potentially wounded spirit of an LD guy. In a society that values intellect, he may believe he isn't valuable. Remind him frequently that he *is* valuable. In fact, God values him so much that it cost the life of his Son. The highest price was paid for each of us. Let the young man know that he isn't defined by what he does, but rather by who God is making him to be. God began a great work in him, and he's constantly perfecting it (Philippians 1:6).

8. Let the LD guy reveal the difficulties he faces. Don't be afraid to ask him specific questions about the frustration. Do this in a safe environment, so as to not embarrass him, and with adequate time for him to process.

9. Help him understand the difference between wisdom and intellect. God promises his wisdom to all who ask for it (James 1:5).

10. Declare your love for this guy. Say it. Show it through acts of kindness and time spent with him. Build him up. Many times an LD guy is "multi-love" lingual. Use all your resources to make sure he understands that he is loved and valued.

SECTION SIX

THE TEENAGE GUY'S FAMILY AND FRIENDS (SOCIAL DEVELOPMENT)

6.1 MALE IDENTITY DEVELOPMENT

The teenage years are a time of incredible self-awareness. Early- and middle-adolescent guys become very conscious of how they look; what they're doing; how they sound, smell, eat, and talk—you name it and they'll find a way of making it all about them.

They're trapped in what David Elkind calls the "imaginary audience" arena.[1] Adolescent egocentrism makes a teenage guy believe he's on stage and everyone is constantly watching him. This self-awareness will give way to self-consciousness, which involves evaluating, assessing, and defining "oneself" against his perceptions of who he is and input from others. A guy will also subconsciously (in early and middle adolescence) and then consciously (in later adolescence) take into account biological factors, cultural norms and ethnicity, gender roles, social influences, and moral and spiritual characteristics as he shapes his identity first as a guy, and second as an individual.

It's important to note here that the goal of identity development is the individuation and a healthy autonomy of a guy. Individuation means he finds his uniqueness. It involves a healthy perspective of who he is, what his roles are, and the contribution he makes to others. Healthy autonomy means he stands sufficient as a man. This developmental task often ruffles the feathers of the theologians within and among us, so I need to qualify what I mean by "healthy autonomy."

We need our guys to learn who they are. We want them to understand the spiritual legacy they're a part of and what they'll leave behind. A guy must "leave his father and mother and cleave to his wife" (Genesis 2:24). This explains the process of identity development. It involves a breaking away or redefining of his connectedness with his family of origin. He leaves the dependence of his family. This is autonomy, but it doesn't stop there. His cleaving to a wife illustrates that he begins another family to duplicate the process. He now sires and raises children of his own. He perpetuates the legacy. The protégé becomes the mentor.

In all of this, autonomy never means he's sufficient apart from community. As a matter of fact, healthy autonomy means that he moves from being a subordinate part of the community to become a confident, active definer of community. Let's examine some of these factors that shape a guy's identity.

BIOLOGICAL FACTORS

We've all heard the phrase "boys will be boys," and maybe we've even said it. Many times this is used to ascribe the powers of testosterone on risk-taking or attention-seeking behaviors evidenced by guys. In effect we are demonstrating the theoretical processes that shape a guy's identity.

Some developmental psychologists, starting with Freud, believed guys were born with a male predisposition toward an identity labeled masculine due to biological factors. Hormonal differences have marked effects on gender. We've already discussed how hormones affect brain differences. The *masculinization* of the fetus with an XY chromosome configuration may in fact do more than just yield male physiological traits. While testosterone does have aggressive effects on a guy, giving him a predisposition for action, there is no conclusive evidence that it affects other masculine-assigned behaviors, nor the

types of behaviors that are aggressive. Nor is there conclusive evidence that links testosterone to violence, though countless studies have been done in an attempt to support this theory. We assume boys will be boys if they fight, throw things in anger, or attempt swan dives off the top bunk bed at camp.

After traveling for two weeks with the Azusa Pacific University Men's Chorale, I had to leave them in order to keep a previous speaking engagement. But during the time I'd spent with them, I grew close to these great guys. On the evening before I was to leave, I had the opportunity to share my heart, observations, and hopes for them with their concert audience, while they stood behind me ready to sing. As I turned around to face them, I was moved to see many of them in tears. I then realized that God had knit our hearts together. These men weren't afraid to be moved publicly. Interestingly, I never hear the phrase "boys will be boys" in reference to behavior like this.

There is more than biology that shapes a guy's identity. William Pollack talks about the dangers of the "boys will be boys" myth, stating, "people assume that they have less power to affect a boy's personality, behavior and emotional development than in fact they do."[2]

MASCULINE IDENTITY THEORY

As a little boy, a guy develops a strong identification and dependence on his mother, asumming she is the primary caregiver. She meets his emotional, physical, cognitive, and relational needs. The majority of the time, she is the primary teacher of spiritual truth and direction for her son, having more day-to-day contact with him. Spiritual truth and the behavior that reflects that truth are instilled through rote, correction, and teachable moments. All of this makes a powerful impression on his identity, making his mother a strong *influencer* of his identity.

In adolescence a teenage guy will begin to pull away from his mother. This initial breaking away may not be an overt rebellious war. It becomes a cognitive awareness of the differences between him and females (primarily represented by his mother and any sisters). He may also distance himself by drawing a line in the sand when he begins to change physiologically. For most guys this becomes a relationship-defining point of resolution for him and his mom.

Now remember that everyone journeys through adolescence differently. I've talked with many guys who said they talked with their mom openly about everything—even their physical changes (including masturbation)—while growing up. There is nothing strange or wrong about that. Yet, in the grand scheme of things, even these guys turn to masculine examples as a frame of reference for their identities as males. This turning to the masculine involves a turning away from the feminine.

Many times a guy turns to his father to identify with him. This can evidence itself in a range of ways from strongly connecting with him relationally to just watching him. In seeking to take on his father's identity, a guy develops masculine traits.

John Eldredge, in *Wild at Heart*, attempts to plot the development of masculine identity in guys. He uses an archetypal model describing men as warriors. He speaks of how a guy needs to overcome obstacles, such as the feminine influences of his mother and the heart wounds from his father. While some of these perspectives are right on, the author doesn't talk about the balance that's necessary if a guy is going to develop a truly masculine identity. Instead, he focuses on stereotypical masculine traits and then universalizes that to all guys.

It's important to note that the unique personal identity development of each guy may override some of the messages he gets from the surrounding culture about what a man is and should be. Not every

man needs a battle to fight, or an adventure to undertake, or a maiden to rescue (and not every maiden needs to be rescued, either). Not every man is rough and rugged; nor is every man sexually driven; nor is every man stoic. You get the picture. Masculine-identity theorists in the last century have presented perspectives that are much more balanced. And if a young man doesn't come to understand that tenderness, love, nurture, emotional sensitivity, and other things that are seen as being feminine are just as important to the makeup and identity of a man, then he'll always live a life that's conflicted and relationally insufficient.

Christian literature on masculinity and mentoring men fails to embrace this point. There's been such an aggressive attempt to address the problem of weak leadership and lack of spiritual initiative in guys that the pendulum has swung fully to the direction of compromising the completeness of men. We've created a Christian strongman culture that advocates raw power as a godly attribute of a man. We forget that in our weakness, God is made strong (2 Corinthians 12:9). In an attempt to address a leadership deficit in the church, pastors and other church leaders become role models of seemingly godly men who live by the "my-way-or-the-highway" rule. They see masculine identity as evidenced in power, control, authority, hardness, and intimidation. These leaders don't know the difference between being *empowered* by God and wielding the sword of personal power. As a result they model a form of *spiritual bullying* that tells guys "this is what a godly man looks like."

I agree that Christian men must be leaders. I agree that we need to help teenage guys in the battle against evil so they can lead their families, the church, and communities in the future and do it well. But I don't believe this should be done at the expense of compromising Jesus' identity in them. In Jesus we see a softer side that nurtures, is affectionate, wins over children, and weeps publicly out of compassion. This is as much a part of the Christ who overturns tables in the temple, stands confronting the religious authorities of the day, and willingly endures pain to the point of death—and does it all to save others. Even Terrell Carver, a skeptic of Christianity, recognizes Jesus as defying the cultural imprinting of traditional masculinity. He says, "[Jesus'] teaching and example recommend and perform an inverted masculinity that runs quite opposite to any recognizable hegemonic conception, of his time or ours, without making Jesus feminine, or woman-centered as such."[3]

Jesus is fully God but also perfect man, one in whom we see masculinity revealed in perfection. Teenage guys need to know that masculine identity is balanced. If we only portray masculinity—and even worse, only Christian masculinity—with archetypes of warrior, champion, gladiator, and so on, but don't consistently present the balance, we create confusion and give a guy license to buy into a worldly identity of masculinity that runs counter to Jesus' example.

In the same way, if we only present masculinity on the other side of the spectrum—not challenging guys to be leaders, to have strength of character, and so on—then we also compromise Jesus' example, too. Those who are responsible for modeling and teaching young men about masculine gender identity should be concerned with showing the existing tension and balance—men are strong but vulnerable; stable but sensitive; warriors but also lovers; leaders and servants; and so forth.

Guys seek appropriate male role models. Internally they know they have this feminine side, but most of the messages they get tell them to downplay that, to suck things up, and so on. In the process of formulating their identities as men, they're taught to live in a denial of how they were created and the men God requires them to be. Models of masculinity need to free guys to be all that they are. In *Dead Poets Society,* John Keating, played by Robin Williams, does this. There is a scene when some of the students

are asking Keating about the Dead Poets Society. He explains that this group of guys would go into the woods and read from master poets and authors.

Obviously confused, one of the boys says, "You mean it was a bunch of guys sitting around reading poetry?"

Keating replies, "It wasn't just '*guys* sitting around reading poetry.'" He continues by saying, "Spirits soared, women swooned, and gods were created, gentlemen. Not a bad way to spend an evening, eh?"

Keating's words free these young men to be all that they are—in balance. Christian fathers must show their sons this same balance. Christian men must model balance to the other men around them.

FATHER WOUND

The literature on masculine identity also has an element of the father wound. This has been played out in various forms. Some guys experience this through the rejection, absenteeism, or deficiency of their fathers. Other guys experience this just from the natural need to break away from their dads to become autonomous men. Regardless, it becomes a part of the process of identity formation in guys.

We need to revisit the definition of healthy autonomy here. Remember, it involves breaking away from that which is safe and familiar in order to stand alone. It also involves choosing to reconnect to something else. By this we perpetuate community. Autonomy is never devoid of connection. This means that a guy—although he looks to his father for connectedness and definition of masculinity—will pull away from his dad in order to become a man himself. That's where the father wound occurs. It's only deeper if the relationship with his dad is deficient or nonexistent. Yet even the best father will be deficient

in some way. That's why God raises up other men to fill in the gap.

The father wound is healed in the context of community. Men need men. It's a natural phenomenon played out in society. Guys love hanging out with just *the guys*. Being the father of two daughters, I often joke about this. I tell my girls I need more testosterone in my life, meaning I need guy time! My wife has also been great to recognize this need in me.

The attributes of God are played out in a community of godly men. No individual man is going to fulfill all that a teenage guy needs in his journey of becoming a man, and a godly one at that. God builds into the soul of a guy a need for deep connectedness to other men. This creates the brotherhood that so many men crave and eventually find. So teenage guys may be wounded from having to pull away from their fathers, but they find healing in the clan or their band of brothers.

I also believe the father wound is less likely to scar a guy's identity if the father releases him into manhood. This can be done in a setting where a rite of passage is initiated. I've noticed that guys who've undergone some rite of passage tend to be less conflicted about their identities as men. They experience more freedom to discover what a man is and should be. The reason for this is because their fathers have given them permission to pull away. In chapter 6.4 we will examine the idea of a rite of passage more closely.

PERSONAL IDENTITY

Erik Erikson identified stages throughout the life span that mark healthy growth. In adolescence, a guy enters into the stage Erikson calls "identity versus identity diffusion."[4] In this stage the teenage guy asks critical questions of himself: *Who am I? What makes me special? Why am I here? What am I going to do with my life? What makes me unique from or*

the same as other guys? Who do I want to be? These questions rise out of the changes that occur during puberty and the rapidly changing expectations or emergent adult roles that are put on them by their community.

Guys need to learn, test, and internalize roles that make them unique. Erikson noted that this stage creates what he called a *moratorium*, or the gap between being a boy and being a man, where a guy can explore who he is.[5] This creates a crisis of sorts, pushing a guy to answer those critical identity questions. If he does so successfully, he will have internalized a process that will continue to inform his identity throughout life.[6] If he cannot navigate through these questions, he experiences identity confusion.

These questions are largely answered in the context of social relationships. The first and most powerfully defining context for a guy is his family. Here he learns about gender roles, social expectations, and his uniqueness. Beyond his family he receives input about who he is and what he does or doesn't do well from school, church, peers, and so on. These sources help form his self-image. Throughout adolescence he'll do things that will shape his identity—he learns he is good at something or he may learn about his spiritual giftedness at church. All of these opportunities will help a guy understand his personal uniqueness, and we should encourage teenage guys to actively pursue them. As we do this, we need to look for the character qualities that will emerge in them.

Too often identity is defined by what men do. This method of labeling a person has tragic results because what a guy *does* will ultimately come to an end. This is why many men live in crisis after their retirement. Instead, we need to help guys see that *who they are* defines what they do. So as a guy takes advantage of new opportunities, such as art, we need to reinforce that he's *creative* and that's what makes him an artist. Therefore, when he can no longer create art in the way that he used to do, he still knows who he is and can redirect and exercise those attributes in another direction.

I've watched teenage guys build their identities around a particular sport or talent. They fail to see the qualities in their character that enhance what they do, pinning it all on their abilities. I've watched as a young man's athletic participation ended through an injury or another guy's talent began to fade, sending his identity, hopes, and dreams into a cataclysmic tailspin. These guys end up confused because, having built their identity around something they did on the playing field or stage, they don't know who they are now. This kind of painful experience forces some men to keep living in the glory days of their past.

It's important for teenage guys to recognize the unique qualities they possess. We need to seize every opportunity to verbalize what we see. Guys need to know they *are* compassionate, and that's why they do loving things; they *are* good, and that's why they stand up for justice; they *are* relational, and that's why they're good counselors to their peers—you get the picture. The input they receive from significant adults—particularly from men—creates an identity-forming anchor for guys.

I once had a mentoring relationship with a guy named Scott, an athlete with an impressive winning record. Scott had built his identity around his sport. But during one of our conversations, Scott expressed to me his fear of losing, saying he was only engaged when someone talked to him about sports. Input from his father or the other significant men in his life usually came in the form of praise for what he'd done well in a game or feedback about how he could improve the next time. While Scott liked to win, he felt relationships should be more important. But he was constantly being defined by what he did, not who God was making him to be.

I told Scott I'd noticed him playing aggressively on the court, yet caring for the well-being of his

teammates and opponents. I also mentioned that I'd noticed him reaching out in kindness to those students in our youth ministry who were marginalized, unpopular, or unlovable. He looked at me in surprise. I explained that I believed he did this because he was compassionate, valuing people above his own agenda and being sensitive to their needs. I told him I thought those were the marks of a great man. Scott became emotionally moved by this and said nobody had ever told him anything like that before. He was now ready to discover the attributes and characteristics that were shaping him into a great man and informing his actions.

6.2 HOW RELATIONSHIPS SHAPE GUYS

The social dimension of a guy's life is very involved. It's in this dimension that two overarching developmental tasks occur. Erikson identifies them as 1) identity versus identity diffusion, and 2) intimacy versus isolation.[1] The logical flow is simple: A guy needs to know and develop who he is first. After he has a sufficient handle on that part of it, he can then give himself away in a committed relationship. While there is significant overlap in the development of these tasks during adolescence, identity always precedes intimacy (see fig. 9). And because development is a successive process, guys are constantly defining and redefining themselves and their relationships.

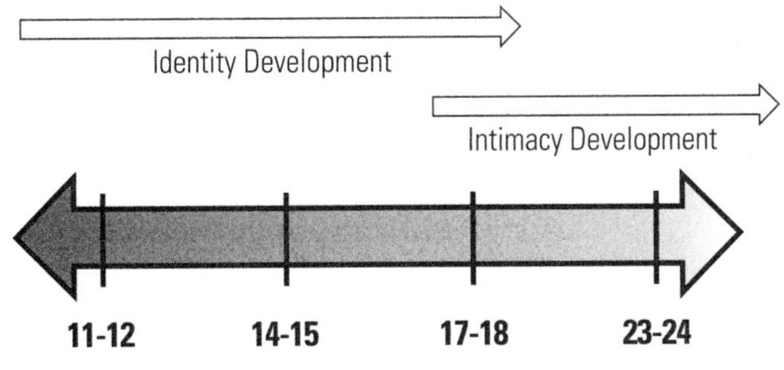

Figure 9

TASK #1—IDENTITY DEVELOPMENT

It's critical for a guy to know who he is in order to become an independent, functioning male adult. Identity development is general. This means he must internalize who he is as a male (even though he's still in the process of becoming a man) in addition to broader societal imprints, such as being American, Christian, and so on. Identity development is also specific, meaning he must internalize who he is personally, as defined by his character traits, personality, skills, roles, talents, and so on.

While identity is developed over the lifespan (beginning at infancy), it becomes more intensely defined during adolescence because a teenage guy has a better cognitive awareness, different physiological perspectives and desires, and a new ability to construct and shape his identity separate from his childhood identity.[2] It's in the social dimension of a teenage guy's life that this process of identity formation is defined. The end result of this process is autonomy.

It's a pronounced process. He starts out very connected to his family, the primary and most influential identity-defining agent in a guy's life. Over the span of adolescence, he must learn and internalize who he is and his life purpose. These messages come largely through his social contexts. Family, church, community, society (in the form of media, technology, education, and so on), and significant relationships speak into and inform who this guy is. Those influences can have a positive result, yielding a stable, secure man in the end. Or they can have a negative result, yielding insecurity, low self-image, or internal conflict. This is why identity development is a byproduct of the social dimension of a guy's life.

As he continues through this process, he loosens the grip of dependence on family and begins to become more independent. In junior high he wants to stay overnight with his friends all the time—a very

sterile and controlled form of independence. He's away from family and his parents, which gives him pseudo-autonomy. In senior high he learns he can make his own decisions, manage his own time, and even have some financial independence. He starts to drive and that enhances the gap of independence. Through his college years, he learns to make significant decisions regarding life goals and choices. These grow out of a more acute understanding of who he is. His connection to past dependencies becomes redefined in that he'll either seek out his parents' advice, or he may simply inform them of his decisions rather than allowing them to control him.

As I mentioned earlier, this process of autonomy does not mean that a guy becomes totally detached from his community, nor does it mean he becomes self-sufficient apart from his community. It means he moves from a child's dependence on adults to the independence of an adult within the authoritative confines of a community and society. He must *individuate*, seeing himself as unique and separate, but not alienated from others.[3]

Unfortunately we've given guys the message that strong men are self-sufficient and need no one or no thing. This creates a crisis of individuation. Teenage guys start to see themselves as separate and unique, but they also get messages that say dependence, neediness, and vulnerability are shameful and perceived by others as being feeble, making a guy less manly. This gender straitjacketing causes the guy to be distant, aloof, alone, and detached.[4] As a result, the trajectory toward autonomy can be off.

I had a former student call me about an issue he was facing. Apparently one of his friends heard him say something very inappropriate to someone else, and this friend confronted him about it. From my perspective, based on how the student described the situation to me, the confrontation was done in a loving, nonjudgmental manner. The friend approached him in order to understand the situation better and

to make him accountable for his actions (or in this case, his words). My student was angry because he "never invited this guy into his circle of accountability." This response came from a wounded male ego. He had internalized a self-sufficiency that mandated that he control all the realms of his world, including who *he* deemed worthy to hold him accountable.

We had a long talk about *shifting dependences* (this is a far better way to understand adult autonomy). Being strong men never means we are self-reliant, self-sufficient, or even self-controlled because our theology defines us as people who are connected in a body. We are accountable to one another and in need of one another (even to help each other with self-control or discipline issues). Being part of a body makes a person connected and accountable to all members of the body. Guys need to learn how to move from being dependent boys to interdependent men.

Because the observations, shaping, and input of others largely define a person's identity, relationships are a significant part of the process. Thus intimacy development becomes the second phase in the social dimension.

YOUTH WORKER TIP

Ever get a phone call from a parent or a male student because war has been declared over the way he cut or dyed his hair, the fact that he pierced his eyebrow, or the style of his clothing? Have you ever felt the shock of seeing one of your guys walk into youth group with his head shaved? Or better still, a guy and his buddies decide to shave their heads at camp—on your watch?

Well, these are all ways a guy may experience *role experimentation,* an essential exercise of identity and autonomy. It involves trying on certain images, looks, and behaviors that give him a sense of independence. You and the guy's parents still need to set boundaries for him. For example, my dad told me that if I got a tattoo, then he wouldn't pay for my college expenses. But you should also expect there will be forms of role experimentation. Learn to choose which battles to fight—or not fight—in order to win the war.

TASK #2—INTIMACY DEVELOPMENT

A guy learns his identity in the context of relationships. In understanding the intimacy development stage, we need to be aware that this doesn't mean that junior highers are incapable of intimate relationships. They can and do have great relationships with peers and adults. It means that depth of intimacy, to the point of giving oneself away in a committed relationship (mostly realized and characterized by marriage), is a learned process contingent and congruent on understanding one's own identity.

While the process is complex, it does play itself out in a tangible and simplified way. Guys learn who they are in the context of sameness first. They have to observe other guys by hanging out, trying new things, holding onto and giving up childhood games, and learning that other guys feel and think the same way they do. Many times stereotypical gender roles and norms are reinforced during this time. This is what Hill and Lynch propose as their *gender intensification hypothesis*.[5]

Simply put, this hypothesis holds that social pressure drives early teenagers, in particular, to behave in more gender-stereotypical ways. While Hill and Lynch say this is an adolescent female phenomenon, others have found it to be evidenced in males as well.[6] Much of the current masculine identity development theory would cite this as a female phenomenon because guys are held to stereotypical masculine roles from birth. Western culture allows girls to have more gender freedom than men. Thus the pressure to conform to masculine gender roles is a constant pressure on guys, not a situational pressure generated from a particular age or stage. Whereas girls choose to act *more* feminine in certain situations (this implies that she can act less feminine much of the time), the opposite is true for a guy. His peers often ridicule him if he deviates from the intense masculine gender role he is expected to maintain.

Phase 1: Guy Groups

Identity begins to take shape as guys find some sense of independence in the bonds of male camaraderie. Have you ever walked into a room full of junior highers? You'll see that all the guys congregate in a pack on one side of the room. Usually the girls are together by default, and they're much more socially engaged with each other, with adults, and across gender. Guys hold their own. They find strength in numbers and in sameness. This is not a cultural phenomenon; it's a developmental one.

I spoke to a junior high youth group in a rather lofty cathedral in London. All of the pews and benches had been moved out of the way to allow room for these early adolescents to mingle. I watched as each

kid came in; the girls mingled, and the guys formed a herd off to the side where the benches had been moved.

I did the same talk for a group of junior highers in Venezuela. I walked into a large conference hall at a boarding school where the kids had already arrived. All the guys were huddled together on the side, while the girls danced and chatted away in the center of the room. I took my rightful spot in the herd with the guys!

Why does that happen? Guys have to find a place where it's safe to learn who they are without letting on that they feel incompetent, unsure, or afraid. They can participate in an intense gender and sexual surveillance[7], watching themselves and others, making mental notes on what a guy should or shouldn't do, be or not be. The *herd effect* provides safety in two ways: first, there is safety in sameness, as we've already discussed; and secondly, there is safety in numbers. The herd allows a guy to be anonymous.

This same-gendered, large herd of guys will soon become unsafe. Guys begin to vie for top-dog status. Competition, bantering, joking, insults, and sometimes bullying (often older guys against younger guys) are required to prove one's maleness. But it creates a dichotomy in guys. On the one hand, they want to maintain their appearance of confidence, collectedness, and control; yet on the other hand, they feel threatened, afraid, and weak.

The best way to regain anonymity and avoid taking hits is to form a pack. The herd then becomes a smaller, same-gendered grouping. The *pack effect* allows guys to form their identities around common interests, problems, abilities, and so on. Later, these packs may get labels such as geeks, jocks, stoners, and other stereotypes. The pack then turns into an even smaller pack of guys as they grow older. The smaller group may allow a guy to be more vulner-

able and open with his search for identity and significance.

This narrowing of his circle of friends pushes a guy toward intimacy. Pollack notes that guys share intimate moments of relating, "but they tend to do so privately, away from the group, where such exchanges might expose them to shame or embarrassment."[8] This process starts at about age 11. And while it may remain throughout adolescence, it shifts somewhere around ages 14 to 15 (see fig. 10).

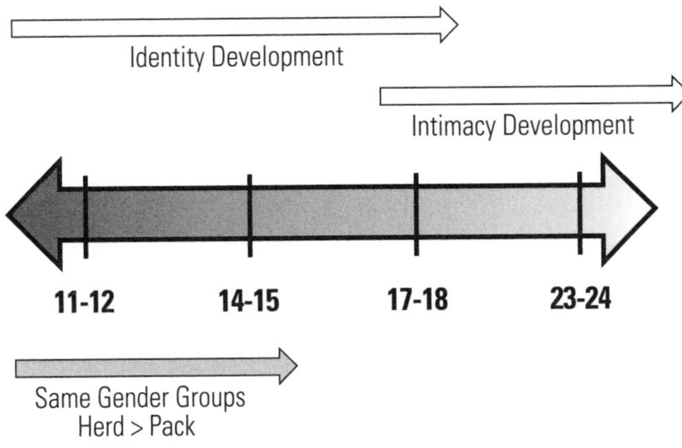

Figure 10

Phase 2: Mixed-Gender Groups

The second noticeable phase in the process is that the pack, within the herd, begins to engage the opposite gender to form a mixed-gender herd. In the middle of that segregated room, the older guys start to allow girls to invade their territory.

Once again this social process takes the form of a larger group experience to smaller group effect. This occurs for the same reasons I stated above: safety in numbers and anonymity can be preserved. This

phase begins to take effect toward the end of early adolescence and at the beginning of middle adolescence. It's much more common to see guys gravitate to mixed-gender groups in the middle of their high school freshman year or the beginning of their sophomore year (see fig. 11). The mixed-gender context gives a guy the opportunity to learn gender and personal differentiation. Once again he can observe and then engage as he gets more comfortable.

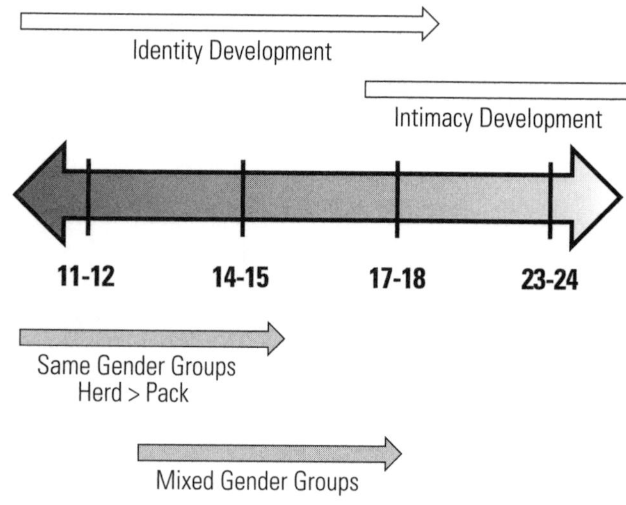

Figure 11

I had a conversation with a sophomore guy who informed me that he was friends with everyone at his school. I questioned him on it because I knew there were about 3,000 kids attending that high school. "Everyone?" I asked. His affirmative reply was steady and sure. He proceeded to tell me he'd crossed the barriers of each demographic group at his school—jocks, preps, geeks, and so on. This young buck was illustrating the point that he'd found new security and confidence in his relational ability; it was shaping *who* he was. He'd found a way to be accepted in the larger, mixed-gender context of his school.

But he was also illustrating another aspect of identity development—*status*. Status allows guys to maintain their uniqueness, even though all the other guys do the same thing. Status comes when a guy conforms to and embraces behaviors or attitudes that give him the appearance of adulthood in front of his peers, while still distancing him from childhood. For this sophomore guy, status meant popularity.

Status can also be achieved by *swearing*, and this is usually the first way a guy will go about it. Swearing is the primary act of independence, as guys can control what they say or don't say. So dropping the F-bomb in front of his friends makes him a real guy (not a boy). And guys get many masculinity-affirming messages about swearing: "He swears like a sailor!" or "That guy's got the mouth of a truck driver." The message is that swearing is manly. So "cursing like a barbarian" gives a guy a tough, manly status.

Other forms of status may include smoking, drinking, driving (even *more* status is allocated if he drives a sports car), fighting, and so on. It may include sexual conquest and losing one's virginity. There's a lot of pressure on guys to achieve status through sexual conquest. While teenage guys know it's acceptable to be a virgin (in part because today's society is more flexible in its views and more respectful of people who wait until marriage), they are still made to feel less than manly if they haven't had a sexual experience. Typical locker-room talk centers on sexual achievement. This masculine status symbol even forces guys to lie or fabricate stories just to save face.

Everything about virginity in the context of a global culture is feminine. Think about it—name a noted male virgin! The word *virgin* is feminine. Every example in history, religion, and even Scripture equivocates virginity with women. The Virgin Mary,

YOUTH WORKER TIP

A guy can achieve status and learn more about who he is through meaningful service. Helping a guy discover his talents, giving him leadership opportunities, and making him a vital part of a ministry and service team can shape his identity. Realize that girls naturally seek out these opportunities, but guys often need encouragement to become involved. This may be the reason girls take more leadership roles in youth ministry. They volunteer more!

the Virgin of Guadalupe, the 12 virgins in Jesus' parable, Greek virgins in mythology—did you ever hear of the "Virgin Tom"? The media also portrays guys who are virgins as inept losers who need to make it their ambition to have sex. It also becomes the driving concern for the virgin guy's friends. The sole climate of the friendship centers on helping the poor virgin score. When he does, there's a celebration. You can probably think of a few movies like that; but I bet you can't name one where the plot line is focused on a female. It's no wonder we have a sexual double standard. Loss of virginity can give a guy a sense of status.

A Christian guy who determines to stay sexually pure must not only fight the sexual temptation, but he must also battle the perceptions that challenge his masculinity. This pressure is great and not easily dismissed. Rites of passages may be a means for helping a guy withstand the pressures that challenge his masculinity. (We will discuss this further in chapter 6.4.)

Status can be achieved through positive means as well. Guys gain status from athletic achievements, getting a job, acts of bravery, and in some cases, academic accomplishments (although this status is attributed to females more than males). Achieving status in this phase of identity development becomes a big deal for a guy.

There's a myth that flies around adult, mixed-gendered circles that single men and women can't be friends. This notion is supported by the idea that men aren't capable of being loving, affectionate, and empathetic apart from a sexual context. In many ways that myth becomes a reality because guys are conditioned to be this way; they don't start out that way. When we see a teenage guy with a girl, we assume he's trying to get a girlfriend, or he's making a move. People always ask if the relationship is romantic. This pressure, along with the other pressures of masculinity, push men to only see mixed-gendered relationships as sexual or romantic opportunities. Even some of the popular Christian dating books have reinforced this false teaching. They

teach guys not to venture into intimate, across-gender friendships in the name of "guarding one's heart." That kind of teaching reduces intimacy to a sexual concept and inhibits healthy identity development.

Guys are capable of having healthy, across-gender relationships. William Pollack notes that his research revealed that not only are guys "capable of forming important platonic friendships with girls, but they're eager to do so and count on these friendships for emotional support and enhancement of their self-esteem."[9]

The large, mixed-gender group helps a guy be an observer. As he becomes more comfortable, the group will narrow and he'll become more of a participant. Around age 16 a guy typically hangs out with a smaller circle of friends—both guys and girls.

Phase 3: Same-Gender Dyadic Relationships.

The third phase is a bold move for a guy. While he's still part of a pack of guys and in the middle of a mixed-gender group, he begins to venture into a single, same-gendered, dyadic relationship (see fig. 12).

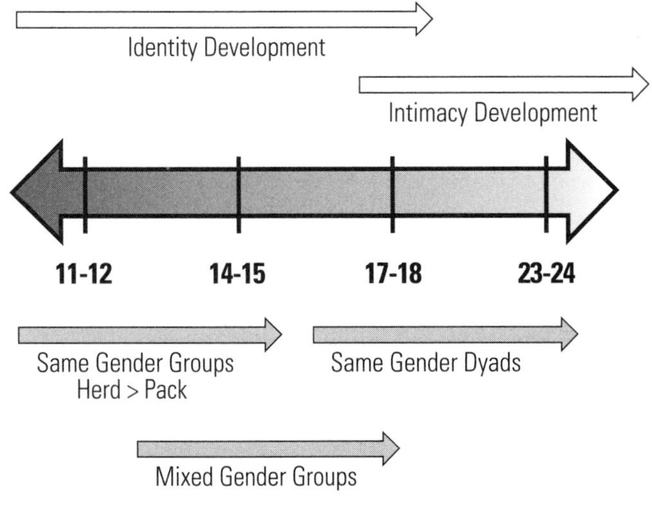

Figure 12

He'll start to narrow down the pack and single out one good male friend. These guys become best friends—a dyadic relationship. At this stage a teenage guy is beginning to better understand intimacy and closeness, but he must practice this where it's familiar—in the context of sameness.

Same-gendered dyadic relationships are safe because of familiarity, on the one hand, but they're also very risky. They're safe because a guy can explore values, interests, talents, and activities with a good friend with whom he feels some affinity. He's allowed to push past the normal bonds of having acquaintances and to venture into a more intimate realm of sharing who he is, his hopes, dreams, hurts, and desires. In this context he gauges some sense of normalcy and differentiation. For these reasons the relationship can be very safe. Yet there is also the gender straitjacketing that impairs "too much intimacy" in a same-gendered relationship. Let's back things up and look at this concept more intently.

First of all, we live in a culture that has difficulty with the word *intimate*. For the most part, this word immediately conjures a sexual image. For guys, *intimate* is the politically correct way of saying he's sexually active with a partner. So using *intimate* in a relational yet non-sexual context is outside of the culturally embedded makeup of a guy. If you take it a step further and make that relational context a same-gendered context, then it becomes even more uncomfortable.

I was having a discussion with a group of guys who were talking about their deep friendships with other guys—their best friends. During the conversation I kept using the words *intimate* and *intimacy*. After doing this a few times, one of the guys interrupted and said he was getting "kind of weirded-out by talking about guys being intimate with other guys."

While guys have this incredible draw toward deep male-to-male relationships, they're conditioned to allow it to go only so far. They're trapped in the gender straitjacket of what their heart and soul needs, versus what their environment and intellectual conditioning mandates. This allows men to bond with each other quickly (men can bond over a ballgame), but it restricts the depth and the desire for the same-gendered intimacy they need. I can't tell you how many times I've encountered guys who are in the middle of a struggle or are already in trouble, yet they say they can't talk to anyone about what they're going through. Guys are taught to keep the masks on and not drop their guards, even in front of their best friends. Intimacy requires an emotional, spiritual, and relational nakedness of sorts that runs counter to a guy's cultural imprinting. Guys need to be given permission and shown by example that they can be vulnerable and have intimate same-gender relationships.

We see great potential for deeply intimate same-gender relationships in Scripture. As a matter of fact, the tangible, relational examples the Bible uses to demonstrate the type of relationships we should have with God are all same-gendered: Jonathan and David; Ruth and Naomi; Paul and Timothy; even Jesus and John, the disciple he loved. If we examine Jonathan and David's relationship, we see they are incredibly intimate. In fact some of the narrative becomes problematic for guys (and also for those women who keep men in the gender straitjacket).

When these two guys meet, Jonathan is considerably older than David. He's the son of King Saul and captain of the army of Israel. David is too young to even fall into the ranks of that army, yet he is old enough to tend to the family business and bear the responsibility of traveling alone. This makes David a teenager. After David kills Goliath, he's brought into the presence of the king. Jonathan is present at this meeting. The narrative tells us that "the soul of Jonathan was knit to the soul of David, and Jonathan loved him as himself" (1 Samuel 18:1, NASB). This soul knitting transcends the boundaries of mere male

bonding. It's a God-induced, God-sanctioned union. These two guys venture into an extremely intimate relationship.

Later in the narrative, Jonathan and David make a covenant with each other. It's the verbal expression of their love and care for each other. Three times they make a covenant, committing to love each other until death separates them (1 Samuel 18:3; 20:16; 23:17-18).

This type of intimacy is difficult for guys. Because men learn to be emotionally restricted (and less in need of emotional connection), this means they'll also be verbally restricted when it comes to talking about something as emotional as love. Guys need to learn that it's good to declare their love to their friends. Jesus reminds us that we should love to the point of death (John 15:13) and that our love will mark us as his disciples (John 13:34-35). It's a manly thing to die for a friend, but tell him you love him—that's a bit girly. But the truth is if we can't say it, then we won't die for it. The bravado of dying for a friend is realized when a guy lives in a way that demonstrates and declares his love for that friend. Jonathan and David do this, and in the end Jonathan does die for his friend and future king David.

Other problematic passages in Jonathan and David's relationship reveal their outbursts and displays of emotion (namely, they cry a lot) and the affection they show each other. These two guys are always weeping when they talk about their relationship. By today's standards they'd be labeled histrionic sissies. As a defensive means, guys learn a *restrictive emotionality*[10] that keeps them from being vulnerable, always distancing them just out of the way of emotional connectedness.

Homophobia also plays a role in a man's restricted emotional intimacy. Loren E. Pedersen states, in *Dark Hearts: The Unconscious Forces that Shape Men's Lives*, "Friendship between men is…burdened by the fear of phallic or genital relatedness, which is also known as homophobia…men are so accustomed to relating emotionally in a phallic way that they fear that, closeness with men will 'turn into' sexuality, as it so often does when they relate to women."[11] The fear of being labeled homosexual affects emotional intimacy so strongly—particularly vulnerability and disclosure—that young guys who've been sexually molested by men often won't report the abuse out of fear of being seen as homosexual themselves.[12] However, Jonathan and David display a deep emotional connectedness that comes with an intimate relationship. They aren't afraid to show their emotions to the point of tears, and Scripture tells us their displays of affection even included kissing (1 Samuel 20:41).

Guys learn that all affection is sexual in nature. From childhood he's conditioned to suppress his need for affection. Watch any movie that predates the '80s, and you'll never see a guy hugging a guy—or worse, a father being affectionate with his son. The Cleaver boys always got a pat on the back, their heads rubbed (comically messing up their hair), or a manly handshake from dad. This conditioning is hard to amend.

First, like the emotional restrictiveness, male-to-male affection is cloaked with the dark shroud of homosexuality. Dads don't want their sons to be gay, so they stop being affectionate with them once they hit puberty. When a guy becomes a teenager, the need for affection and reassuring touch is considerably necessary and greatly desired. While he may desire and need it, a guy can't admit he has a need for affection out of fear of being perceived as weak or soft, so he suppresses that.

Secondly, he experiences new sexual desires and a new freedom to engage in dating. He starts to get attention from girls. This combination blurs the line between affection and sexual touch. Maybe this is why the number of sexual crimes is so high—guys are living their lives affectionately repressed and sexu-

DAD AT THE DOORSTEP

Every guy my daughters date has had an in-depth conversation with this very protective Italian father. I had lunch with one of my daughter's boyfriends at the beginning of their relationship. I knew he'd read a popular Christian dating book that advocated not kissing or having any kind of affectionate contact until the couple stood before each other on their wedding day. The book's directives equated remaining pure with the avoidance of kissing until the couple says, "I do," and are pronounced husband and wife. The challenge was to keep oneself pure for their partner so that the only person you ever kissed would be your spouse.

In the course of the conversation, I told this teenage guy that I would have a problem if he *didn't* kiss my daughter. Now I know that sounds dangerous—believe me, it was very difficult to say! The guy looked at me in amazement. He was overjoyed and he even let out a sigh of relief, giving one of those "Yes!" responses under his breath, as if he'd just scored a touchdown. I quickly assured

CONTINUED >

ally charged. The only outlet for their affective needs is sexual. Maybe this is also why the father wound suffered by so many guys is such a prolonged, painful, debilitating thing. The only place where a teenage guy could theoretically feel a reassuring, strong and safe affection (without worry of it being sexual) should come from his biological father. When this doesn't happen, the woundedness is great. William Pollack writes:

> The gender straitjacket, combined with the absurd link that is often made between boyhood affection and adult male homosexuality, creates a restrictive environment. Boys are frequently pushed away from one another when they exude even a modicum of overt genuine love or affection for one another. This misguided perception—a form of homophobia—is perhaps the most regrettable because it may lead us to undermine boys' friendships before they've even taken hold.[13]

At this point the dilemma worsens. Now a double jeopardy effect kicks in: guys can't experience any physical affection from other guys because it's perceived to be homosexual; and he can't receive affection from girls because it's perceived to be lustful, impure, and inappropriate. Once again, the most popular Christian dating books reinforce a detrimental view that reduces all physical contact as being sexual. These authors are writing out of—and generating an atmosphere of fear in—a desperate attempt to keep kids as far away from sexual sin as they can. Their directive: avoid any physical contact because physicality is unwise at best, and (according to some authors) immoral at worst. I agree we must teach kids to abstain from *sexual* contact, and they must live purely. But I don't believe we should reinforce a position with the lie that all touch leads to sex.

When teenage guys enter into the third phase of identity and intimacy development, they learn and

practice intimacy in the context of sameness. So it's not too surprising that many men experience failure in their friendships and marriages. Their restrictedness precludes them from intimacy. Guys must learn that they need and can give affection in opposite- and same-gendered relationships and that affection is not sexual. We allow girls this luxury. Go to any airport and watch women and men respond to the people who come and go. Women are much more affectionate and freer with touch—even in same-gendered relationships. On the other hand, guys are much more guarded.

Take one last look at Jonathan and David. So great was the intimate bond between Jonathan and David that at Jonathan's death, David laments and eulogizes him, saying:

> How have the mighty fallen in the midst of the battle! Jonathan is slain on your high places. I am distressed for you, my brother Jonathan; you have been very pleasant to me. *Your love to me was more wonderful than the love of women.* How have the mighty fallen, and the weapons of war perished! (2 Samuel 1:25-27, NASB; emphasis mine)

David isn't talking about a homosexual relationship; he's talking about a deeply intimate love relationship that transcended even the natural sexual relationship he had with his wives (one of whom was Jonathan's sister). I don't want to run commentary on this passage, but I hope it spurs you to dig into God's Word and discover the deeper meanings yourself. While this passage tends to be problematic and makes us uncomfortable, it does illustrate the point. Guys begin to form natural, same-gendered dyadic relationships even by God's design. Those relationships can be sabotaged if we don't coach and mentor guys to break beyond their fears and distorted perspectives and to battle the lies they've been fed.

CONTINUED >

him that our conversation wasn't finished and that he should remain intensely focused on what I was about to say.

I love my daughter, but I also loved this guy. I wanted him to learn that there is a difference between affection and sexual touch. I wanted him to know that he needs affection and so does my daughter—a woman who may someday be someone's (if not this guy's) wife. We have to bust the myth that all touch is sexual. Guys need to break the conditioning that says affection leads to sexual conquest. Wives would agree that sometimes affection is called for without it ending up in intercourse. A guy also needs to realize that if his affective needs are met (from women and from men), then he may not be as sexually directed as he sometimes finds himself. Yet the "no affection" stance entrenches a guy's already distorted view of affection, turning it into something that is sexual and is now spiritualized as a form of impurity. And I explained all of this to a very intent teenage guy.

CONTINUED >

CONTINUED >

After I gave my impassioned lecture, I told him he *could* kiss my daughter—but I also told him *how* he could kiss my daughter! Affectionate touch is acceptable in *public contexts* where it's visible, yet comfortable for other people to witness. I said he could kiss, cuddle, and embrace my daughter, but only in a way where he'd be comfortable doing in front of me. I didn't mind if he affectionately kissed my daughter goodnight. He could do that in front of me. But I did mind if he swallowed her face. He quickly got the picture and understood the boundaries between affection versus sexual touch.

Phase 4: Mixed-Gender Dyadic Relationships

As intimacy is learned and identity is defined, a guy begins to feel more comfortable in a dyadic relationship with a member of the opposite gender. This level of comfort usually comes in late adolescence (see fig. 13). The very first problem to arise is a common one. I've heard many late-adolescent guys say they think it stinks that their roommate or best friend got a girlfriend and now his guy friends never see him anymore. Those guys who complain also vow on their mother's grave that they'll never do that to their friends—but then along comes a girl, and they do it, too.

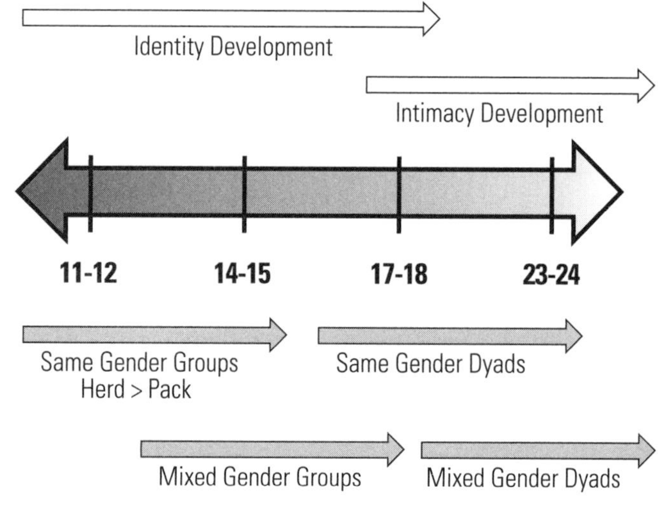

Figure 13

This is common because mixed-gender dyadic relationships are new and intimacy is learned in the context of these relationships. Guys learn in the context of sameness first, and then they have to shift and learn in the context of difference (mixed gender). As a guy learns intimacy in the context of difference, he forgets he still has to give some attention to his buddies. Guys become single-minded until they get the task down. In addition, at this stage in life a guy ventures into a relationship with a girl in hopes of finding a compatible life mate. The prospects of romance and love charge the relationship, whereas that element doesn't exist in his relationship with his buddies. As loyal as a guy can be to his boys, man-woman love takes longer to learn. It also takes more of his focus and energy because he wants to do it right, and there is more riding on this relationship, as we will see. Guys may need accountability in their guy-guy relationships, while their buddies need to be patient and more understanding toward a hopeless romantic.

It's also important to note here that across-gender relationships, dating relationships, and even marriages are better when a guy has and maintains guy time with his friends. I believe the Jonathan and David effect is still a very strong spiritual connection that allows men to have hearts bound in communion with each other. This can empower them and recharge them to bring more back to their girlfriends or spouses.

The mixed-gender dyadic relationships phase begins right around ages 18 to 19, which would tell us that a guy this age is probably not ready to get married, but he starts to prepare for it. Dating changes when a guy gets past high school. He starts to get more serious about whom he dates. He wrestles through concepts such as mate selection and commitment. Guys don't fear commitment; they've just never practiced it in a relationship before because they haven't been allowed to do so.

Dating is a luxury of the Western culture. We are a society that allows our children to select their own mates. While we complain about dating—and often fear our guys are going to use it as a platform for sex-

GUY-GIRL DIFFERENCES

In his book *Real Boys*, William Pollack discusses the differences between the way girls and guys form intimate friendships. While girls see intimate friendship as involving a deeply emotive, face-to-face conversation, Pollack says that guys "follow their own formula for friendship: start with action and energy, throw in loyalty and laughter, and 'doing together.' Add covert verbal expressions of caring, earnestness and hidden physical touching—and you get a good friend. This formula may differ completely from that for a girl's friendship, but it may be no less real or intimate."[14]

WHY ARE GUYS SUCH JERKS TO GIRLS?

When girls ask this question, what they mean is that guys tend to have an attitude, say mean things, and sometimes deliberately do things that are inconsiderate. The reason is because guys are conditioned to believe that nice guys finish last and never get the girl. So they have to put on a bit of toughness and aloofness around women so girls don't see them as weak momma's boys.

This issue isn't just a guy thing though. Girls *do* gravitate toward bad boys. They tend to flirt more with the bad boy and have great brother-sister conversations with the nice guy. If a guy is nice to a girl, then he feels as though his chances of having a deeper relationship with her are doomed. One guy actually told me he was tired of being the nice guy because all the girls in his life—the ones he thought could be a great girlfriend—all saw him as their "big brother." We need to empower our guys to be "nicer," but we also need to encourage girls to desire nice guys over the bad boys.

ual experimentation—we fail to see that it's a great way to select a mate.

As a guy becomes more in tune with who he is and learns the roles he plays as a male (along with learning the roles girls play as females), he can then find companionship in girls and ultimately with a special woman to whom he may one day commit as a life partner. Through the natural social process, this usually happens in post-late adolescence or early young adulthood.

By the time a guy gets to late adolescence, he'll have begun internalizing personal values, morals, and ethics. He'll have some sense of life and a career direction. He'll understand his personal strengths and weaknesses, his needs and resources. He may have future dreams, goals, and ambitions. And he should have the problem-solving skills he needs to accomplish those things.

When he gets all of this stuff straight about himself, a guy may feel more comfortable giving himself away and committing to a marriage relationship. But at the same time, he now discovers that it all needs to be tweaked, compromised, and meshed with his partner. While this is difficult work, it evidences healthy identity and intimacy formation because a guy will have come to know himself well and be able to identify the negotiables and non-negotiables that will make a healthy relationship work.

Dating helps a guy define those things. If we look back at the timeline (see fig. 13), we can see that the most natural age for real dating to occur happens after a guy has entered into a comfort zone with mixed-gender dyadic relationships and when he is in the zone of intimacy development. For the most part, that may be after age 18 for some guys.

But I've encountered many stable, socially confident, and engaging late-adolescent guys who disclosed that they never really dated in high school.

They didn't see the need, pushed past the pressure to prove their manliness and virility, and just developed friendships with girls. They followed their natural instincts to build their relationships out of who they were. The funny thing is that usually when a guy discloses this information to me, he comes confidentially to find out if he's relationally healthy or normal. The societal message says he isn't normal if he hasn't dated or been sexually active from an early age.

When guys date before the age of readiness, they often do so to fulfill other kinds of personal needs, such as status, sexual desire, acceptance, security, fun, and so on. These are normal and not necessarily all negative, but true dating (what dating was designed for: mate selection) won't occur until the later adolescent years. Now before we restrict dating altogether, let's remember that dating can function to help a guy (and a girl) define who he is and what he desires, to define what he can relationally offer a partner, and to define the practice of forming, maintaining, nurturing, growing, and even terminating relationships. So often we don't want our kids to date because we want to spare them the pain of broken hearts. For a guy, this is the worst idea. Face it—a guy with a broken heart also suffers a broken and humiliated spirit because he's supposed to be invincible. He believes he should be resilient to relational pain because he's competent. Guys need to learn that pain is a part of relationships. Pain in relationships helps a guy learn that he's not invincible but he can weather through it. And that pain becomes a marker for the antithesis of sweet joy once he's worked through it and survived.

Guys really want to do relationships right. They seek out models and mentors in men who are in long-term relationships. Many guys have watched their parents deal with the complexities of marriage. They may have seen right and wrong ways to do it. Maybe the majority of guys have seen those relationships fail. From my personal observation, I've noticed that guys have an ability to separate themselves from their

parents' tragedies. They see the mistakes and vow not to have a marriage like that. Others come from homes where the marriage is intact and thriving. These guys often have a realistic perspective on the good and the bad, as well as the do's and don'ts they've observed. Regardless of their background, guys seek honest appraisal of the difficulties and joys in building good marriages. Many aren't afraid of the hard work that comes with building a relationship, once they get over the significant hurdle of a fear of rejection.

Guys truly desire to love and be loved. They're wired with deep intimate needs. Yet throughout his life, a guy is on a trajectory that informs and rewards him if he's a man who is strong, competent, self-sufficient, and who needs very little. When he's faced with a deep love relationship, the rules change. He's required to give his heart away. This vulnerability is the most feared thing for a guy. In *Raising Cain*, Dan Kindlon and Michael Thompson describe it well:

> The reason a boy fears dependence on a girl is that he fears her rejection and the pain and humiliation that go with it. A boy's desire to be powerful isn't as much about muscle as it is about heart and the fact that if you allow yourself to be dependent on someone—for a smile, for love, for sex, for self-respect—then you can be devastated by her as well.[15]

Some guys can't manage the complications and tough work of deep, committed relationships. They'd rather play video games than face the fear of rejection. This minority may end up in countless shallow relationships, never committing to anyone; or they may be exploitative in their relationships. Yet the majority of guys *will* work at breaking down the bravado, giving their hearts away, and working hard to make their relationships work.

6.3 GUYS AND FAMILY

Craig is a 19-year-old college sophomore trying to figure out who he is. Like most guys, he has areas of his life where he feels relatively confident and other areas where he feels more insecure. This bothers Craig a lot because he compares himself to the guys around him. He begins to measure himself by who he isn't rather than who he is.

One of the primary topics of Craig's discussions with me was his home life. Craig grew up in a Christian home. His parents are active in their local church, and Craig has never known life apart from this. Craig's parents have always been together because divorce was never an option. He watched them operate in the good times and struggle through the bad and painful times. Craig's father worked hard to provide for his family. His mother stayed home with the kids until Craig and his sister went to school, then she joined the work force to supplement the income.

In the end, Craig's comparative nature negatively affected his outlook on his family. After reading some of the popular literature on masculinity, Craig announced that he'd suffered a deep father wound. This wound was keeping him from being the man he needed to be because he was always trying to gain his father's approval and never getting it. A few weeks later he came to the conclusion that his mother was emasculating him. He claimed that her grip was so strong on him that he was resentful. Not only was she emasculating, but she was also "castrating" because her demands and expectations were feminizing him. As evidence of this, he cited the fact that she always wants him to talk about his feelings and says she can hear it in his voice when he's sad and discouraged,

but he still won't talk about it. I asked Craig if her perceptions were accurate. He said they were, but he shouldn't have to run to his mommy like a little girl.

YOU CAN'T CHOOSE YOUR RELATIVES

Family is a powerfully defining influence on a guy, but we must keep something straight: families don't lock in anyone's future, destiny, character, or the quality of their life experiences. I've met guys who came from hellish family situations, but they now have quality lives with quality relationships. I've also seen guys who came from exemplary families end up in jail.

I hear guys like Craig play blame games or scramble to cover their bases by finding some fault they can pin their failures to when life goes south. They have a father wound or an emasculating mother; they weren't breastfed or their diapers were too tight as an infant; they masturbated too much as a young teenager—anything to give them a reason for their lack of fulfillment. The tragic thing is that the Christian community is also responsible for perpetuating these kinds of attitudes. We give the impression that events in a person's life, deficiencies from the family, even past sins all affect our futures.

I am a clinically trained therapist. I am also a Christian. Because of my psychological training, I have problems with popularized psychobabble. As a mental health professional, I know that even the most tragic events can be worked through, but I don't agree with the humanistic principles of my field that hold that humanity has all the tools and capability of solving its own problems. As a Christian my theology informs my science. The theology of an omnipotent, sovereign, and Almighty God mandates belief that there is nothing greater than he. The theology of complete redemption also mandates that there is nothing that cannot be remade by a God whose redemption is complete for all eternity. That means

God is bigger than any wrongdoing, trauma, or sin; his redemption can make anyone new; and he can break through any stronghold of our past, present, or future. Past sexual sin isn't going to sabotage a person's future marriage if God is allowed to redeem and transform. The perpetual woundedness that follows a tragic event in a person's life doesn't have to leave a person defeated because God makes all things new. The deficiencies of our families don't have to limit us because God provides for our every need.

We need to start with this basic premise: God is bigger than anything we might encounter. He will sufficiently meet every need. No family, father, or mother will meet all of our expectations or do it all right all the time. No spouse will meet every need. God won't allow it because he wants us to trust him more than anyone else in our lives. I asked Craig, "If your family met every need and did everything right, what would you need God for?"

Regardless of a guy's family situation, God has provided deliverance from anything that would keep him in bondage—whether it's imagined or realized. So as we look at families, remember that the greatest thing we can teach guys is to trust a good God who is bigger and breaks the power of anything that has a stronghold on them.

GUYS AND FATHERS

Whether present or absent, a father plays a very crucial role in a guy's life. If the father is absent, a teenage guy must work through some painful issues and find resolution in order to be healthy. When a guy gains the cognitive skills to understand circumstances, attitudes, motives, and relational dynamics, then he questions, analyzes, and reasons through why his father may have abandoned him or is detached (absent). This process usually starts with the guy attempting to figure out what he did or what's wrong

with him—what keeps his dad from desiring to connect with him? He may also analyze his father in an attempt to find out what is wrong with Dad as well.

This is a more difficult step in the process because every teenage guy still wants his dad to have it all together so he can coach his son through some of the perils of adolescence. Analyzing one's father for flaws is a last resort for a teenage guy because he doesn't want to find anything dramatically and conclusively wrong, just in case the connection can be restored. It's a form of hope that keeps the guy from seeing the true picture.

Guys in this stage tend to act out frequently—in a self-fulfilling prophecy kind of way—in order to prove that they are problematic, or to seek the attention of others, or to vent the hurt (which they ultimately turn into anger—the acceptable male emotion). Studies have shown a correlation between father absence and delinquency, crime, poor self-esteem, suicide, academic failure, and gang involvement (among other things) in teenage guys.[1] It's crucial for many men to come alongside a teenage guy in need of a father figure.

While I say this, I must qualify an observation I've made regarding this issue. I've encountered many single mothers who've been concerned, and rightfully so, that their sons don't have some prominent male figure in their lives. These wonderful women attempt to fill the father role for their sons, but soon realize they fall short. At her own emotional expense, the single mom seeks to have her son connect with a male role model and detach from her. To me this is a powerful example of a mother's love, which we will discuss more fully. Many times these moms panic a bit because they don't believe their sons have any such models in their lives. I usually advise these mothers to "chill."

From my observations guys tend to seek out male models on their own. They just gravitate toward them—it's a part of the internal mechanism of being a guy. Therefore, instead of finding a role model for her son, a single mother may need to be more concerned with helping him screen the models he's already pursuing. This gravitational pull is not just indicative of guys who lack a central male figure. Guys who have great relationships with their dads also do this. It fills the internal desire of a guy to be a part of a tribe of men, a band of brothers, or a fraternity of generational manhood. While a guy has internalized the "Boy Code"[2] that requires him to be strong, competent, and secure, he's constantly on a mission of espionage, scoping out how other men think, act, work, play, feel, and so on. All men, especially male youth workers, need to recognize that they are a part of this great fraternity. They need to be aware that they impact the development of every guy.

What's more, fathers who have good relationships with their sons need to see the value of other men coming alongside their sons without feeling jealous or fearful about being replaced. This phenomenon exemplifies the basic tenet of the church as Christ's body. Each member plays a vital role in supporting, nurturing, and developing others. Older men need to take to heart the surrogate or additional father roles they play in the lives of younger men. This *generative* perspective (a perspective passed from generation to generation) is vital to the continuous development of healthy, God-honoring men.

Fathers of the Past

Fathers relate to guys differently than mothers. Whereas a mother is more verbally expressive, pampering, and less inhibited emotionally than a father, fathers tend to nurture, care for, and engage their sons in different ways. At one point on the generational landscape of father-son relationships, fathers were more disengaged in the nurture of their sons. The prewar and immediate post-World War II generations of fathers were not the same as fathers of present and

emerging generations. Many fathers from the war generation were attempting to redefine their roles as men and fathers. They may have been sons of immigrants who came to the United States, and many had to work hard to make a life for themselves and their families while attempting to be American. They may have suffered through the Great Depression that left families crippled from financial ruin and wounded a man's sense of strength and provisional power for his family. They were all part of a relatively new era of an industrialized modern culture that decentralized a father from his home, as his work became a separate event from the rest of his life. All of these factors played into a man's need to be the strong, stabilizing agent in the life of his family.

With all of that on his plate and the desperate hopeless feeling that decentralization and war created for a generation of men, a mythological self-made, invincible man emerged. He painted on a smile, wore the mask of stability, and never let anyone know the uncertainty he faced or the inept hopelessness he may have felt. Strength was defined as emotional stoicism. This father concentrated all of his energy into the appearance of not being fazed by any trauma or calamity. In fact, a historical review shows the men of that time clamoring with great enthusiasm to go "over there" and fight a glamorous war. Men didn't fear war or see the travesty of it. They rushed to enlist as if they were going to miss out on securing tickets for a world-class, once-in-a-lifetime event. If they were disqualified from the "war effort," they presented as though they were discouraged. The movies, music, and media of that era are characteristic of this masculine invincibility.

And to top it off, many women were called on to fill the roles vacated by men in shipyards, power plants, construction, and labor. This compromised the feminine role of being a homemaker (or "housewife," as she was called then). But women saw this change as only being for a season—until their strong men returned home. Nonetheless, this displaced gender experience also shaped a woman's influence on her young sons. After all, mom was only doing a man's job because dad was winning a war. It takes a lot of effort to be invincible; something must be compromised.

Many men returned home from war having seen the atrocities that come with battle, but in the literature there is little to no mention of the post-traumatic stress or the effect that war had on those men. It wasn't until they reached their twilight years that they started to expose the horrifying toll it took on them. Their efforts to maintain their invincible, problem-free, competent strongman image came at the expense of distancing themselves from the emotive nurturing their sons needed, which their wives were then called upon to do.

They became emotionally disengaged fathers. This difficulty of becoming close to their sons birthed boys who perpetuated the sins of their fathers. Second and third generations of fathers never had an example of a dad who engaged or was close in the way they needed him to be. This pain and longing also generated a *father hunger*[3] in men that forced a recent generation of fathers to give their sons what they'd missed.

Fathers of Today

Today's fathers tend to be more engaged. They work to be involved in the fabric of their sons' lives. They desire to stay close to their sons. This is mostly done in active ways. Dads connect with their sons' hearts through activities. Everything from sporting events to chores becomes an opportunity for fathers and sons to connect when a father comes alongside his son. Pollack reinforces this. He says:

> Fathers, I've found, often discover they can most effectively tap into a boy's emotional world by joining their sons in this

> kind of work-related, goal-oriented activity or supporting them in their efforts. Because our society places tremendous emphasis on the conventional female approach to bonding verbally by sharing feelings through words, we often lose sight of what my research illuminates—that fathers frequently show that they care and nurture their sons through action.[4]

This idea is vividly illustrated in the movie *Life as a House* (New Line Cinema, 2001). The plot centers on the relationship between a father and son. The father (played by Kevin Kline) is absent from his teenager's life because of a divorce. The son (played by Hayden Christensen) is angry, defiant, and acting out, which becomes more than his mother and stepfather can handle. When the biological father learns he has a terminal illness, he desires to connect with his son. As an act of desperation, the mother (played by Kristin Scott Thomas) releases custody of the teenager to his father who makes his son work alongside him as he demolishes a dilapidated shack (which was a family inheritance) and rebuilds a dream house on the ocean shore. The intense human drama and resolve between this father and son are played out as they engage in action intimacy. The house becomes the representation of their relationship.

The brilliance of this movie is that the father sees how he and his son relate through doing. The action offers them the opportunity to share their hearts with each other, to learn life lessons in teachable moments, and to be genuinely real. It also shows that just doing—while effective in breaking through to a teenage guy—is not enough.

I grew up with a post-war father. And I can recall those impactful, intimate moments I spent with him while we were engaged in something: learning to shoot a rifle at sunset on a lake in Wisconsin; standing in the deafening pits of the nitro-fueled, supercharged, funny car speedway as they burned out; or

Christmas shopping for a gift for my mother. I remember one distinct moment when my dad took me to a midget car drag race at Soldier's Field in Chicago. We sat in the second row off the wall, and our seats were located on the curve at the end of the straightaway. As the cars came around that turn, they got so close you could feel the power against your body when they roared passed. About midway through the race, a car missed the curve and plowed into the wall directly in front of us. It happened so quickly that I didn't know what was going on. I only remember my dad's body coming over his seat to shield me from flying debris. And a sharp piece of metal from the rim of that car landed right in my lap.

I think about that incident now as a father, and it sends a chill down my spine as I imagine what could have happened. Yet all I knew at the time—and still know now—is a father's love that instinctively protected me. My dad would have died for me. I kept that piece of metal for years after that incident.

Research shows that fathers who are actively involved in the lives of their sons turn out guys who are less aggressive and competitive, are better able to express their feelings of vulnerability and sadness, have more flexible attitudes about gender and life, have a healthy self-esteem and fewer incidents of depression, have greater academic and career success, are better equipped for intimacy, and have better problem-solving skills.[5]

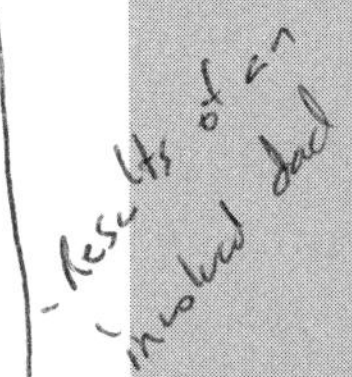

Dads who learn an emotional vocabulary take intimacy with their sons a step further. Guys need to see a man's heart, but they need to hear it as well. This is driven home in the book of Proverbs. Proverbs, the book of wisdom, is written from the perspective of an older man who is mentoring a younger man. The mentor refers to the protégé as "son" throughout the book. Often throughout the first nine chapters (which serve as the foundation of the book), the mentor tells the son to listen (Proverbs 2:2; 5:1, 7; 8:32, 34, NASB) to his impassioned appeals; to

hear his words (Proverbs 1:8; 4:1, 10, NASB) and to *receive* his instruction (Proverbs 2:1; 4:20; 8:33, NASB). Such desire from a father to his son implies that if the son is listening, then the father is speaking.

The Language of Fathers

Men have an uncanny way of communicating love, nurture, care, and concern without saying a word. While this is all well and good, I always encourage older men to verbalize their compassion for, their dreams regarding, and their adoration to their teenage sons. It's not enough to leave a teenage guy guessing; he needs to be affirmed beyond a shadow of a doubt.

I spoke to a father who desired to do this with his son. He was afraid because he didn't know how his son would receive it. I told him the best way to do this was to be straightforward with his boy. He should tell his son he wants to say some things, but he doesn't expect the son to respond. Then he can verbalize that he believes the son might think it's weird, but he feels strongly that he must say what he needs to say. But I cautioned him not to belabor that point because a teenage guy can get freaked out by all the preparation leading up to the actual conversation, as if something tragic is about to occur.

After we got over that hurdle, the dad articulated his second fear. "I don't know if I'll know exactly what to say," he said. I asked him to shift gears and tell me what his son meant to him. The man verbalized the sweetest and most powerful description of love and adoration for a boy that I've ever heard. As he spoke his eyes welled up, and he got choked up. "See, I don't want to do that in front of my son," he said.

"WHY NOT?!" I encouraged him to allow his son to see and hear his heart.

Some fathers feel uncomfortable doing this because they still buy into the invincible man myth that their fathers passed on to them. They fear they will appear wimpy and soft in front of their sons. Some men even believe this behavior may encourage their sons toward weakness, making them susceptible to bullying, effeminate behaviors, and even homosexuality. Fathers who come alongside *and* who verbalize their care are powerfully affirming to their teenage guys. We see this practiced throughout the Old Testament in the form of the "blessing," where the patriarch would declare his love to his son, share his hopes and dreams for his son by recognizing the boy's full potential, embrace and kiss him, and invoke God's blessing upon him.

GUYS AND MOTHERS

The oldest theories about the mother-son relationship and identity development grow out of Freudian psychoanalytic schools. Freud proposed a theory of masculine gender identity development based on his belief that the male child develops a strong erotic or sexualized love for his mother. This love (which leads to many other emotions, such as jealousy, fear of abandonment, anxiety, and so on) is repressed into the unconscious. The young boy's desire to possess his mother as the object of his love, along with the threat his father poses ("castration anxiety," as termed by Freud), is the Oedipus complex.

Freud believed the Oedipal attitude germinated in the heart of the young boy between the ages of three and five, while he's in what Freud called the "phallic phase" of life. Seeing the affection the father has for the mother, the boy fears his father will castrate him. The anxiety over the possible castration and the incest taboo leads the child to abandon his desire to erotically possess his mother. He then turns to the father and begins to identify with him. In seeking to take on the father's traits, the boy develops a masculine identity.[6]

While much of the psychological community disagrees with the sexual overtones of Freud's theory, they do agree that it does create a framework in understanding a dynamic between mothers and sons in the formation of masculine identity. The Oedipal triangle (father, mother, and son) creates some complications that precondition the gender struggles that guys will face in identity development.

A male infant, like all infants, is dependent upon his mother as the primary caregiver; most importantly, she nurses the child. She meets the boy's emotional, physical, cognitive, and relational needs in crucial formational years. This has a powerful influence on the emerging identity during the developmental years of adolescence. As the boy begins to pull away from his mother, there is conflict between his strong need for emotional intimacy (attachment) and an equally strong need for identity (autonomy).[7] These *attachment battles* exemplify a teenage guy's need and reluctance to connect with his mother.[8]

Mothers become aware of these attachment battles. She knows them intuitively, and she feels them acutely as they occur. This intuition or instinct is a built-in, God-designed part of mothering sons. Most mothers, unless they have some compulsive disorder, give up their sons. The greatest struggle she faces is to know when and how to let go. I believe that within the scope of the literature that came out of the men's movement, moms got a bad name. At times it is misogynistic (hateful of women) in nature.

Much of what's written today attempts to regain some sense of machismo that swings the pendulum back to believing that guys are feminized or tamed by society, and it all starts with the influence of mothers. This notion runs counter to strong moral standards, basic controlled behaviors of a civilized people, and even godly character. John Eldredge gravitates toward this view:

> The idea, widely held in our culture, is that the aggressive nature in boys is inherently bad, and we have to make them something more like girls. The primary tool for that operation is the public school system. The average schoolteacher faces an incredible challenge: to bring order to a room of boys and girls, and promote learning. The main obstacle to that noble goal is getting the boy to sit still, keep quiet, and pay attention…for an entire day. You might as well hold back the tide. That's not the way a boy is wired, and it's not the way a boy learns. Rather than changing the way we do male education, we try to change males.[9]

Teaching the disciplines of order, anger management, reasoning skills, social graces, emotional literacy (reading emotional responses), empathy, caring, nurturing, and uninhibited love and affection all run against the natural wiring of a guy. Internalizing these things won't feminize him; it will make him a civilized gentleman. It will give him character and *quality of heart.* Don't change the education—change the guy! Most of the time these virtues and ideals are taught while he's at home under the care and tutelage of his mother (albeit a feminine influence) and long before a guy gets to school.

A mother's strong influence and teaching is essential to the shaping of masculine identity. It's the foolish man who shuns the influential teaching of his mother. The writer-mentor of Proverbs warns his protégé over and over not to forsake his mother's teachings (Proverbs 1:8; 6:20). He even takes this a step further and compares wisdom to a woman who influentially and even alluringly calls out to guys. At the end of Proverbs 1, she has a little monologue where she tells a foolish guy that he scoffs at her teaching, neglects her counsel, and did not want her correction, so calamity comes on him and she is no longer there. Her final words at the end of the chapter are,

"For the waywardness of the naïve will kill them, and the complacency of fools will destroy them. But he who listens to me shall live securely and will be at ease from the dread of evil" (Proverbs 1:32-33, NASB).

No Place Like Home

Many guys find their mothers to be a refuge. She becomes the force that shapes his self-esteem. She provides the grace and nurture, which she instills in him. Mothers personify love to many guys. She is often the first line of engagement for a teenage guy when he's struggling with an emotional issue, because she can lovingly guide, teach, and even correct him without damaging his heart. She is the trusted one in his life. When everyone fails him, he knows his mom will be there. When these things don't happen, the devastation is paramount. A guy's relationship with his mom is a deep heart relationship that goes through a series of trials. He needs the connectedness, but at times he despises it.

The mother tension comes out of the messages she receives from the masculine voice of society as well. She hears, "Stop babying the boy!" "Quit being so overprotective." And, "He's going to become a mama's boy." As a result, moms play an engage/disengage game. William Pollack points out that "she is held responsible for a boy's emotional growth and development, and yet she is also expected by society to push him away so he can learn to survive in a culture that may shame him for showing the very feelings she's teaching him to express."[10]

Let's go back to the Oedipus thing—is there a point when a guy needs to "cut the apron strings"? Yes, but this doesn't mean his mother stops being an influential force. It doesn't mean he walks out on her. It doesn't mean she must cease being a caring, loving, empathetic voice in his life. When a guy separates from his mother, it's not because of gender; it's because of autonomy. As the primary caregiver, a mother represents all the things that make a guy dependent. She becomes the object of his repressed freedom. Her directives are interpreted as an inability to take care of himself. Her empathy and concern are viewed as prying into his personal life.

A mother once told me she was at the end of her rope. She felt as though she were raising her son alone, and she wasn't getting any support from his father. She said she felt as though her son was beginning to resent her. Her assessment of the situation was that this was a gender issue—the boy needed a man to be the strong arm in his life. She was missing the point. As we examined the situation, it was evident that the boy's father was supporting and leading on the same page. The difference was that the mother was the more immediate and constant voice in the boy's day. Thus her son would challenge her. She represented his dependence and he was exercising his autonomy skills by creating friction with her. He was testing her *authority*, not because she was a woman and he was becoming a man, but because she was the authority and he wanted to be released from that.

Guys need to learn that there is independence within the boundaries of authority. Mothers become a strategic instructor in that line of learning. And this mom in particular needed to hold her line, but she also needed to discern which battles to fight in order to win the war.

Mothers need to learn how and where to let go, and how to embrace their son's independence as well. This process is learned. But women still struggle with the independence of their sons because they fear the relationship will be damaged. The relationship won't be lost, but it must be redefined. I believe men find this easier to do than women. That's why dads can usually recognize autonomy in their sons more acutely than moms can. But while men may read the situation accurately and have an easier time letting go, they often make it a gender thing and in-

FEMALE YOUTH WORKER TIP

Don't be afraid to give a young guy a female perspective—even if he gives you grief over it. Remember, he doesn't want to be viewed as incompetent, but he needs to know a woman's viewpoint. Women are so aware of gender equality that many *don't* see the gender perspective differences. You greatly assist a guy when you coach him to understand things the way a woman does. In addition, you are insuring his success by helping him to be a man who will be liked and sought after by women.

terpret it incorrectly. They'll say a mother is making her son soft, or she's too overprotective, and so on.

Women play an important role in the development of a guy's identity. When a mother is absent, other women must step in and become a godly female influence. Just like the men in his life, it takes more than one woman to shape and develop a guy's identity. In the journey to find out who he is and how to give himself away, a guy must pull away from his parents. This doesn't mean that a mother needs to totally separate herself from her son. It just means she must learn to discern and then redefine the way she's mothered the boy during his life so far.

A guy's disconnect from his parents prepares him for a reconnect with a spouse. There is never a true independence, as we have already noted, but rather *inter*dependence. He leaves his family to start a family. The strong feminine voice in his life is not replaced as much as it is changed. This is a delicately learned dance between mother and son and that son and his wife. But it should be noted that it's no different between a father and daughter. The constant voice in the life of a child will always be the voice of the same-gendered parent. The dance occurs when a spouse moves in as a new primary influence.

6.4 RITES OF PASSAGE: BLESSING

Jake's dad unexpectedly woke him up at 5 a.m. on a Saturday. "Get up, buddy! Something huge is going to happen today. You and I are going on a little trip; I have a surprise for you."

Jake had turned 14 about two months prior to this, so he knew this wasn't a birthday surprise. Groggy and totally caught off guard, Jake didn't know whether he should be excited or irritated that he was awakened at such an early hour. Jake thought it might be a dream, so he just rolled over and started to doze off again.

A few minutes later his dad came back in, flipped the lights on, and started bouncing the bedsprings. "C'mon, buddy. We have to be on the road in 10 minutes." Jake inquired about this whole mystery event, but his dad didn't yield a single hint. Instead, he threw a pair of jeans and a T-shirt in Jake's face, telling him that the sooner he got dressed, the sooner he'd find out.

When they pulled the car out of the garage, it was barely light outside. Jake was slumped in the front seat of the car. He pulled his baseball cap over his eyes and attempted to fall asleep. They didn't get far before his dad started poking him and talking. Jake's mom had packed a few snacks (granola bars and some bananas, only enough to make you hungrier in the morning), so his dad encouraged Jake to reach in the back seat and break them out. As they ate, his dad started to tell Jake about the qualities he'd seen in him. He told him about the dreams he had for him

as a man. They laughed about some of the childish things Jake had done as a "little boy."

Three hours flew by, and Jake started to recognize the scenery. They were on their way to the family cabin. As they pulled onto the wooded, country road about two miles from their destination, Jake's dad asked, "Do you know your way from here, son?" Jake replied in the affirmative. His dad stopped the car. "I'm confident that you know your way. I want you to trust me now and get out of the car. Walk to the cabin and I'll meet you there." Jake was confused, but he got out and started walking.

The road was silent and beautiful. Jake looked around him intently. Sometimes he didn't recognize the terrain, so he would stop, get his bearings, and press on. After a short distance, Jake noticed a man standing next to a tree. A kind of creepy feeling came over him. As he got closer to the man, he recognized him. It was his grandfather. He stopped Jake and they talked—about Jake. Grandpa told Jake about the great man he'd watched Jake become over the years. When they were finished, Grandpa asked, "Do you know your way to the cabin?" Jake answered that he did. Grandpa said, "I'm confident that you know your way; I'll meet you there."

Jake began to walk again, leaving his grandfather behind. Something very cool was happening. Jake couldn't figure it out, but he knew he would be changed by this experience. As he walked, Jake's youth pastor emerged from behind a tree. It scared Jake, and they both had a good laugh. The conversation they shared was similar to the ones he'd already had with his dad and his grandfather. His youth pastor told him about the godly qualities he saw in Jake, and how God had made Jake into a great man. He ended the conversation the same way as before, "Do you know your way to the cabin? I'm confident that you know your way. I'll meet you there."

Next, Jake's other grandfather met him; then a close family friend he'd always called "uncle"; his long-standing soccer coach; a college-aged cousin he'd always looked up to; and two of his uncles. Each man shared his perspectives and identified different qualities he saw in Jake. Jake realized these were men he looked up to, men who had impacted and shaped his life.

When Jake arrived at the cabin, they were all there. A breakfast feast awaited them. They ate together and prayed together. After the meal was finished, there was a ceremony that his father had planned. All of the men gathered around Jake. His grandfather read from Scripture about putting away childish things and embracing Christ. Jake's dad had him take off his T-shirt (the symbol of his childhood), and then he was given a new shirt to wear (as a symbol of his manhood). Jake's dad asked him to tear apart the old shirt, which Jake did. Then the men gathered around him and each one presented him with something symbolic (a stone, a knife, a light, and so on) that illustrated the characteristic they'd observed in him. When the ceremony ended, each man welcomed Jake into manhood.

Jake experienced a rite of passage.

THE IMPORTANCE OF RITES OF PASSAGE

At a recent retreat, I asked a group of college guys, "When did you first know that you'd become a man?" The response was interesting—only silence. Then one guy broke the ice by saying, "I don't know that I *am* a man yet." Slowly but surely each guy admitted he had no recollection of ever having passed from childhood to manhood.

They were all products of their American Western culture, which thrives on the obsession and perpetuation of youth. Marketing and media keep icons in front of them in roles and situations that glamorize youth and minimize adult responsibility. Industrial-

ization and modernity have also affected the generations that preceded them. It used to be that fathers taught their sons a trade. They spoke of passing the mantle of authority so when the boy came of age, he would be charged with the family trade and his father would work alongside him. This became lost in the decentralization of the home. Modernity individualized society. Through the uses of technology and the enculturation of humanistic self-sufficiency theories, the power of a community was lost.

These guys were also a product of a Christian culture that has generated an avoidance of symbols and rituals (something that had once been a strong part of church history), so as not to be offensive or intimidate the seekers. As a result we've produced a few generations of men who have slid somewhat into manhood. Maybe this is why so many men have mid-life crises. They never really know they are men, so at age 40-something they make one last-ditch attempt to frantically hold onto the youth they never left behind.

As I dialogued with these guys, it became more and more evident that they were sliding into manhood. They identified things that they thought were steps toward adulthood, such as getting a driver's license, going to college, having a job, or even having their first sexual encounter. None had received any kind of confirmation that he was a man. None had experienced a definite point of passage where he left childhood and moved into manhood.

Three Reasons Why a Rite of Passage Is Important

1. It creates an inward realization that a guy has crossed over. He must consciously see things in a new light of responsibility, or he must consciously choose to ignore that responsibility. It's so easy for a guy to hide behind the mask of irresponsibility because we have fed them the line that "boys will be boys," keeping them in a constant state of capri-

ciousness. This line was used recently when a group of late-adolescent guys was being hosted for lunch at a friend's home. They sat throughout the house eating their lunches and having a great time enjoying each other's company. When it came time to go, the host found plates left on the living room floor and watermark rings on her furniture. Her gracious remark was, "Boys will be boys."

Well, sometimes boys want to *stay* boys. When we are intentional about making them cross the line through a rite of passage, they face the music and know that men are more responsible, conscientious, thoughtful, and protective. They're also challenged to take initiative instead of waiting to be told when to act.

Mark was a star athlete on his varsity soccer team. He knew and played the game with amazing instinct and skill. Mark also had great leadership ability because his peers, especially his teammates, sought him out. But he constantly found himself in a frustrating situation with the coach who couldn't get Mark to organize the guys on the field during the game. In Mark's mind, he was still just a boy, so he would do everything that was required of him. His controlling father often told him exactly what was required, how to accomplish things, and the timing in which it was to be done. So Mark didn't have to think or take initiative. It was all done for him.

Mark said he didn't like taking the initiative because then he'd have to be responsible all the time. Mark wasn't lazy, nor was he irresponsible with directives. And Mark was already a leader—so what was the problem? He was a boy sliding into manhood. A rite of passage will help a guy generate a perspective of initiation or a frame of mind that he is now a man.

2. It validates him in the community of men. We've already established that guys are bombarded with the notion that they must be the Lone Ranger or Superman. They tackle life from an aloof, introspective, and isolated stance. The validation of a community of men welcomes him into the community. A guy gets to see that he becomes a strategic and vital part of something that is greater than he is. The interdependence he learns will positively affect a guy's esteem, confidence, problem-solving ability, and interpersonal dynamic. Validation informs a guy that he takes his rightful place in the ranks of men. He becomes part of a legacy—a band of brothers or a God-honoring, multigenerational fraternity. It gives him a sense of belonging.

The validation from a group of men—that a guy has now become a man—is also very confirming. From this point on, he's no longer stuck between childhood and adulthood. Many of the contemporary rites of passage that guys point to in their lives are all experiences without a community around them—buying their first car, conquering some obstacle, or, most commonly, losing their virginity.

Loss of virginity for a guy is a rite of passage in this society. He becomes a man when he sexually conquers. Almost every coming-of-age movie reflects this experience as being a rite of passage. A guy can tell his friends who validate him that he's a "real man" now. I've even encountered high school guys whose *fathers* encouraged them to have a sexual experience because it would make *real men* out of them. Having a son do this reassures this kind of father that his son isn't gay. So the term *real man* has more than one meaning here. When there is no validation of manhood by a community of men, a sexual experience informs a guy that he has crossed the boundary into manhood.

When a guy does experience a rite of passage like the one Jake did, he knows he's been examined and "approved" by a body of men whom he respects, admires, and appreciates their influence on his life. He learns he has joined their ranks. The men in his life have created closure on his childhood. They give him the privileges and hold him accountable for being a man. This is an important form of empowerment that is lost when a guy doesn't have a rite of passage. He's empowered to take initiative and to stand in his rightful place alongside a company of men.

3. It connects manhood and spirituality. In a God-centered ritual that informs a guy that he's now a man, he comes to understand that he can also be a godly man. Ritual has always been a part of God's design for his people in worship and in their interactions with each other. From the days of Moses and the Tabernacle to the glimpse of the throne room in John's account in Revelation, we see ritual. A rite of passage ushering a guy into manhood should be a ceremony that notes God's design on his masculinity.

Elements of a Rite of Passage

Rites of passage can be as unique as the guy. There is no set way to do this. Here are some principles surrounding rites of passage that may inform you on how you can craft a rite of passage into manhood for a guy you know.

1. Recognize and verbalize a guy's potential, qualities, and character. There is great power in verbal expression. We even see it in the validation of salvation on our lives: "If you confess with your mouth, 'Jesus is Lord,' and believe in your heart that God raised him from the dead, you will be saved" (Romans 10:9). There is power in naming the characteristics that mark a guy as a great man. Speaking this truth into a guy's life sets him on a trajectory that will inform his actions as a man for the rest of his life. Many men have gained the necessary confidence to play out particular life qualities because someone saw them and told him about them. Many times in ancient and primitive rites of passage, boys were given

new names based on characteristics they exhibited. They became their names as men.

2. Raise the level of expectation; he's passing from boyhood into manhood. Paul encapsulates this in 1 Corinthians 13:11, saying, "When I was a child, I talked like a child, I thought like a child, I reasoned like a child. When I became a man, I put childish ways behind me." A rite of passage is the putting away of childish things. While that doesn't mean he must cease to be fun-loving, it does mean he's now expected to take the initiative and be responsible, to see life through a different lens.

3. Personalize it; make his ceremony unique to him. Many times the rite of passage had a secret component or an element of mystery that signified for the guy the uniqueness of this event and a respect for him, on the part of the community of men, to carry the secret like a man. We tend to have an aversion to this type of mystery because we're afraid it will seem cult-like. Yet there is an overwhelming sense of value and authority that comes with being the bearer of a secret.

4. Symbolize it; add a new page in a guy's story. Symbols become markers or anchors for a guy. The gifts that were given to Jake were symbolic of the things his mentors saw in him. They became the reminder of those qualities. This past year, the group of guys I mentor decided that they'd mark this year by focusing on being loving men. For a year we looked at what Scripture says about love and compassion and how to use it in our lives. They practiced it, prayed about it, and held each other accountable for it. At the close of the year, we had a rite of passage that marked them as loving men. Stations were set up in the sanctuary, each one illuminated with a candle. The guys were asked to visit each station, to silently read the Scripture there, and then to follow the directions as a symbol of their journey in becoming compassionate men. The first station had Scripture denoting that loving men are to be poured out. There were six goblets filled with red water. When each guy read through the Scripture and had time to reflect and pray, they were asked to empty the goblet as a symbol of their desire and commitment to be poured out as loving men. The three other stations…well, those are a secret. You get the point.

5. Make it deeply and profoundly God-centered. This ceremony can have a rich sense of liturgy. Reading Scripture, identifying godly characteristics from the archetypes of men in Scripture, praying over a guy, laying hands on him, and anointing him with oil all become a profound way of making this a God-centered celebration. Remind a guy that God made him a man, and God will continue that good work in him.

6. Challenge his manhood. Rites of passage often involved an element that was dangerous but within the acceptable range of risk. In Jake's case it was taking a two-mile hike alone. He wasn't securely confident that he knew the way to the cabin, but he trusted his resourcefulness. The men around him also affirmed their trust in his ability. This element of danger symbolizes accomplishment and plays into his innate ability as a man to overcome.

7. Recognize and authenticate that this is bittersweet. The guy needs to know that something (childhood) is being left behind. In some ways change like this can be painful. Some cultures have rituals where pain is actually inflicted upon the person, such as tattooing, piercing an ear, pulling a tooth, circumcision, or cutting oneself to become blood brothers—*not that physical pain is being advocated here.* The nation of Israel remembers the bittersweet during the season of Passover by eating bitter food.

Regardless, that is the bitter part—reminding the guy of what he's leaving behind and showing him that he's man enough to walk through painful trauma. Often the pain that was inflicted left a mark (tattooing),

a scar (piercing), or a permanent redefining of the body (as in circumcision) that served as a reminder and an indicator to others that this guy is now a man. In Jake's case his kid shirt was taken and torn. He experienced the vulnerability of not wearing his shirt and the disappointment of having it destroyed. These symbols give closure to childhood.

The sweet part comes when the guy steps into manhood. Jake was given a new shirt, which he wore with pride. This becomes another symbol that he's now a man. It's important to note here that this may also be a bittersweet moment for his father (who should disclose this fact to his son). It's wounding because he's losing his little boy. Rites of passage both heal and empower the boy to be what he needs to be, and it also formalizes the father's need to let go of his son. Dad recognizes that other men must help to inform his son's masculinity, so he releases him. This is a powerful act of love and a strong example of manhood for his son. He illustrates that men don't need to be threatened by the attributes of other men who will win places in the heart of his boy.

8. Provide mentors and models. In this ceremony, welcome him to the ranks of having and becoming both mentor and model. A guy needs to be reaffirmed that real men seek the counsel of wise men. He needs to know that he's in the company of men who trust God together. He needs to know that he's interdependent, like all of the other men in that room. He also needs to be aware that he has become a model and a mentor to younger guys.

I know a family who crafted rites of passages for their children. One day the oldest son (18 years old) came into my office all excited because his 14-year-old brother had selected him to be one of the mentors in his rite of passage. This illustrated the cycle of manhood being passed on from generation to generation.

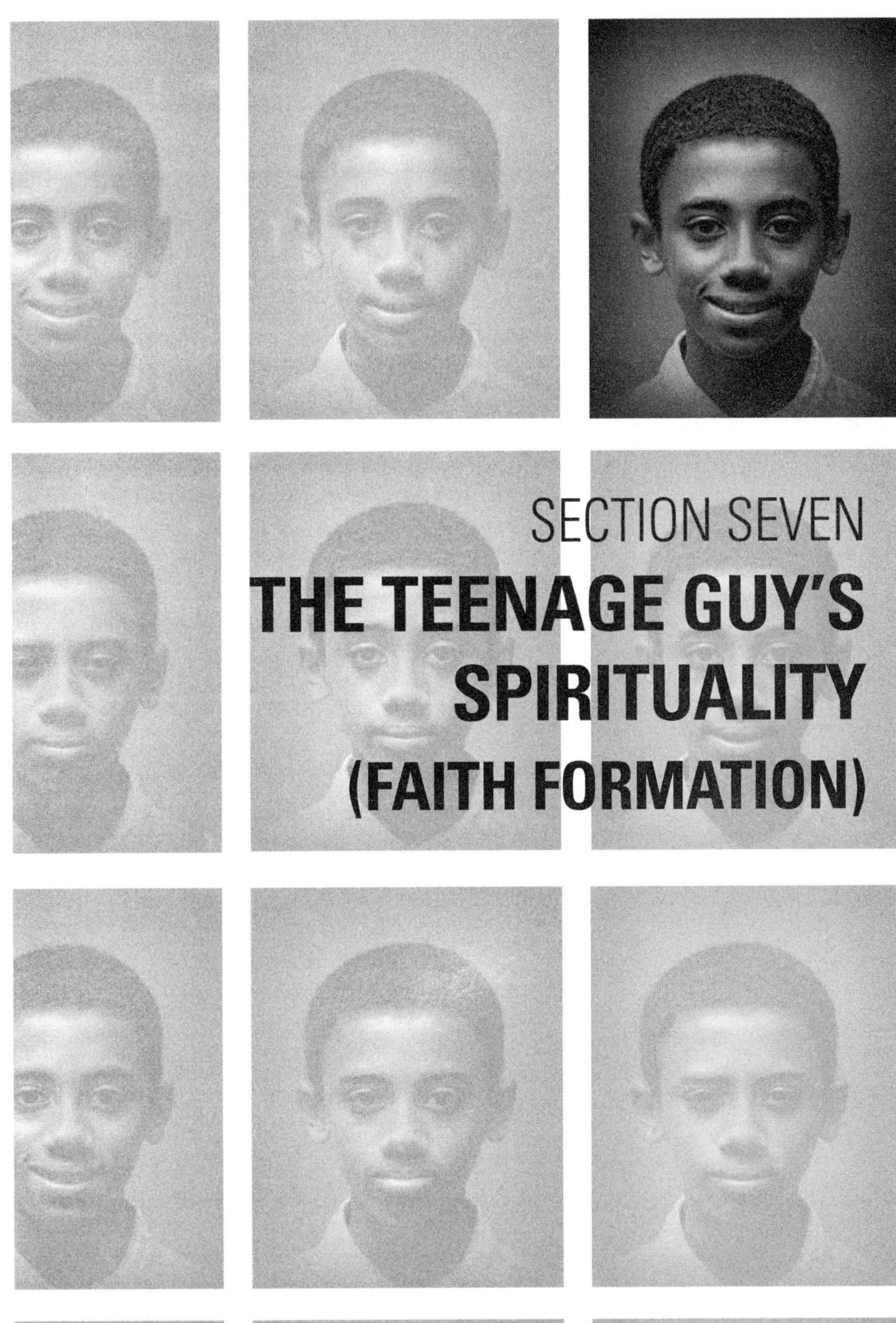

SECTION SEVEN

THE TEENAGE GUY'S SPIRITUALITY (FAITH FORMATION)

7.1 SPIRITUALITY

It was pre-season training for the Azusa Pacific University men's soccer team. The guys had come back to school early to train. There were very few new players added to the roster because the team was strong and young with many great players returning to the team. This was going to be a dynamic year. The Cougars would definitely be the team to beat.

At my first meeting with them as chaplain, I thought it would be interesting to figure out the heart of this team. I asked the guys to get into small groups of about four to five players each. Then I asked them to discuss the question: "How do you want this team to be known?" Each group was given a piece of paper to write down their list and then formulate statements. Overwhelmingly, each group stated that their number-one desire was to be known as a team of guys who were God-honoring men of character and integrity. I knew the hearts, passions, and desires of these guys, and I believed their statements were true. But the season would prove the test.

This team really was the team to beat. They were high on the hit list of every team in the conference. That meant the Cougars had to compete hard, play tough, and fight to win. Often their character was challenged, but their spiritual integrity and masculinity was also in conflict. The game became a mild version of war; the field was a battle zone. The guys would face some of the common tensions of spirituality and masculinity. Can a guy be tough and compassionate? Can he fight and care? Can he compete hard and turn the other cheek? Many times the guys were faced with these questions. When another team came at them with ferociousness, could they assert

themselves but not destroy? It's hard to be a Christian and an athlete; for that matter, it's hard to be spiritual and masculine!

Guys receive the message that spirituality is a soft, feminine characteristic while society informs them that masculinity is tough, aggressive, and stoic. Masculinity and spirituality are in constant conflict for guys.

SPIRITUALITY AND MASCULINITY

The best way to describe spiritual formation in guys is that it's like walking in a terrible blizzard with the wind and snow blowing in your face—uphill. You can make progress, but it's difficult to see where you're going. You're running counter to all the natural forces, and it's not very warm or engaging.

Herein lies the dilemma: there seems to be a bipolar pull on guys when it comes to faith formation. On one hand, the messages they get from culture, including a Christian culture, is that masculinity involves conquest and control. This is played out in power situations, sexual encounters, and relational detachments, all of which run counter to true spiritual formation and conformity to the person of Christ. On the other hand, he is faced with a spirituality that's presented as being *feminine*. A guy constantly finds himself in the dilemma of having to deny being a man or being a Christian. For a teenage guy in the developmental stage where identity and spirituality are still being formed, this dilemma becomes an internal storm.

Church Is for Girls: A History

Patrick Arnold, author of *Wildmen, Warriors, and Kings: Masculine Spirituality and the Bible*, makes this observation about guys and spirituality:

> [Men] really aren't very good at spiritual or emotional things like religion. When males

> do get involved with the local church, it seems they gravitate once again to the practical affairs: church maintenance, administration, and long-term financing. But the life of the Spirit? Spirituality, prayer, and worship belong somehow to the world of women; stained-glass windows, elaborate rituals, lacy weddings, and dainty sermons make a Real Man uncomfortable. So Real Men not only eschew quiche, they avoid church, too. And the only times a Real Man goes to church are at his baptism, wedding, and funeral: the "carried, married and buried" syndrome.[1]

Over the centuries, Western cultural influences have shaped masculinity to run counter to spirituality. The Age of Enlightenment elevated the rational minds of men. Science and reason superseded any aspiration or association with the spiritual or mystical. A man's strength was validated by his knowledge and logical powers, rather than his faith.

The Industrial Revolution came along and decentralized the family, taking the dominant masculine role model (father) out of the home. The mantle of spiritual mentoring and leadership fell upon mothers. With the Industrial Revolution also came the rise of materialistic consumerism and rugged individualism. Men became valued by what they produced and were forced to be self-made. This individualization and quantifiable productivity left little room for faith community or the intangibles of faith formation.

Prior to the turn of the twentieth century, there came the new male-dominant phenomenon of fraternal orders or lodges. The formation of these orders put masculinity back into the context of community. Men would congregate together to be men. Complete with secret rituals, quasi-religiosity, and a reinforced "guys only" bravado, men congregated in these orders, abandoned their leadership, and reduced their presence in the church.[2] Church became a place for women and

children. Mary Stewart Van Leeuwen, in her book *Fathers and Sons: The Search for a New Masculinity*, notes that of a population of about 19 million men in America during the late 1800s, more than six million were involved in some fraternal order or lodge.[3]

Between 1880 and 1920, the men's freethought movement became dominant. These men perceived the church as *feminized*, squelching free and critical thinking in men who needed to be liberated from "Christian superstition, clerical domination and biblical tyranny."[4] Led by Robert Ingersoll, this atheistic movement presented men as strong, intelligent, loving, family-centered, rugged men who acted in "gentlemanliness" without the need for a feminine belief system.

There is still a pervasive overtone of this in America today. The wildman movement of the late 1980s and early 1990s recaptured the spirit of the former fraternal orders almost a century later. Men looked to free themselves from being domesticated and from losing their unique differentiating power, which was being embraced as the androgynous characteristics of the women's liberation movement. The wildman weekend was born, bringing men into a closed community to reclaim their masculine power. Once again the wildman weekend came complete with secret rituals, quasi-religiosity, and a reinforcement of the "guys only" bravado. It brought men into community again.

But unlike the fraternal orders, there was a new spin to this movement—men were challenged to get in touch with their feminine side. It's not too surprising to learn that the feminine side was the side that embodies the spiritual. Fathers were encouraged to connect with their sons and free them from the bondage of domestication. Thus, prior to the turn of the 21st century, guys were once again given the message that spirituality is not the natural predilection of a man, rather it lies in the deep recesses of his being that is...soft.

The Church Strikes Back

So while spirituality was presented as being feminine and unnatural for manly men, the only logical responses for a man were to 1) compromise his manhood and embrace a feminized spirituality; 2) walk away from spirituality altogether, which many men did; or 3) swing the pendulum in the opposite direction to create the other pole in this bi-polar dilemma.

As a counteractive measure, the church took a muscle-up, strongman approach to Christianity. Activists arose in reaction to the feminization of spirituality and to fight the exodus of men from church. These activists believed that men could function as men in a feminine church by reclaiming it and instilling in it a renewed manhood marked by moral and spiritual fervor.

Evangelists such as Charles Finney (a former member of the Masonic Order) and denominational leaders such as Jonathan Blanchard spoke against the lodges and orders, calling men back to the church. Anti-lodge organizations such as The National Christian Association were formed. In 1911 under the direction of Fred Smith—the general secretary of the Youth Men's Christian Association (YMCA)—a countermovement known as the "men and religion forward movement" was designed to combat the atheism of the freethought movement. They organized evangelistic campaigns targeting men and boys (similar to Promise Keepers) with the aim of seeing over three million American males become Christians. They would then be integrated into the life and leadership of the church. They used slick marketing tactics associated with sports and entertainment to reach boys and men. The organization saw its mission as rescuing an effeminate church by generating a muscle or "strongman Christianity."

Christianity became militantly disciplined and warlike in strategy, matter-of-fact, dominating, and stoic in nature. Smith was viewed as the embodiment of the Christian manliness that was described in many Christian periodicals of the day as "virile, direct, pungent, fearless, unwearied, undismayed, possessing great vision, steady persistence, remarkable executive ability and undaunted courage—men think of a man's religion when they think of him, and they think of him as the striking exemplification of the message."[5] The manifesto of the men and religion forward movement heralded "harnessing our strong manhood to the big problems of the Church of Jesus Christ—a putting of our strong manhood back into the program of Jesus Christ."[6] God and men came together in a show of force to confront the problems that Christendom faced.

A Present-Day Movement: Compromise

Today, Promise Keepers uses some of the same approaches as movements in the past. But the difference between Promise Keepers and its century-old predecessor, the men and religion forward movement, is that Promise Keepers has bought into the feminine-side mentality of the late twentieth century men's movement, allowing men to be vulnerable and breaking down some of the bravado. Although the brokenness just frees men to be more of the muscle Christians they need to be in order to take back the church as leaders. *Wild at Heart* also embraces the mythopoetic gender dichotomy of a man's soul so as to liberate him to really tap into the *warrior* he was designed to be:

> A man must have a battle to fight, a great mission to his life that involves and yet transcends even home and family. He must have a cause to which he's devoted even unto death, for this is written into the fabric of his being. Listen carefully now: *You do*. That is why God created you—to be his intimate ally, to join him in the great battle.[7]

Once again, almost 100 years later, we see that God and men come together in a show of force to stare down the problems that Christendom faces. Let's pause for a moment to say there are many great things that have grown out of the Christian men's movement. It has freed men to break down the walls of invincibility and allowed them to be vulnerable for healing and support. It has also brought men back into a community with other men to seek after the heart of God. It has called men to live responsibly and with integrity. And it has given many men direction and hope from being feminized.

But like the movements of the past, it stands in the way of helping teenage guys formulate their faith during their developmental years. This new Christian men's movement leads young guys to believe that a *real* Christian man is an in-your-face, confrontational, virile, direct, pungent, fearless, unwearied, undismayed, undaunted, no-nonsense, bulldozing machine for God. Like Fred Smith, pastors and leaders of the church today become examples of this type of man who relentlessly takes lives apart as dominating CEOs of the church—but all in the name of Christ. This is done to grow the church, build the kingdom, reclaim a manly leadership—in short, "a putting of our strong manhood back into the program of Jesus Christ."

SPIRITUALITY ISN'T MALE OR FEMALE

All of the aforementioned movements reinforced the premise that spirituality in general, and Christianity in particular, are feminized and must either be defeated or dominated. All offer a stronger masculinity as a solution, either by bucking up and being a real man apart from spirituality or by muscling up and being a real man by dominating it. They all begin with the notion that their perception of masculinity is correct and that the church is feminized because it runs counter to a man's internal identity. They advocate that masculinity should inform the work and direction of spirituality, rather than the opposite.

Spiritual formation is transformational. That means God changes guys at the very core of their beings—their identities. It might be that over the last few centuries God has been patiently and methodically changing masculinity, not spirituality. Those who hold on to the bravado of a male identity in the name of *real* manhood may be missing the power of God. Those who run from a perceived "feminine" church may be turning their back on him. And those who're "in your face" may be fighting him.

FAITH FORMATION

As I said before, spiritual formation is transformational. God started a great work in the hearts and lives of guys and he will be faithful to complete it. That work is a *process* of becoming more and more conformed to the image of Christ. It's not about the *product*. It's less about arriving and more about the journey. This concept is difficult for a teenage guy to grasp because he's still not in a place where he can wrap his mind around the abstract of that statement: "conformed to the image of Christ." As a result he learns it only within the confines of the concrete, then carries that with him into adulthood because he is taught *what* to believe, not how to think theologically. That means his trajectory is slightly off, making it difficult for him to hit the mark. All of this may seem a little nebulous, so let's break it down.

In a concrete, conceptual form, guys learn that being like Jesus means mimicking him. They learn they must constantly measure themselves against an icon that was fully God and perfect humanity. It soon becomes a defeating exercise, if we're being honest about it. As a result, they resolve that this is the journey—striving to perfect a god-like character similar to Jesus. What Would Jesus Do? (W.W.J.D.?) becomes the gimmicky mantra. They adopt the premise that godly men strive to be perfect—sinless. The eradication of sin—sinful habits, sinful thoughts, sinful conversations and attitudes—becomes the focal point of their Christian living. And while Scripture calls us to live pure lives, it also tells us that Christ eliminates our sin as far as the east is from the west. So their trajectory gets off at the point where guys learn to make *sin* the focal point of their Christian living—whether it's embracing it or eliminating it.

Christ needs to be the focal point. The writer of Hebrews challenges us to "fix our eyes on Jesus, the author and perfecter of our faith" (Hebrews 12:2). Satan doesn't want guys to formulate faith, so by getting the trajectory off—making guys constantly fixate on their sin—they never know the power of godly living. Godly men don't eliminate sin in their lives; godly men *deal* with sin in their lives. They come to understand that this is the very thing that makes them run to God, rely on him, and live in him.

If the trajectory is off, it produces Christian teenage guys (who later become Christian men) who see Jesus as a Halloween costume. They put on the mask of Jesus and work hard pretending to be like him. They believe that acting like him will make them become like him. They learn that their action (doing) defines who they are (being), instead of understanding that who they are (a good work in process) defines what they do. In reality they may never see that they've conformed God's Son into *their* image, rather than being conformed into his.

This can be confusing because doesn't the apostle Paul tells us to imitate Christ (Ephesians 5:1)? Yes, but not in a way that seeks sinless perfection. Paul is clear to say that we imitate Christ in love—like loving children. The imitation process is described for guys. This is doable and not defeating. Now a guy can look to Christ's example and love his enemies, those who are caught in sin, and those who are seemingly unlovable, just as Jesus did.

But doesn't Paul also say to "clothe yourselves with Christ" (Galatians 3:27; Romans 13:14)? Yes, once again this passage doesn't mean that a guy

should wear him like a garment or costume; it implies that a guy needs to consciously understand that he's covered like a blanket by Christ's finished work at Calvary. This becomes a reminder when his flesh and lusts flare (Romans 13:14), and also in the context of baptism (Galatians 3:27).

Being conformed to the image of Christ is an ongoing process, not a means to an end. The trajectory is corrected when guys learn that being Christlike means Christ lives *through* them, not when they try to *be* him. People need to see Jesus in godly guys and men, not guys trying to be like Jesus. Guys need examples of men who see themselves as conduits through which Christ flows. This is a very humbling process because a man's flaws become visible as the light of Christ shines in him. It becomes evident where man stops and where God begins in his life. It makes 2 Corinthians 12 a reality—our weaknesses become the contrast against the full power and perfection of God in us, so that there is no mistake as to who is being seen. We can truly understand John the Baptist's words that Christ "must increase, but I must decrease" (John 3:30, NASB).

Older men need to model what it means to "fix their gaze on Jesus." A guy will walk in a manner worthy of his calling if he's constantly looking to Jesus, not striving to eliminate something Jesus has already eliminated. Teenage guys need to be surrounded by men who love Jesus more than anything else. They need to see that Christ is the purpose for living and that he's actively and continuously transforming a man into something good. They need to see God's power against the backdrop of that man's weaknesses. They need to understand that as a conduit through which Christ flows, a man will also experience pain and sorrow because Christ will conform us to his suffering, as well as his joy. They need to know that being like Jesus is less about what they do and more about who they are.

ARCHETYPES OF FAITH FORMATION

We have discovered that archetypes are a great tool to help guys understand their spiritual development as it's played out in character. This is not a new thing, as we have discussed in previous chapters. Developmental psychologists, such as Jung, have drawn on archetypes to help guys understand identity development. Men such as Robert Bly have drawn from mythology and poetic literature to create archetypes that help a guy navigate through masculinity. John Eldredge also uses the archetype of a warrior to help guys navigate through faith formation.

Archetypes such as Warrior, King, Wildman, Sage, Trickster, Healer, and so on give guys a picture of the multifaceted dimensions of a man's spiritual life. In addition we have also personalized some of these archetypes by emulating them as examples, such as William Wallace from *Braveheart*.

While it's good to use archetypes to help a guy formulate faith, we have to be aware of the danger of gravitation toward power icons. We often present guys with archetypes of fighters, not lovers. We forget that many guys are not called to battle but may be called to heal. They may not be called to lead, but they may be called to listen.

I rarely hear of Jesus being emulated as the archetype of masculinity. We look at Joseph, David, Daniel, and Paul, but we bypass Jesus. In Christ we have a complete picture of all that he's making men to be. That means he's the only archetype who completely embodies all characteristics that men can become. It doesn't mean we are completely like him. Guys can see in Christ the different characteristics that he's perfecting in them. A community of guys being the body makes a composite picture of Christ.

While Christ embodies all archetypes, no one man embodies all that Christ represents. Therefore, it's irresponsible for anyone to universalize a single archetype (such as a warrior) as the icon for guys to become. Some may be warriors, while others are prophets, and still others are healers, and so on. This helps a guy find his uniqueness in the body of Christ. It also makes him less sufficient in himself and more interdependent upon the community of God. And finally it doesn't erode his esteem when he realizes he doesn't fit the archetype that has been universally imposed on all men, implying he is less a man if he isn't conformed to that type.

STAGES OF SPIRITUAL DEVELOPMENT

Earlier I alluded to the fact that spiritual development parallels cognitive development. As a guy begins to understand the abstracts of faith, such as redemption, sanctification, and even faith itself, he moves through the distinct stages of spiritual development. These theories can be synthesized into three distinct stages during adolescence.

Stage 1: Accepting Beliefs

As a concrete operational thinker, many early-adolescent guys are trying to wrap their minds around the abstracts of faith as they are presented in concrete contexts. Redemption, transformation, grace, and so on, only have meaning when they understand it in the narrative of Scripture. They hear of David's faith and only know faith in the light of the action that faith generates. Because of this, an early adolescent guy can be very accepting of his beliefs. Sometimes those beliefs may be imposed upon him from birth, making his belief system a cultural imprint upon his soul, rather than a spiritual imprint. This doesn't mean that it's wrong or powerless, it just means he may not know anything else but that which his parents, church, and community have taught him. As long as he's in a concrete operational stage of cognitive development, he will accept the imposed beliefs that have shaped him (see fig. 14).

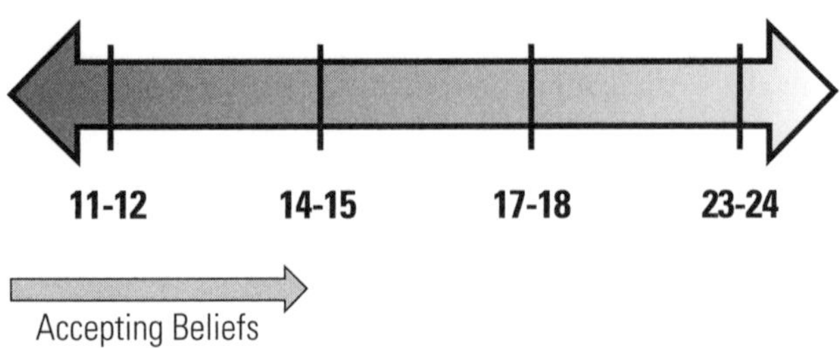

Figure 14

He will also watch the way in which these beliefs are played out concretely in the lives of the men around him who say they are Christians. While he's watching women live out faith distinctives, the men in his life are also helping him to put those distinctives into the context of masculine identity formation. Many guys can come to faith in Christ, but their understanding of that may be limited. They may respond out of a fear of hell, or a life crisis, or a desire to be like a friend or mentor. All of these are essential and good because they assist a guy in his spiritual journey.

Stage 2: Challenging Beliefs

As a guy becomes more cognitively aware, he'll start to dissect and analyze the things he believes and has been taught to believe in order to see if they are true. In fact he'll test these things with God's blessing (see 1 John 4). If a guy is going to own his faith, then he has to test it.

Unfortunately, we become more afraid of that than we need to. Youth workers, parents, teachers, and mentors get a bit ruffled when we hear a guy testing. We want to reel him back into the zone by correcting him and telling him what to believe. The period of time when a guy challenges beliefs is during his middle adolescence (see fig. 15). During this

time he's also fighting for autonomy, adopting aspects of adult manhood, and working through complex abstract feelings such as guilt, shame, relief, and so on. All of these development issues inform and challenge his beliefs. As a result, he evidences—either internally or externally—a form of rebellion.

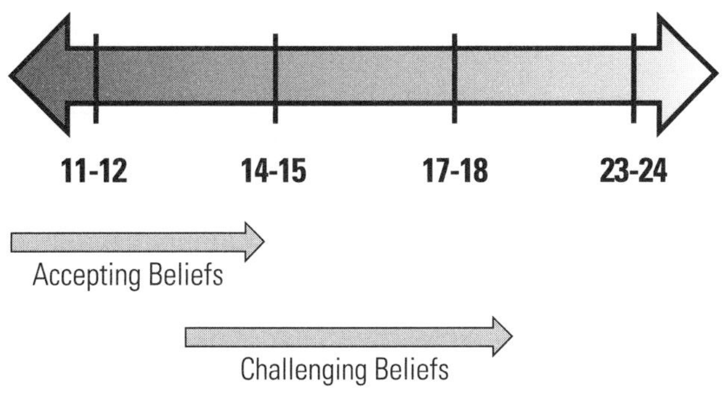

Figure 15

A Planned Rebellion

Rebellion can take on many forms, from overt disregard for his imposed beliefs and values to an intellectual debate about them. It's during this time that we must help a guy plan his rebellion. A *planned rebellion* evidences wisdom on the part of those who are helping a guy navigate through faith formation. Instead of squelching his need to challenge his beliefs, we should start the process for him and guide him through it. The way this is done is by raising questions that make him articulate tenets of faith and put them into action. We can play devil's advocate and not allow him to hide behind spiritual pat answers. We can give him hypothetical situations and ask him to respond, and then question him as to how and why he came to those conclusions. We can also give him the freedom to make decisions and then hold him accountable for those decisions.

I see a lot of guys hit the ditch when they come to college (even a Christian college) because they never had an environment that allowed them to test beliefs. Having been kept within rigid boundaries, the new freedoms of college life don't make him as accountable for his values as he would have been in a more controlled environment.

For example, I want to see guys become men who will walk out of a theater because the movie violates acceptable morals. A guy will never do that if he's never given the opportunity. Here's how we, as youth leaders and parents, can help guys practice to live what they believe in each stage of the spiritual formation process:

- Early adolescent—I would hold the boundary of no R-rated movies because he's not old enough to watch them in the theater, and he's in the process of accepting beliefs and values. When he moves into the challenging stage of faith formation, I would raise issues as the devil's advocate, asking questions such as, "What's wrong with seeing movies that are R-rated? They're only movies!" I may even complicate the issue by asking, "Why is it okay to see an R-rated movie such as *Schindler's List*, but it's wrong to see an R-rated movie such as *Wedding Crashers*?"
- Middle adolescent—As he got older, I would tell him that he could see that movie, as long as we watch it together and he has a conversation with me about it afterwards. I would want to know what he identified as moral-violating content. I would want to know what content he thought made the movie R-rated. I would test him to see if he found anything offensive enough to walk out, and why he would (or wouldn't) have done that.

- Late adolescent—As he became even more autonomous, I would allow him to choose the movies he sees while he's still under my direct care, and I would expect him to be accountable for his decisions. In short, I want to know that he'll be able to make God-honoring decisions before he steps into an environment that offers him greater freedoms. Help him challenge his beliefs and plan his rebellion.

We should also know that planned rebellion takes a lot of wisdom on the part of the guy's mentor or parent. We need to understand that a guy doesn't have to experience something to know if it's right or wrong. I've encountered parents who've said they know their son is going to drink, so he might as well do it in their presence instead of sneaking around and doing it where he may endanger himself. That isn't planned rebellion; it's unbridled liberty that's lacking wisdom. The teenage guy in that situation isn't held accountable for the complexity of values that accompany that situation (such as the law for underage drinking). The lack of wisdom comes when the adult fails to see that there is no accountability, but mistakenly believes they're holding him accountable when in fact they are just monitoring him. The guy never challenges anything; he just indulges.

Many guys have told me they will never know if something is right or wrong until they've experienced it. For example, a guy may say, "How do I know that smoking pot is really wrong unless I try it?" They may also believe the inverse of that logic by asking how *you* know something is wrong if you've never experienced it. When this happens to me, I'm quick to make it a cognitive issue rather than a moral issue. That line of logic is faulty and is not applied consistently in our lives. I usually challenge the guy to think by asking him to stick a paperclip in a socket to see if electricity is there. After all, he needs to experience it to know it exists. Or maybe he can explain how someone is an expert on suicide but

has never experienced it personally. Does an oncologist have to have cancer to know how to treat it? Or can a male gynecologist be an expert? That line of logic is faulty.

Stage 3: Internalizing Beliefs

In this stage a guy owns his beliefs. He'll begin to understand *what* he believes and *why* he believes it. He'll continue to challenge and refine his values and beliefs as they intersect his daily living and practice. This stage parallels the cognitive stage of idealism in later adolescence (see fig. 16).

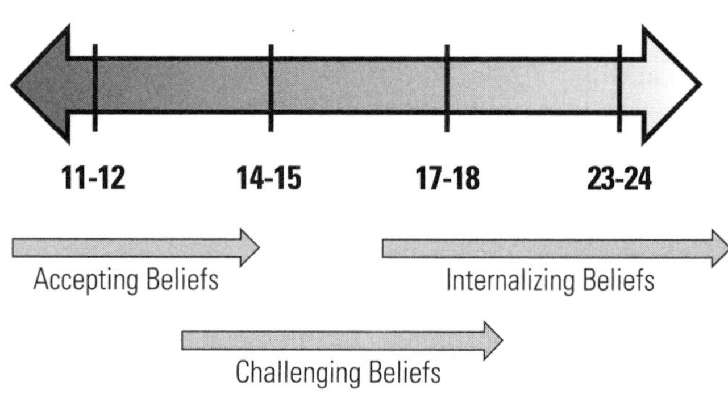

Figure 16

It's also in this stage of faith formation that he can understand competing values and beliefs, diverse values, and beliefs held by others. He may become frustrated when he cannot put his beliefs into a life application context or when they don't fit that context in the way he expects them to. He may experience internal conflict over personal values that clash, such as justice and mercy. He'll begin to see that he cannot separate himself or his actions from his beliefs. He'll realize that he has developed a world and life view.

If he's a Christian, then his internalized values will require him not only to act like a Christian, but also to think theologically Christian as well. He'll begin to consciously draw on his beliefs and values to shape his daily practice and inform his decisions. In this stage of spiritual development, he's able, for the most part, to articulate his beliefs. He'll also begin to understand that his identity as a man and the quality of his character are rooted in his values and beliefs.

GUYS HAVE SPIRITUAL NEEDS

Teenage guys don't need to see a powerful man work for God; they need to see a powerful God work *through* men.

They need to see God give fearful men courage to take a stand, not reckless men taking a stand for their own spiritualized agenda.

They need to see men who, out of deeply compassionate, merciful hearts, rescue those caught in injustice and unfairness.

They need to see men who will be measured by Christ's highest commandment to love, not for muscling-up and kingdom building.

They need to see that real spiritual men are marked as Christ's disciples by their love, not by being strong and right.

They need to see that love bears all things, believes all things, hopes in all things, and endures all things. And they need to see that when God alone empowers that love, it becomes a force to be reckoned with.

They need to know that love is not a feminine characteristic but a God-characteristic.

They need to see leaders who will be shepherds, not CEOs; conciliators, not generals; and servants, not dominators.

They need to see men who are confident because of *whose* they are, not *who* they are.

They don't need to see men who are called virile, direct, pungent, fearless, unwearied, undismayed, or undaunted as the embodiment of the God message. Rather, they need to see men who are loving and joyful peacemakers who are patient, kind, good, faithful, gentle, and self-controlled because they are empowered by the Holy Spirit, the Seal and Hope of the God message.

They need to know that in their weakness (no power), God is made visible and strong.

They need to see that spiritual blessing comes on men who are meek, who mourn, who hunger and thirst after righteousness, who are pure in heart, and who are persecuted not because they are "girly" but because they are godly.

They need to see men fall in fear and trembling before an Almighty God whose name alone quakes the earth, not a man who comes alongside a pitifully powerful God who needs men to help him by putting their manhood back into his programs.

They need to know that purpose and fulfillment come in communion with their Savior, not in a battle to fight, or an adventure to live, or a maiden to rescue.

They need to walk humbly with their God in a reverent understanding that he's holy beyond comprehension and that in all of his awesome majesty he chooses to be mindful of something that he formed from dust—a *real man*.

If this is feminized Christianity, then we have a really warped sense of masculinity.

APPENDIX A

MORE ON GUYS' PHYSIOLOGY

THE HYPOTHALAMIC-PITUITARY-GONADAL AXIS (HPG AXIS) CHAIN REACTION

The hypothalamus begins secreting a gonadotropin-releasing hormone (GnRH) and follicle stimulating hormone (FSH). *Tropic* forms of hormones largely trigger other hormonal activity through the endocrine system. This begins the *hypothalamic-pituitary-gonadal axis* (HPG axis) chain reaction. The gonadotropins are released in a regularly timed series of bursts. They, in turn, trigger the pituitary gland (also at the base of the brain) to secrete a lutenizing hormone (LH). The high level of lutenizing hormone in a guy's system stimulates the leydig cells in his testicles, which begin the mass production of testosterone (see fig. 4, p. 46). On an average a guy's testicles will produce about 6 milligrams of testosterone daily.

A GUY'S PUBECESCENT EXPERIENCE

It's broken down into two stages known as *adrenarche* and *gonadarche.*[1] Andrenarche involves the releasing of the hormone cortisol from the adrenal glands above the kidneys. This also creates a surge of the growth hormone somatotropin from the pituitary gland and thyroxin and triiodothyronine from the thyroid gland, all of which stimulate pronounced and rapid physical growth in mass and stature. While the hormone production of the thyroid and adrenal glands figures into the process of puberty, they are not necessarily a part of the HPG axis. Yet the thyroid and adrenal glands work concurrently with the activation of those other glands in the endocrine system. Adrenarche manifests itself with the development of secondary sex characteristics in a guy.

Gonadarche follows adrenarche and is manifested by the development of primary sex characteristics. A primary sex characteristic involves the physical changes and maturation of the reproductive system,

the *primary* sexual system—whether internal or external.

Secondary sex characteristics are influenced by somatotropic hormones largely produced by the pituitary and thyroid glands. In order for primary sex characteristics to develop, the hypothalamus must begin to methodically release a gonadotropin-releasing hormone (GnRH) about once every hour. This triggers the pituitary gland to make gonadotropins which trigger the development of the adrenal gland to make androgens (estrogen, progesterone and testosterone) and the testes to produce more testosterone.

TESTICULAR DEVELOPMENT

A physician may use an orchidometer to measure testicular development. An orchidometer may look like a spoon-like device, or it may be a gauge in which the testicle can be inserted. For the most part this is rarely used unless there is evidence of some developmental problems. Yet the science surrounding the orchidometer is an accurate gauge of understanding and assessing pubertal development in guys. By the way, the Greek word for testicle is *orchido*. This is largely used in the medical community when identifying disease, procedures, and general health care of the testicles.

RECENT CIRCUMCISION HISTORY

Boys who were born in the late 1940s and 1950s were routinely circumcised in the United States. The medical community believed that the removal of the *prepuce* or foreskin (the procedure known as *circumcision*) prevented some diseases, including urinary tract infections and penile cancer, and was better for hygiene. The hygiene issue correlated directly to the accumulation of *smegma*—oil and dead skin cells—under the foreskin of uncircumcised guys. This is easily cared for with proper washing, and it

can also occur in milder forms on a circumcised guy if he does not have proper hygiene.

The medical community also believed that the nerve endings of an infant's penis were not fully developed and therefore immune to pain. This has since been disproved, and there is still controversy as to the effectiveness of the topical anesthetic creams that are used on infants for circumcision today.

But earlier, the immunity to pain theory and the belief that circumcision prevented disease made circumcision a necessary medical procedure in the U.S. Parents were given options only to NOT circumcise their sons.

In 1975 the Task Force on Circumcision for the American Academy of Pediatricians (AAP) concluded that circumcision was not necessary for the prevention of disease, nor adequate for good hygiene. Despite this, physicians still advised parents against NOT circumcising their sons. In 1989 another task force from the AAP concluded that parents should be given options and presented with the risks of circumcision. Finally in 1999 the AAP task force on circumcision concluded that there is no scientific evidence suggesting that circumcision is even a necessary procedure and that parents should be presented these facts without exaggeration. As the result, beginning in the 80's and 90's many parents did not elect to have their male children circumcised. Some insurance companies also do not see this as a necessity and therefore do not cover the procedure. As the result there are more and more guys who will not be circumcised in the United States. This can have a defining effect on guys.

SPERM PRODUCTION

Sperm travels from the testicle and matures in the *epididymis*, a small sack located at the top of each testis. If a guy does a testicular self-exam, he should be able to feel the epididymis on each testicle. From there sperm is moved through yards of coiled tube in the epididymis into a single tube known as the vas deferens or spermatic cord. The *vas deferens* runs from the epididymis through the abdomen, over the bladder, and joins with the seminal vesicle at the *ampulla*, where both pass into the prostate. The *seminal vesicle* emits fluid, the beginning of semen, into the vas deferens. About 70 percent of the fluid that comes from the seminal vesicles will make up semen. This, along with a hair-like cilia, assists the mobility of the sperm through this journey into the prostate.

At puberty the prostate will begin to increase in size. Prostate development starts about the same time the testes begin to develop. By the time it fully matures it will be the size of a walnut. The prostate is the gland that produces the other 30 percent of the fluid that makes up semen. *Semen* is the clear-to-milky white liquid that is visible at ejaculation. The fluids from the prostate and seminal vesicle mix with the sperm in the prostate so that the sperm has a mobile environment.

When a boy ejaculates through an orgasm or nocturnal emission, the visible mixture is called *ejaculate*. The ejaculate will leave the prostate through the urethra, the same passageway through which urine passes. When a guy's body begins to orgasm, the sphincter muscle closes the urethral opening to the bladder so that semen does not mix with urine or pass into the bladder.

Just below the prostate is the *bulbourethral gland* or *Cowper's gland*. At about the size of a pea, this gland releases an alkaline fluid that neutralizes the acidic environment of the urethra so that sperm can pass protected.

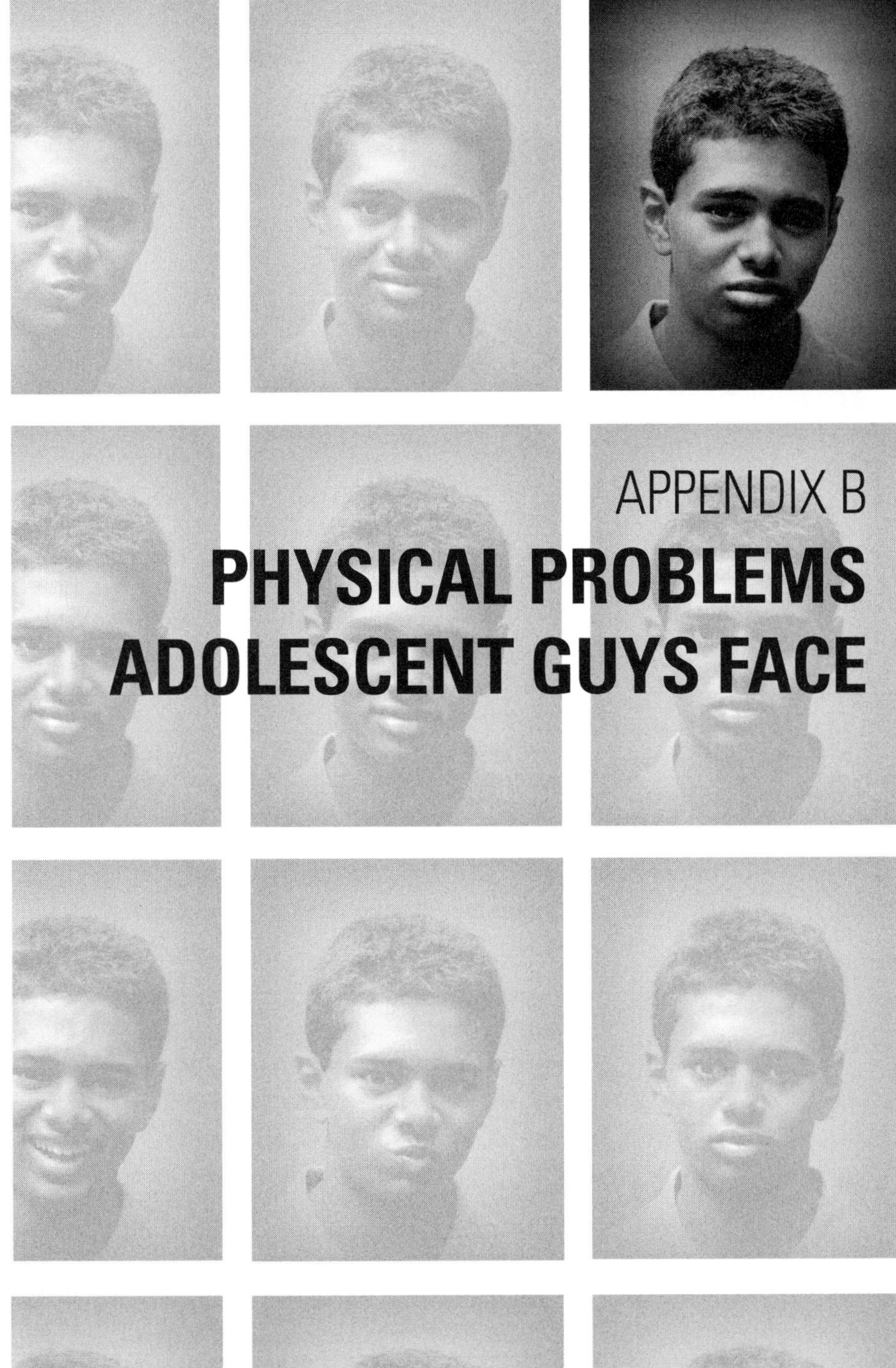

APPENDIX B

PHYSICAL PROBLEMS ADOLESCENT GUYS FACE

Youth workers experience moments when a guy or his parents will call to let them know about some physical problem, disease, or disorder he's experiencing. Being on the front lines with teenage guys, a youth worker needs to be informed about the physical issues and problems they may face. Many times knowing a bit about the problem can open up doors to deeper conversation. Adolescents, in general, believe they're invincible; adolescent guys believe they're indestructible. When a problem occurs, they need you to be knowledgeable.

I've begun the knowledge-gathering process for you by listing many of the physical problems you may encounter with a teenage guy. Some of these problems occur during development, while others may carry on beyond their teenage years. For the most part, a teenage guy may have already sought help from a health professional before he decides to tell you. So he may share the news with you because he needs your support, reassurance, or understanding. However, occasionally a guy may come to you *before* he seeks medical help. If he trusts you, he'll come because he may be worried and unable to talk to his parents for some reason. Your first-hand knowledge about some adolescent-guy issues will serve you well.

It's also important to note here that a minor can seek medical help from a health care professional without his parents' knowledge. Every state allows minors to give consent for treatment of sexually transmitted diseases, emergencies, drug abuse, and contraception—apart from their parents' knowledge. The courts also allow adolescents to give permission for their own medical care under the following guidelines: 1) If he is an emancipated minor, meaning he's under the age of 18 but is married, or is a parent, or is serving in the armed services, or is living separately from his parents and is managing his own finances; 2) If he is a mature minor, meaning he's generally between the ages of 14 and 18, who, in the judgment

of the health professional, can understand the risks and benefits of his treatment.

PHYSICAL CONCERNS

This first part deals with common teenage problems. Sometimes you may hear a guy say, "My doctor said I have—[fill in the blank]." Hopefully, the following list will give you a frame of reference for some typical (and not-so-typical) teenage medical conditions so you can engage the guy in further conversation about what's going on with him in particular.

Acne: Almost every teenage guy deals with acne in some form. A simple zit can throw a guy's world into a tailspin (although he'll never show it). Nonetheless, his entire love life can rise or fall with the state of his complexion. Our culture sells fast-acting products that promise to help, and they do improve things a little bit. But for the most part, acne just goes with the territory of being a teenager.

The guy who deals with *severe* acne is the one you should be concerned about. Some teenagers have acne not only on their faces, but also on the chest, shoulders, back, and even legs and buttocks. Many guys realize that a condition this severe can be undesirable to others. They may feel alienated because people are isolating them. They may also avoid hugs or any kind of touch that puts them in close contact with others because they want to avoid making people feel uncomfortable and receiving possible rejection.

This pervasive kind of acne can scar a guy's body and his esteem. There are prescribed medications, such as *erythromycin*, that can help to decrease the acne bacteria, but these may not clear up his complexion totally.

I've encountered guys who contemplated *suicide* because of their acne. They lost their self-confidence and any hope for relief or a future relationship.

PATIENT'S BILL OF RIGHTS

Laws that are passed to give patients certain rights also apply to minors. Those rights include appropriate emergency care that cannot be withheld; participation in treatment options; and strict confidentiality between the patient and the health professional. This means that even if a parent signs off on insurance payments for medical treatment of the minor, the physician is not allowed to break confidentiality if the minor doesn't allow it.

This can have a domino effect, resulting in a loss of dreams for the future. In short, he could lose heart to the point of committing suicide. This guy needs you to come alongside him, love him, and build up hope in his character and his future.

Alopecia (a fancy term for "hair loss"): Alopecia is genetic. If there is a family history of early balding and hair thinning, then chances are a guy will also experience this. Most of these guys begin to experience alopecia in late adolescence. There are topical treatments, such as *minoxidil*, that can help. Sometimes, as a means of avoiding the embarrassment of balding, a guy can compensate by cutting his hair very short or shaving his head. This doesn't eliminate the problem, but it's an acceptable fashion statement.

Asthma: This is a bronchial disorder that many guys experience. It's an allergic reaction that constricts the airway. Guys with asthma can function normally with inhalers containing anti-inflammatory agents that dilate the airway. Sometimes exercise, smoke, or changes in the weather can aggravate this condition.

Chronic Fatigue Syndrome: This is very hard to diagnose. A guy with chronic fatigue syndrome will complain of extreme fatigue all the time. He may also run low-grade fevers and experience muscle soreness. Regardless of the amount of sleep he gets, he still seems to be tired and loses energy quickly. Many other problems, such as depression, anemia, mononucleosis, various sleep disorders, and even the mere physical toll that adolescence takes on a guy, must be ruled out before chronic fatigue is diagnosed. This can take a long time and can be very disheartening. He may feel as though no one believes him and he may even question himself at times. Let him talk about what's ailing him. Be understanding.

Crohn's Disease: This is an inflammatory bowel disorder that causes severe cramping and diarrhea. Rectal bleeding, weight loss, and fever may also occur. Sometimes the inflammation of the intestine can

cause a blockage leading to ulcers and sores. It's not known what causes this disease, which is sometimes aggravated by stress, but physicians believe it's the result of an immune deficiency that fights bacterial infection in the intestines. A guy with Crohn's may not be a regular attender in your youth ministry. He may also miss a lot of school, which often leads to alternate educational options such as homeschooling or private tutoring. This can affect a guy's social life and be very discouraging for him.

Dermatitis: This is an itchy skin rash that usually presents itself in warm or hot weather. It's often visible and can make a guy very self-conscious. Topical steroid treatments, antihistamines, and some prescribed medications can help to eliminate this.

Diabetes Mellitus: This is a chronic condition where a body doesn't produce the insulin it needs to regulate blood sugars. Since there's no cure, a person with diabetes has to learn to deal with the problem. In this case a guy will have to learn to read his blood sugar levels and give himself regular insulin injections. This doesn't have to get in the way of normal functioning. Most people with diabetes live very active lives. Just be aware that he'll have to bring syringes and insulin with him to camps, on retreats, and on mission trips.

Eczema: This is an itchy, red, dry, flaky condition of the skin. Sometimes it appears as skin rashes or dry splotches. The disorder can have genetic roots or it can be an allergic reaction to irritating substances, such as detergents, that come in contact with the skin. It's a chronic disorder. This might cause a guy to go into hiding if he has a severe bout with it. He may also wear inappropriate clothing (such as long-sleeved shirts in the summer) to hide the condition. Treatment of this disease is often done with topical creams and medications. It's also reduced through the continued use of skin moisturizers and lotions. This may be a blow to a guy's ego, especially if he has to use creams that are marketed to women.

Enuresis (a fancy term for "bed-wetting"): This disorder mostly occurs with adolescent guys. It usually starts in childhood and may continue until about age 15. In rare cases it can last longer. This can become very frustrating to parents who may not understand the pathology of the disorder. Countless methods to eliminate the problem range from behavior modifications—such as not drinking after certain hours—to chemical therapies comprised of medications that limit the production of urine. As hard as a guy tries, he cannot shake this disorder. He usually wets the bed shortly before waking up in the morning. As he gets older, this becomes embarrassing and discouraging. He may never go on a retreat or overnighter because he's too fearful of the risk.

I encountered a situation with a 12-year-old guy whose frustrated parent made him go on a weekend retreat. I was the guy's youth pastor and his mother didn't inform me of the problem. The parents thought that by making their son go on a retreat, it would jolt him into taking some action to correct the problem. Instead, this kid kept everyone awake all weekend because he was afraid to fall asleep. Many times when puberty begins and primary sex characteristics develop, a guy's bedwetting problem ends. In short, a guy grows out of this problem, but this can be a long and emotionally painful road.

Hematuria (blood in the urine): This may come from bleeding in the kidneys, bladder, or prostate. A guy may experience this if he begins to do any kind of running workout or goes biking. It results from the repeated jarring of the bladder during these kinds of activities. A physician should be consulted if this occurs.

Hernia: Sometimes referred to as an "inguinal hernia," this is a condition in which the weak areas of the abdominal muscles can tear or split, allowing the intestines to bulge through. Heavy lifting, strenuous sports, or even straining to pass a stool can result in a hernia. Symptoms can include a visible lump in a

guy's groin area, pain in the groin, and in extreme cases—blockage and strangulation of the intestines. Guys are usually checked for this whenever they have a physical, especially sports physicals. This is the procedure where the doc says, "Turn your head and cough." He places a finger behind the scrotum and pushes up into the abdomen to feel if there is any inconsistency in the muscle. Coughing forces a guy to bear down and constrict the muscle, allowing the physician to feel any tears or bulging. If a guy has a hernia, it's usually corrected through surgery.

Hypothyroidism: This is when the thyroid fails to produce enough hormones to activate growth and the sex characteristics of puberty in a guy. It also fails to maintain the metabolism of the body. A guy with an underactive thyroid may experience delayed puberty. At first, people may believe he's a late bloomer. But if puberty hasn't begun by age 14 or 15 (evidenced by growth and mass increase), then a physician should be consulted. A guy who is diagnosed with hypothyroidism often undergoes hormone therapy.

Jock Itch: During warmer weather a guy can develop a red, scaly, itchy, and sometimes painful rash on his groin and inner thighs. This jock itch is a fungus that can be treated with over-the-counter anti-fungal medications. Sometimes this can be prevented if a guy dries off well after showering and uses a medicated powder.

Meningococcal Disease: This is caused by a bacteria that's transmitted via saliva through sneezing, coughing, kissing, and sharing food or drinks. This can put teenagers who share close quarters—such as at camp, in boarding schools, or in college dorms—at high risk. This disease can first appear as a rash, then lead to bleeding under the skin, headaches, stiffness in the neck, joint aches, shock, and ultimately meningitis—an inflammation of the covering of the brain. If not treated in a timely manner, it can result in brain damage, hearing loss, loss of limbs, kidney failure, and even death. If someone in your youth group is di-

agnosed with this, it's essential that you notify all affected families immediately. There are vaccines that reduce the risk of this disease. In 1997 the American College Health Association issued a statement recommending that all college-bound teenagers consider receiving this vaccine.

Migraine Headaches: These can render a guy immobile. Oftentimes the headache is so severe that it leads to dizziness, sweating, sensitivity to light and sound, fatigue, nausea, vomiting, or any combination of these symptoms. These headaches are caused by the constriction of blood vessels in the brain, due to overactivity of the nervous system. This may be due to anything—from stress to foods to hormone activity. Some guys only experience this during adolescence, while others first experience it in adolescence and then it follows them throughout their adult lives. Guys may experience various types of migraine headaches too. One is called a *cluster migraine*, in which a guy may feel sharp, random, shooting pains in his head. A physician should be consulted regarding any severe headaches.

Mononucleosis: At one time this was known as the "kissing disease." It's common among adolescents, and the Epstein-Barr virus causes it. Symptoms include nausea, on-and-off fevers, continuous sore throat, chronic fatigue, and loss of appetite. This disease needs to run its course, which can range from a few weeks to a few months. There is no sure treatment for mono, except for lots of bedrest.

A guy with mono can end up missing a lot of school and will have to drop out of extracurricular activities. This could cause him to spend a great portion of the year without opportunities to exercise the talents he's been developing (in athletics, music, drama, art, and so on). He may be afraid he's compromising future scholarship opportunities. And because of the amount of rest that's required to get better, this disease could also kill his social life. There's a time when a person with mono is no longer contagious.

Home visits at this point will keep a guy feeling connected and cared for.

Osgood-Schlatter's Disease: This primarily affects the knees of young athletes. It produces swelling, pain, and constant tenderness in the joints. The pain usually occurs just below the kneecap down the shin. Many times rest from a sport is required and this can last anywhere from two weeks to an indefinite period of time. This disease can devastate a guy who hinges his identity or his college scholarship possibilities to a sport. But the pain can make it difficult to walk, let alone participate in athletics. Anti-inflammatory medications, pain inhibitors, and rest help to reduce the discomfort until he outgrows the problem.

Precocious (Early) Puberty: This is a hormonal disorder that can have some hereditary connections. A guy with this problem can begin puberty anytime between the ages of six and eight. That means he'll begin to develop pubic, facial, and body hair; experience the enlargement of his testicles and penis; acquire strong sexual drives; and all other changes that come with puberty before he reaches the age of 10. When puberty stops, then his adult growth does, too, which means he won't mature to an adult height. There is also the potential for psychological damage. He'll experience teasing and rejection from his peers, as well as inappropriate expectations from adults who, based on his appearance, believe he's older and more emotionally, socially, and intellectually mature than he is. Many times depression and low self-esteem follow this guy. This disorder can be treated with hormonal blocks.

Pubertal Gynecomastia: Many times a guy will start to notice that the area around his nipples is protruding. As puberty progresses he may become aware that it's increasing. When a guy hits age 12 to 14, his testicles produce estrogen as well as testosterone. If there's a hormonal imbalance, it can cause *pubertal gynecomastia*, which affects up to 40 percent of all adolescent guys during puberty. Within about two

years after puberty begins, about 70 percent of those affected will notice it disappearing. If breast buds don't disappear within three years of the onset of puberty, then treatment by a physician is a possible option. Within three years 90 percent will no longer suffer from it.

The remaining 10 percent suffer from the commonly misunderstood disorder known as *gynecomastia*. Many people believe this condition would be eliminated if a guy lifted weights to build up his chest. This is a myth because the problem is not muscular but hormonal. Lifting and dieting will not correct the problem. While a guy is going through this awkward physical disorder, he may avoid taking off his shirt. What complicates the problem is that he may be too embarrassed to talk about it. The potential for ridicule about having breasts (the ultimate physiological assault to his masculine anatomy) is far too great for a teenage guy to risk exposure—verbally or visually. And if he can hide his condition by wearing an oversized shirt and being careful not to run or jump too much, then he's certainly not going to willingly share this problem with anyone. This limits his involvement in summer sports, camps, retreats, and other outdoor events. Youth workers need to be sensitive to this, especially if they plan activities that allow guys to go shirtless.

Scoliosis (an *S* curvature of the spine): It's often evidenced during adolescence when bone development begins, although it's more common in girls. If a guy is diagnosed with this condition, it can be corrected by wearing a brace (underneath his clothes) for long periods of time. The brace is designed to keep his spine stable so it will grow straight. If it cannot be corrected this way, then surgery may be necessary. This can limit a guy's activities. *Lordosis* is another spinal problem that evidences itself as a sway back. It can be treated in the same way as scoliosis.

Sleepwalking/Talking: Sometimes the activity on an adolescent guy's mind can continue into his sleep-

ing hours. While you are on an overnight retreat, you may find a guy walking or talking in his sleep. Some experience this episodically. Usually it's nothing to be concerned about. Guys typically outgrow it. But it can freak out everyone on a youth group retreat if a guy abruptly yells or has loud conversations by himself in the middle of the night.

Strep Throat: Because of the activity and changes in a guy's body, he can become susceptible to a variety of germs. Strep is a bacteria that causes a severe sore throat, making it difficult to eat or drink because swallowing is painful. This problem is treated with antibiotics.

SEXUAL PROBLEMS

Sexual problems are physical issues a guy may experience in his reproductive development or system. Some of those issues are:

Bloody Ejaculation: Sometimes after masturbation a guy may detect blood in his semen. This alone can be traumatizing, but many times his guilt may escalate the problem. Blood in a guy's ejaculate can be the result of a broken capillary—a very small blood vessel—in the reproductive tract. This isn't harmful. Out of contrition a guy may talk to his youth worker about this occurrence before he tells anyone else. You need to assure him that it's not a problem. But if it continues, then he should consult a physician immediately. Also reassure him that God is not punishing him.

Epididymitis: This is an infection and the subsequent inflammation of the coiled tubes of the epididymis. And it's one of the most common causes of scrotal pain. A guy with this infection will experience testicular pain, fever, chills, testicular swelling and sensitivity to touch or pressure, abdominal and pelvic pain, burning during urination, painful ejaculation, and discharge from the penis. Epididymitis can be a side effect of a sexually transmitted disease, although

a guy can have this problem apart from sexual contact. It's usually treated with antibiotics.

Hematocele: A blood-filled cyst or mass that forms on the testicle. Guys experience this when they get hit in the groin and the testicle is injured. Normally, it will disappear on its own, and the blood will be reabsorbed like a bruise.

Hydrocele: This is fluid in the scrotum. A cyst can sometimes form in the membrane of the scrotum and fill with a yellowish fluid that enlarges the scrotum abnormally. It can feel like a testicular mass when it begins to develop. Usually diagnosed by ultrasound, this problem is harmless. It doesn't impair sexual function. If the cyst's appearance bothers a guy, then a physician can aspirate the liquid. (This means the doctor will remove the cyst by inserting a syringe and drawing the fluid out). Many times the fluid will return. Sometimes the problem will go away by itself and the guy's body will reabsorb the fluid. There is no known cause.

Orchiectomy: The medical removal of the testicle. Trauma can occur to a testicle from a sports injury, falling, or getting hit. If irreparable damage is done, then the testicle may be removed. The loss of a testicle doesn't necessarily compromise a guy's sexual abilities or his ability to sire children. Often a prosthetic testicle can be inserted inside the scrotum, giving the look and feel of a real testicle.

Orchitis: A painful infection in one or both testicles. Usually it's accompanied by some inflammation of the testicle as well. Orchitis can either be bacterial or viral. The most common form of viral orchitis is mumps. If an adolescent guy gets the mumps during his teenage years, it can inflame his testicles.

Pearly Penile Papules: These are small skin bumps that run around the corona (rim) of the glans (head of the penis). These papules can become noticeable in late adolescence and they occur in about 10 per-

cent of all guys. Sometimes a guy can mistake these for tiny genital warts. They're not infectious, nor will they compromise a guy's sexual pleasure or performance. They don't grow and they don't require any treatment.

Penile Fracture: This problem is extremely rare. A penile fracture can occur when there is trauma to the erect penis, causing the corpus cavernosum to rupture. A guy may hear a snapping sound and experience pain, followed by extreme swelling and bruising afterward. Most often this occurs during sexual intercourse, but it could also occur if a guy is engaged in "dry sex" or grinding. A physician should be consulted immediately. Many times this problem is surgically correctable.

Phimosis: This problem only occurs in uncircumcised guys. Phimosis is the inability of the foreskin to retract. Puberty brings frequent erections, as well as the enlarging of the penis. If the foreskin is tight, constricting penile growth and erection, then the pain can be constant and great. The only way for this to be corrected is for the foreskin to be surgically loosened or completely removed.

Prostatitis: This is a painful infection or inflammation of the prostate. It has two forms: one is bacterial, which yields infection but can be treated with medication. The second is referred to as *congestive prostatitis*. In effect, this is an engorgement of the prostate (the prostate gets too full), also known as *blueball*. Guys can experience this problem when they're sexually aroused, as well as from the day-by-day production of sperm and semen without regular emission.

Contrary to popular belief, a guy's body doesn't always release ejaculate through wet dreams. The myth that every guy will experience wet dreams if he stops masturbating is a damaging lie that can have painful consequences for some guys. Many young men never experience wet dreams. [*Disclaimer: I'm*

not saying masturbation is right, nor am I saying it's wrong. I'm just saying we can't lie to guys regarding the functions of their bodies to try to make them stop masturbating.]

Congestive prostatitis can result in a painful condition that can be relieved one of three ways: frequent intercourse, frequent masturbation, or through a procedure done by a physician called "palpating the prostate," where the doctor inserts a finger rectally and puts pressure on the prostate until it forces ejaculate out of the urethra.

Peyronie's Disease: A condition in which fibrous scar tissue can form on the corpora cavernosa or the spongy tissues that make up the shaft of the penis. This scar tissue produces a firm area known as a "plaque," causing the penis to curve up, down, or sideways, depending on where the scarring is located. The problem is noticeable during erection because when the erectile tissue fills with blood, the scarred part doesn't expand, causing the penis to bend. A guy can still have intercourse and can reach orgasm without difficulty. The causes of this disorder are not completely known, but they consist of a range of things from poor development of the corpora cavernosa during puberty to an injury or trauma to the penis. It can be surgically corrected.

Spermatocele: This is a small cyst that forms on the epididymis. It can often be detected from a testicular self-exam. It's usually filled with a milky fluid containing dead sperm. It's harmless and painless. Sometimes it's so small that it is undetectable.

Testicular Cancer: Testicular cancer is not common, but it's the most common form of cancer found in young men between the ages of 20 and 34. About 75 percent of all testicular cancer cases occur in men between the ages of 20 and 50. Testicular cancer is one of the most treatable cancers, with almost a 100 percent cure rate if it's detected in time.

The best prevention is for guys, beginning at age 15, to do monthly testicular self-exams (TSE). Women have drastically reduced the threat of breast cancer by teaching adolescent girls to do breast self-exams. Now guys should follow this example. Effective ministry to male teenagers means we are concerned for the welfare of every guy. This demands a holistic approach to ministry, so youth workers need to challenge guys to learn how to do a self-exam—their doctors can show them how during a routine physical. This challenge should be a part of every formal "guys only" talk that a youth group has.

Testicular Torsion: The scrotum is not divided into two distinct compartments, allowing the testicles freedom of movement. But a problem can occur when the testes twist or turn within the scrotum, entangling the spermatic cords on each testicle. This is a highly painful condition and it can even cut off the blood flow in one or both testicles. It can happen at any time without warning, but it often occurs after some strenuous activity. A guy will feel sharp pain in his testicles, followed by nausea, vomiting, fever, and swelling. He could also pass out from the pain. Treatment usually requires immediate surgery.

Urethritis: This is when the urethra, the canal between the opening of the penis and the bladder, becomes infected. The urethra allows urine and ejaculate to pass from a guy's body. Symptoms of urethritis include painful or burning urination and ejaculation; itchiness; puss or mucous coming out of the penis (it leaves a stain that may be noticeable on a guy's white underwear); and the opening at the end of the penis (meatus) may be red and stuck together by the dried secretions. Causes of this infection can include anything from soap irritation to sexually transmitted diseases.

Varicocele: This is the swelling of the veins around the testicle. It usually affects the left testicle, causing a dull pain in the scrotum and making it feel like a "bag of worms." It's a vascular problem that can lead

to infertility. The problem can often be corrected if it's caught early.

APPENDIX C

GUYS AND SEXUALLY TRANSMITTED DISEASES

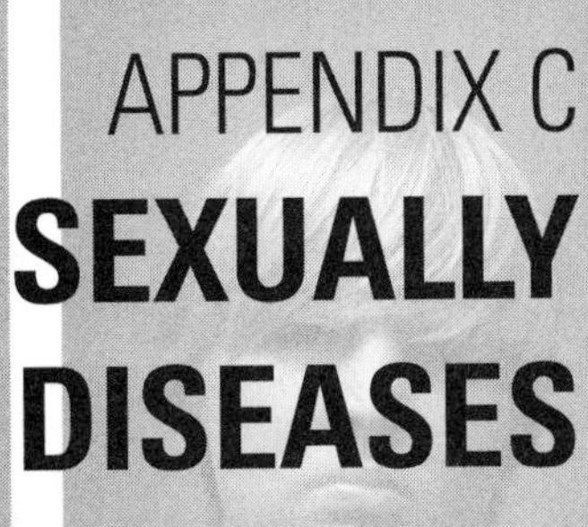

Sexually transmitted diseases (STDs) or sexually transmitted infections (STIs) are acquired through sexual contact, including intercourse, oral sex, and anal sex. Some STDs create great discomfort while others can result in death. There are about 15 million new cases of STDs reported each year.[1] More than two-thirds of those cases occur in people under the age of 25.[2] Each year one in four sexually active teenagers contracts an STD.[3]

STDs can be divided into three categories: viruses, bacterial infections, and parasites. (Just for the record, many diseases and infections can attack a guy's reproductive system without sexual contact, but they are also contagious if he is sexually active. We won't discuss them. The STDs noted here are more commonly associated with sexual contact or infectious needle use.)

VIRAL

A small, complex molecule that survives in the fluids of a host. When it enters the body it begins to multiply rapidly. There is no cure for a viral STD, but medications can slow the virus' reproduction, which in turn can eliminate some symptoms and keep it under control. A guy with a viral STD will always have that virus in his system and can infect anyone he has sex with.

- **HIV/AIDS:** Human Immunodeficiency Virus (HIV) destroys the body's immune system by multiplying in the body's white cells and destroying the T-cells (which kill infected cells and activate the immune system). Once in the body, HIV may take a long time before it causes any noticeable symptoms. Early signs of HIV may include fatigue, fever, night sweats, nausea, swollen glands in the groin, neck and armpits, diarrhea, dry cough, mouth sores, sore throat, and unexpected weight loss. When a guy is diagnosed with HIV, he is said to be

"HIV-positive," and the virus never leaves his system. Once the immune system starts breaking down, the infected person has AIDS (Acquired Immune Deficiency Syndrome). In the late stages of AIDS, the infected person is susceptible to flu, pneumonia, cancer, or any other opportunistic diseases that result in death.

- **Herpes:** Sores that may appear on a guy's penis, scrotum, thighs, buttocks, and anus. Many guys with herpes report a tingling or burning in the genital region before sores start to appear. Herpes sores usually disappear after two to three weeks. This may lead a guy to believe the virus is gone, but it isn't. Sores can return throughout his life—there is no cure for this STD. But there are medications that can keep it under control.
- **Genital Warts:** Clinically known as Human Papilloma Virus (HPV), it begins with small, hard, fleshy bumps around the corona of the penis or around the anus. These bumps look like common skin warts and are usually painless at first. If they are not treated, they can grow into larger, coral-like lumps. Again, this STD cannot be cured, but it can be controlled with topical drugs, oral medications, inferno injections that boost the immune system, cryosurgery (freezing and surgical removal), or in some cases, traditional surgery.
- **Hepatitis B:** There are many strains of Hepatitis, but the "B" strain is most common—and it's passed though sexual contact. Unlike the other viruses, the body can develop antibodies to fight off this infection. There are also vaccines that help treat and prevent this virus. While a guy's infected body is trying to fight off Hepatitis B, he may experience joint pain, nausea, vomiting, fever, loss of appetite, headaches, and fatigue. This may be misdiagnosed as the flu. If his body activates antibod-

ies within six months, he is said to have "acute hepatitis B"; if it goes beyond the six-month period, it is "chronic." Because this virus causes flu-like symptoms (and is sometimes not symptomatic at all), it's called the "silent infection." Advanced stages of Hepatitis B attack the liver, resulting in severe vomiting and nausea, jaundice (or a yellowing of the skin and eyes), and a swollen or bloated stomach. If untreated it can result in cirrhosis of the liver, liver failure, cancer, and death. A person with chronic hepatitis B can manage the infection and live a long and healthy life.

PARASITIC

A parasite is a small organism or bug that lives on or in the infected person, known as the host. Pubic lice or crabs and scabies are the most common parasites. These sexually transmitted infections can be treated with topical medications or, when extreme, with internal medications.

- **Pubic Lice:** Commonly called "crabs" because they look like crabs. Pubic lice are passed through sexual contact but also can be contracted from dirty bed linens, towels, or clothing. Pubic lice attach to the base of pubic hair and lay eggs. As pubic lice mature they suck their host's blood, which results in itching, irritation, rashes, and inflammatory skin reactions. Often the skin becomes raw after scratching. Treatment for pubic lice ranges from topical prescriptions to medicated shampoos.
- **Scabies:** Much smaller than pubic lice (which can be seen with the naked eye upon inspection), scabies are eight-legged parasites that burrow under the skin where they lay eggs and live for about a month. A guy can get scabies from prolonged skin-to-skin contact with an-

other infected person. Often symptoms include a rash and itchiness on the webbing between the fingers and toes and in the folds of skin surrounding joints (such as elbows and knees), and in the loose skin of the penis. Many times the itching will produce skin sores that can become infected.

BACTERIAL

Single-cell organisms that chain together to form an infection in a guy's body. They can be treated with antibiotics and eliminated.

- **Chlamydia:** The most common STD. It can cause a burning or itching sensation in the urethra of a guy's penis, especially during urination. Often a guy discharges a milky white substance from his penis. He often notices them as spots that stain his underwear.
- **Gonorrhea:** Like chlamydia, it can cause burning and itching in and around the penis. A constant, puss-like, foul-smelling discharge known as "gonorrhea drip" often is a symptom. This can make urination very painful and difficult. Penicillin is the powerful antibiotic administered to eliminate this STD.
- **Syphilis:** It's often undetected because the symptoms are usually mild and go away quickly. Syphilis can appear as small, painless sores or lesions on or around the penis, in or near the mouth, anus, or hands. If not treated, syphilis can run its course over many years and can result in death because it attacks the nervous system and heart. The earlier advanced stages of syphilis can result in a scaly red rash on a guy's hands and feet. As the infection progresses, the rash appears on his chest and back.
- **Chancroid:** This STD starts as a soft bump on the penis or anus about 10 days after sexual

contact. Eventually this pimple-like bump becomes an open, puss-filled sore accompanied by swollen lymph glands in the groin. Chancroid can be very painful because the sore stays open and oozes puss. Contact with clothing can often keep it irritated. Unlike herpes (witch which chancroid is often confused) chancroid is treatable if detected. But a qualified medical doctor must rule out the possibility of herpes before treatment occurs.

COMMON STD SIGNS/SYMPTOMS

- Puss-filled, foul-smelling, yellow or green discharge from the penis
- Pain during sex or when urinating
- Constant itching/burning of the urethra or tip of penis
- Sore throat in those having oral sex
- Pain in the anus for those having anal sex
- Chancre sores (painless red sores) on the genital area, anus, tongue, and/or throat
- Scaly rash on the palms of hands or soles of feet
- Dark urine; loose, light-colored stool; yellowish eyes and skin
- Small blisters that turn into scabs on the genital area
- Swollen glands, fever, body aches
- Unusual infections, unexplained fatigue, night sweats, weight loss
- Soft, flesh-colored warts around the genital area

PREVENTION

There are three ways to avoid STDs/STIs. The first and best prevention is sexual abstinence. Secondly, sex in a monogamous relationship with an uninfected partner. If a partner has had a bacterial or parasitic STD and has been treated, then they are no longer infected. But if a partner is diagnosed with a viral STD, it can be contagious. The third way to curb the spread of STDs is through condom use, however it does not prevent STDs if a guy engages in oral sex. If a teenage guy believes he's been exposed to a sexually transmitted disease or infection, he should consult a physician. Timely treatment and care for STDs is critical.

NOTES

SECTION 1

Chapter 1.1

1. L. Cooper, trans., *The Rhetoric of Aristotle* (New York: Appleton-Century-Crofts, 1932), 134.

2. Ibid.

3. Nancy Cobb, *Adolescence: Continuity, Change, and Diversity,* 5th ed. (Boston: McGraw Hill, 2004), 23.

4. R.J. Havighurst, *Developmental Tasks and Education,* 3rd ed. (New York: McKay, 1972).

SECTION 2

Chapter 2.1

1. Harrison G. Pope Jr., Katharine A. Phillips, and Roberto Olivardia, *The Adonis Complex: The Secret Crisis of Male Body Obsession* (New York: Simon & Schuster, 2000).

2. John Condry, "Gender Identity and Social Competence," *Sex Roles* 11, no. 5 (1984): 485-511. This theory was also found in earlier writings; cf. H. Kaye, *Male Survival: Masculinity Without Myth* (New York: Gossett & Dunlap, 1974).

3. M. L. Collaer and M. Hines, "Human Behavioral Sex Differences: A Role for Gonadal Hormones during Early Development?" Psychological Bulletin 118 (1985): 55-107.

Chapter 2.2

1. John W. Santrock, Adolescence, 10th ed. (New York: McGraw-Hill, 2004).

2. Mark A. Goldstein and Myrna Chandler Goldstein, *Boys into Men: Staying Healthy through the Teen Years* (Westport, CT: Greenwood Press, 2000), 68-69.

3. A. Peterson and B. Taylor, "The Biological Approaches to Adolescence: Biological Change and Psychological Adaptation," in *Handbook of Adolescent Psychology,* ed. Joseph Adelson (New York: Wiley, 1980).

4. Online at http://www.teenpuberty.com/index.php?section=male&page=stages

Chapter 2.3

1. Michael Gurian, *A Fine Young Man: What Parents, Mentors, and Educators Can Do to Shape Adolescent Boys into Exceptional Men* (New York: Jeremy P. Tarcher/Putnam, 1998), 33.
2. Online at http://www.teenpuberty.com/index.php?section=male&page=stages
3. W. Robson and A. Leung, "The Circumcision Question," *Postgraduate Medicine* 91 (1992): 237-244; C.S. Kikiros, S.W. Beasley, and A.A. Woodward, "The Response of Phimosis to Local Steroid Application," *Pediatric Surgery International* 8 (1993): 329.
4. Scott F. Gilbert, *Developmental Biology,* 4th ed., (Sunderland, MA: Sinaur Associates, 1994).
5. Richard D. McAnulty and M. Michele Burnette, *Exploring Human Sexuality: Making Healthy Decisions* (Boston: Allym & Bacon, 2001), 96.
6. I explain these views in depth in a book on masturbation. (See Steve Gerali, *The Struggle* (Colorado Springs: NavPress, 2003).) This book uncovers some of the baggage that has made masturbation a shaming experience and has perpetuated a silence about it in the church. It also looks at some of the myths and lies that are propagated in the name of moral rightness. Exposing these lies doesn't mean that masturbation is okay; it just means that it may not be wrong.
7. Steve Gerali, *The Struggle* (Colorado Springs: NavPress, 2003), 76.
8. Stephen Arterburn, Fred Stoeker, and Mike Yorkey, *Every Young Man's Battle: Strategies for Victory in the Real World of Sexual Temptation* (Colorado Springs: WaterBrook Press, 2002), 130.

SECTION 3

Chapter 3.1

1. Stephen Arterburn, Fred Stoeker, and Mike Yorkey, E*very Young Man's Battle: Strategies for Victory in the Real World of Sexual Temptation* (Colorado Springs: WaterBrook Press, 2002), chap. 13.
2. Ibid., 130.
3. Ibid., 108, 135.
4. Frank Hajcak and Patricia Garwood, "Quick-Fix Sex: Pseudosexuality in Adolescents," *Adolescence* 23, no. 92 (1988): 755-759.

5. R. Albert Mohler Jr., *Commentary by R. Albert Mohler Jr.*, "Pornified America—The Culture of Pornography," August 22, 2005, http://albertmohler.com/commentary_print.php?cdate=2005-08-22 (accessed December 22, 2005)

6. Steve Gerali, *The Struggle* (Colorado Springs: NavPress, 2003), 122.

Chapter 3.2

1. See A.R. D'Augelli and S.L. Hershberger, "Lesbian, Gay, and Bisexual Youth in Community Settings: Personal Challenges and Mental Health Problems," *American Journal of Community Psychology* 21 (1993): 421-448; and S.L. Hershberger, N.W. Pilkington, and A.R. D'Augelli, "Predictors of Suicide Attempts Among Gay, Lesbian, and Bisexual Youth," *Journal of Adolescent Research* 12, no. 4 (1997): 477-497.

2. Gabe Kruks, "Gay and Lesbian Homeless/Street Youth: Special Issues and Concerns," *Journal of Adolescent Health* 12 (1991): 515-518.

3. Ritch C. Savin-Williams, *Mom, Dad. I'm Gay: How Families Negotiate Coming Out* (Washington, D.C.: American Psychological Association, 2001).

4. Robert T. Michael, John H. Gagnon, Edward O. Laumann, and Gina Kolata, *Sex in America: A Definitive Survey* (Boston: Little, Brown & Co., 1994).

5. See R.H. DuRant, D.P. Krowchuk, and S.H. Sinal, "Victimization, Use of Violence, and Drug Use at School Among Male Adolescents Who Engage in Same-Sex Sexual Behavior," *The Journal of Pediatrics* 133 (1998): 113-118; R. Garofalo et al., "Sexual Orientation and Risk of Suicide Attempts Among a Representative Sample of Youth," *Archives of Pediatrics & Adolescent Medicine* 153 (1999): 487-493; G. Remafedi et al., "The Relationship Between Suicide Risk and Sexual Orientation: Results of a Population-Based Study," *American Journal of Public Health* 88, no. 1 (1998): 57-60. These articles describe population-based sample studies that substantiate that gay teenagers are more at risk of committing suicide than heterosexual teenagers.

6. Jonathan Nicholas and John Howard, "Better Dead than Gay? Depression, Suicide Ideation and Attempt Among a Sample of Gay and Straight-Identified Males Aged 18 to 24," *Youth Studies Australia* 17, no. 4 (1998): 28-33.

7. Belinda Hanlon, "The 1999 Massachusetts Youth Risk Behavior Survey," Massachusetts Department of Education (2000), under "Chapter 4—Illegal Drug Use," http://www.doe.mass.edu/hssss/yrbs99/chapter4.html

8. G. Remafedi, J.A. Farrow, and R.W. Deisher, "Risk Factors for Attempted Suicide in Gay and Bisexual Youth," *Pediatrics* 87, no. 6 (1991): 869-875.

9. J. Selekman, "A New Era of Body Decoration: What Are Kids Doing to Their Bodies?" *Pediatric Nursing* 29, no. 1 (2003): 77-79.

10. S. Carroll, R. Riffenburgh, T. Roberts, and E. Myhre, "Tattoos and Body Piercings as Indicators of Adolescent Risk-Taking Behaviors," *Pediatrics* 109, no. 6 (2002): 1021-1027.

SECTION 4

Chapter 4.1

1. William Pollack, *Real Boys: Rescuing Our Sons from the Myths of Boyhood* (New York: Henry Holt and Company, 1998).

2. Ibid., 23-24.

3. G. Stanley Hall, *Adolescence: Its Psychology and Its Relations to Physiology, Anthropology, Sociology, Sex, Crime, Religion, and Education*, 2 vols. (Englewood Cliffs, NJ: Prentice Hall, 1904).

4. L. Dorn and F. Lucus, "Do Hormone-Behavior Relations Vary Depending Upon the Endocrine and Psychological Status of the Adolescent?" (paper, presented at the meeting of the Society for Research in Child Development, Indianapolis, IN, March 1995).

5. Miller Newton, *Adolescence: Guiding Youth Through the Perilous Ordeal* (New York: W.W. Norton & Company, 1995).

6. Nancy Eisenberg and Bridget Murphy, "Parenting and Children's Moral Development" in *Handbook of Parenting: Applied and Practical Parenting*, ed. Marc H. Bornstein, (Hillsdale, NJ: Erlbaum, 1997), vol. 4, chap. 10.

7. John M. Robertson and Robert Freeman, "Men and Emotions: Developing Masculine-Congruent Views of Affective Expressiveness," *Journal of College Student Development* 36, (1995): 606-607.

Chapter 4.2

1. Janet Holland, Caroline Ramazanoglu, and Sue Sharpe, *Wimp or Gladiator: Contradictions in Acquiring Masculine Sexuality*, WRAP/MRAP Paper 9 (London: The Tufnell Press, 1993), 14.

2. Trevor Lloyd, *Let's Get Changed Lads: Developing Work with Boys and Young Men* (London: Working With Men, 1997).

Chapter 4.3

1. Terrence Real, *I Don't Want to Talk About It: Overcoming the Secret Legacy of Male Depression* (New York: Simon & Schuster, 1997).

2. Ibid., 172.

3. R. Latzman and R. Swisher, "The Interactive Relationship Among Adolescent Violence, Street Violence, and Depression," *Journal of Community Psychology* 33, no. 3 (2005): 355-371.

4. United Nations Fund for Population Activities, "Supporting Adolescents and Youth: Fast Facts," http://www.unfpa.org/adolescents/facts.htm

5. Howard N. Snyder, Ph.D. and Monica H. Swahn, Ph.D., "Juvenile Suicides, 1981-1998," *Youth Violence Research Bulletin* (March 2004), Office of Juvenile Justice and Delinquency Prevention, http://ncjrs.org/html/ojjdp/196978/contents.html

6. U.S. Census Bureau, "Section 2. Vital Statistics," *Statistical Abstract of the United States: 2004-2005*, http://www.census.gov/prod/2004pubs/04statab/vitstat.pdf

7. Dave Capuzzi and Douglas R. Gross, eds., *Youth at Risk: A Resource for Counselors, Parents and Teachers* (Alexandria, VA: American Association for Counseling and Development, 1989), 282.

8. Dean Borgman, *Hear My Story: Understanding the Cries of Troubled Youth* (Peabody, MA: Hendrickson Publishers, 2003),.

Chapter 4.4

1. James E. Shaw, *Jack and Jill, Why They Kill: Saving Our Children, Saving Ourselves* (Seattle: Onjinjinkta Publishing, 2000).

2. School Violence Watch Network, "USA School Violence Statistics," http://www.cyberenforcement.com/schoolwatch/svstats.asp#2001

3. Allan M. Hoffman and Randal W. Summers, eds., *Teen Violence: A Global View* (Westport, CT: Greenwood Press, 2001).

4. Center for Disease Control and Prevention, "Youth Violence," *Injury Fact Book 2001-2002*, http://www.cdc.gov/ncipc/fact_book/31_Youth_Violence%20s.htm

5. National Center for Education Statistics, "Indicator 7: Violent and Other Incidents at Public Schools and Those Reported to the Police," *Indicators of School Crime and Safety 2004*, http://nces.ed.gov/pubs2005/crime_safe04/indicator_07.asp#here (This site combines data collections by federal departments and agencies such as the National Center for Education Statistics

(NCES), the Bureau of Justice Statistics (BJS), the Federal Bureau of Investigation (FBI), and the Centers for Disease Control and Prevention (CDC).)

6. January 29, 1979: A 16-year-old girl in San Diego opened fire on children as they arrived at their elementary school across the street from her house, killing two adults and injuring eight students and a police officer, http://www.cybersnitch.net/schoolwatch/svstats.asp

7. Edwin S. Schneidman, *The Suicidal Mind* (New York: Oxford Press, 1996).

8. S. Verlinder, M. Hersen, and J. Thomas, "Risk Factors in School Shootings," *Clinical Psychology Review* 20, no. 1 (2000): 3-56.

9. Dan Kindlon and Michael Thompson, *Raising Cain: Protecting the Emotional Life of Boys* (New York: Ballantine Press, 2000), 223-224.

10. The Commission on the Status of Women, "Future Perspectives on the Promotion of Gender Equality: Through the Eyes of Young Women and Men" (panel discussion at the United Nations Headquarters, New York, the forty-ninth session, from February 28 to March 11, 2005).

11. Media Awareness Network, "Violent Video Games and Stimulus Addiction," http://www.media-awareness.ca/english/resources/educational/handouts/video_games/violent_video_games.cfm (Adapted from *Screen Smarts: A Family Guide to Media Literacy* (Boston: Houghton Mifflin, 1996) by Gloria DeGaetano and Kathleen Bander.)

12. Dean Borgman, *Hear My Story: Understanding the Cries of Troubled Youth* (Peabody, MA: Hendrickson Publishers, 2003), 189.

SECTION 5

CHAPTER 5.1

1. J. Giedd et al., "Brain Development During Childhood and Adolescence: A Longitudinal MRI Study," *Nature Neuroscience* 2, no. 10 (1999): 861-863, http://www.nature.com/neuro/journal/v2/n10/full/nn1099_861.html

2. Ruben C. Gur, Ph.D., "Declaration of Ruben C. Gur, Ph.D." (affidavit in habeas corpus petition on behalf of Toronto Patterson who was scheduled for execution by the State of Texas on August 28, 2002, http://www.abanet.org/crimjust/juvjus/Gur%20affidavit.pdf

3. Michael D. De Bellis et al., "Sex Differences in Brain Maturation During Childhood and Adolescence," *Cerebral Cortex* 11, no. 6 (2001): 552-557.

4. Ibid., "Declaration of Ruben C. Gur, Ph.D."

5. Bennett A. Shaywitz et al., "Sex Differences in the Functional Organization of the Brain for Language," *Nature* 373, (1995): 607-609.

6. K. Kansaku and S. Kitazawa, "Imaging Studies on Sex Differences in the Lateralization of Language," *Journal of Neuroscience Research* 41, no. 4 (2001): 333-337.

7. Michael Gurian, *A Fine Young Man: What Parents, Mentors, and Educators Can Do to Shape Adolescent Boys into Exceptional Men* (New York: Jeremy P. Tarcher/Putnam, 1998).

8. S.A. Brown, S.F. Tapert, E. Granholm, and D.C. Delis, "Neurocognitive Functioning of Adolescents: Effects of Protracted Alcohol Use," *Alcoholism: Clinical and Experimental Research* 24 (2000): 164-171.

9. M.L. Wolraich, J.N. Hannah, A. Baumgaertel, I.D. Feurer, "Examination of DSM-IV Criteria for Attention Deficit/Hyperactivity Disorder in a County-Wide Sample," *Journal of Development and Behavioral Pediatrics* 19, no. 3 (1998): 163-168.

10. Michael Gurian, *The Wonder of Boys: What Parents, Mentors and Educators Can Do to Shape Boys into Exceptional Men* (New York: Jeremy P. Tarcher/Putnam, 1996).

11. Ibid., 17.

12. G.M. de Courten-Myers, "The Human Cerebral Cortex: Gender Differences in Structure and Function," *Journal of Neuropathology and Experimental Neurology* 58, no. 3 (1999): 217-226.

13. R.F. Eme, "Sex Differences in Childhood Psychopathology: A Review," *Psychological Review* 86 (1979): 574-595.

14. K. Kansaku and S. Kitazawa, "Imaging Studies on Sex Differences in the Lateralization of Language," *Journal of Neuroscience Research* 41, no. 4 (2001): 333-337.

15. Virginia Berninger and Todd Richards, "Dyslexic Children Have Abnormal Brain Lactate Response to Reading-Related Language Tasks," *American Journal of Neuroradiology* 20 (1999): 1393-1398, http://www.washington.edu/newsroom/news/1999archive/10-99archive/k100499.html

16. James R. Brasic, "Pervasive Developmental Disorder: Asperger Syndrome," eMedicine.com (use "Pediatrics" and "Developmental & Behavioral" links), http://www.emedicine.com/ped/topic147.htm

17. The National Dissemination Center for Children with Disabilities (NICHCY), "Autism and Pervasive Developmental Disorder," *Fact Sheet* 1, January 2004, www.nichcy.org/pubs/factshe/fs1txt.htm

Chapter 5.2

1. John W. Santrock, Adolescence, 10th ed. (New York: McGraw-Hill, 2004), 123.

SECTION 6

Chapter 6.1

1. David Elkind, *All Grown Up and No Place to Go: Teenagers in Crisis* (New York: Addison-Wesley Publishing Co., 1984), 33-36.
2. William Pollack, *Real Boys: Rescuing Our Sons From the Myths of Boyhood,* (New York: Henry Holt and Company, 1998), 53.
3. Terrell Carver, *Men in Political Theory* (New York: Manchester University Press, 2004), 6.
4. Erik H. Erikson, *Identity: Youth and Crisis* (New York: W. W. Norton & Co, 1968).
5. Ibid.
6. Erik H. Erikson, "Identity and the Life Cycle," *Psychological Issues* 1 (1959), 50-100. Erikson believed that life stages, including identity development, were an "epigenetic" process. This means that each stage is contingent upon the successful completion of the previous one. It also means that each stage is a part of a whole that must be mastered. Erikson, speaking of the epigenetic principle, said, "[It] states that anything that grows has a ground plan, and that out of this ground plan the parts arise, each having its time of ascendancy until all parts have risen to form a functioning whole," (p. 52).

Chapter 6.2

1. Erik H. Erikson, *Identity: Youth and Crisis* (New York: W. W. Norton & Co, 1968).
2. J.E. Marcia and J. Carpendale, "Identity: Does Thinking Make It So?" in *Changing Conceptions of Psychological Life*, ed. Cynthia Lightfoot, Chris A. Lalonde, and Michael J. Chandler (Mahwah, NJ: Lawrence Erlbaum Associates, 2004).
3. Michael L. Jaffe, *Adolescence* (New York: John Wiley & Sons, 1989), 182.
4. William Pollack, *Real Boys: Rescuing Our Sons from the Myths of Boyhood* (New York: Henry Holt and Company, 1998), 184.

5. J. Hill and M. Lynch, "The Intensification of Gender-Related Role Expectations During Early Adolescence," in *Girls at Puberty,* ed. J. Brooks-Gunn and A.C. Petersen, 201-228 (New York: Plenum Press, 1983).
6. T. Alfieri, D.N. Ruble, and E.T. Higgins, "Gender Stereotypes During Adolescence: Developmental Changes and the Transition to Junior High School," *Developmental Psychology* 32, no. 6 (1996): 1129-1137.
7. The Commission on the Status of Women, "Future Perspectives on the Promotion of Gender Equality: Through the Eyes of Young Women and Men" (panel discussion at the United Nations Headquarters, New York, the forty-ninth session, from February 28 to March 11, 2005).
8. Pollack, 182.
9. Ibid.
10. J.L. Orlofsky, "Intimacy Status: Theory and Research," in *Ego Identity: A Handbook for Psychosocial Research*, ed. J.E. Marcia, A.S. Waterman et al. (New York: Springer-Verlag, 1990).
11. Loren E. Pedersen, Dark Hearts: T*he Unconscious Forces that Shape Men's Lives* (Boston: Shambhala, 1991), 196.
12. Stephen D. Grubman-Black, *Broken Boys/Mending Men: Recovery from Childhood Sexual Abuse* (New York: Ivy Books, 1990).
13. Pollack, 187.
14. Ibid., 195.
15. Dan Kindlon and Michael Thompson, *Raising Cain: Protecting the Emotional Life of Boys* (New York: Ballantine Press, 2000), 197.

Chapter 6.3

1. William Pollack, *Real Boys: Rescuing Our Sons From the Myths of Boyhood,* (New York: Henry Holt and Company, 1998), 124.
2. See Pollack, *Real Boys.*
3. James M. Herzog, "On Father Hunger: The Father's Role in the Modulation of Aggressive Drive and Fantasy," in *Father and Child: Developmental and Clinical Perspectives*, Stanley Cath, et al., eds. (Boston: Little Brown & Co, 1982), 163-174.
4. Pollack, *Real Boys*, 120.
5. Ibid., 119.

6. Sigmund Freud, "Some Psychological Consequences of the Anatomical Distinction Between the Sexes," in *Sex Differences: Cultural and Developmental Dimensions,* Patrick C. Lee and Robert Sussman Stewart, eds. (New York: Arisen Books, 1925).
7. Nancy Chodorow, *The Reproduction of Mothering* (Berkeley: University of California Press, 1978).
8. Samuel Osherson, *Wrestling with Love: How Men Struggle with Intimacy with Women, Children, Parents and Each Other* (New York: Fawcett Columbine, 1992), 4.
9. John Eldredge, *Wild at Heart: Discovering the Secret of a Man's Soul* (Nashville: Thomas Nelson, 2001), 80.
10. Pollack, *Real Boys*, 87.

SECTION 7

Chapter 7.1

1. Patrick Arnold, *Wildmen, Warriors, and Kings: Masculine Spirituality and the Bible* (New York: Crossroad Publishing Co., 1991), 12.
2. Mark C. Carnes, *Secret Ritual and Manhood in Victorian America* (New Haven, CT: Yale University Press, 1991).
3. Mary Stewart Van Leeuwen, *Fathers and Sons: The Search for a New Masculinity* (Downers Grove, IL: InterVarsity Press, 2002).
4. Evelyn A. Kirkley, "Is It Manly to be Christian? The Debate in Victorian and Modern America," in *Redeeming Men: Religion and Masculinities*, Stephen B. Boyd, W. Merle Longwood, and Mark Muesse eds., 80-88 (Louisville, KY: Westminster John Knox Press, 1996).
5. Ibid., 84. Kirkley cites a number of descriptive passages on Fred Smith taken from Messages of the *Men and Religion Movement*, vol. 7 (New York; London: Funk & Wagnalls Company, 1912).
6. Fayette L. Thompson et al., *Men and Religion* (New York: Young Men's Christian Association, 1911), 6.
7. John Eldredge, *Wild at Heart*, 141.

APPENDICES

Appendix A

1. Susman, E., & Rogol, A. (2004). "Puberty and psychological development." In R. Learner & L. Steinberg (Eds.), *Handbook of Adolescent Psychology*. New York: Wiley.

Appendix C

1. American Social Health Association (ASHA). http://www.ashastd.org.
2. Discovery Health, http://health.discovery.com/centers/teen/relationships/sex-stds.html.
3. Alan Guttmacher Institute, *Sex and America's Teenagers* (New York: Alan Guttmacher Institute, 1994), 38.